The
Young
Scientists

The
Young
Scientists

America's Future and the Winning of the Westinghouse

Joseph Berger

Foreword by Dr. Leon M. Lederman
Winner of the 1988 Nobel Prize in Physics

ADDISON-WESLEY PUBLISHING COMPANY

Reading, Massachusetts   Menlo Park, California   New York
Don Mills, Ontario   Wokingham, England   Amsterdam   Bonn
Sydney   Singapore   Tokyo   Madrid   San Juan
Paris   Seoul   Milan   Mexico City   Taipei

The material from the booklet "Creature Features" by Dr. Richard M. Plass, which appears on pages 69–70, is reprinted by permission of Dr. Plass.

Many of the designations used by manufacturers and sellers to distinguish their products are claimed as trademarks. Where those designations appear in this book and Addison-Wesley was aware of a trademark claim, the designations have been printed in initial capital letters (e.g., Alka-Seltzer).

Library of Congress Cataloging-in-Publication Data

Berger, Joseph, 1945–
    The young scientists : America's future and the winning of the
Westinghouse / Joseph Berger ; foreword by Leon M. Lederman, winner
of the 1988 Nobel Prize in Physics.
        p.   cm.
    ISBN 0-201-63255-1
    1. Westinghouse Science Talent Search. 2. Science—Study and
teaching (Higher)—United States. 3. Science—Study and teaching—
New York (State)—Bronx (N.Y.) 4. Research—Methodology.
    I. Title.
    Q182.3.B47   1994
    507'.1'273—dc20   93-25339
                                                                                    CIP

Jacket design by Barbara Atkinson
Text design by Barbara Cohen Aronica
Set in 10½-point Century Old Style by Jackson Typesetting, Inc., Jackson, Michigan

1 2 3 4 5 6 7 8 9-MA-96959493
First printing, December 1993

To Annie

For reminding me about the pleasures of learning

Contents

Foreword

Dr. Leon M. Lederman,
Nobel Laureate

Charles Townes did the essential physics that made the laser possible. John Bardeen and some colleagues applied the quantum theory to the properties of electrons in semi-conductors and came up with the transistor. James Watson, along with Francis Crick and Maurice Wilkins, reasoned out the structure of the DNA molecule, the key to genetics. Individual scientists, working alone or in teams, have made discoveries that have changed the way humans live on this planet. Not in the seventeenth century, with Galileo and Newton, or in the nineteenth century, with Dalton and Faraday, or even in the early twentieth century, with Einstein, Rutherford, Bohr, and Heisenberg, but in the late twentieth century, these men became scientific pioneers.

Where did they come from? What schools did they attend? What influenced them? How many scientific discoveries—a cure for cancer, the theory of everything, the origin of life—were missed because the requisite talent was lost due to an unfortunate early environment: poor teaching, insensitive parents, poverty?

For centuries the world has accepted its gifted scientists as it accepts natural events—hurricanes, earthquakes, lightning strikes. However, as humans began to translate knowledge into utility, science into technology, the pace of science began to accelerate. Curiously, the number of technological problems also grew. Breakthroughs in the sciences of medicine, nutrition, and general health care led, in part, to exploding population growth. Low-cost power, whether generated by nuclear reactors or the burning of trees, led to global warming, the ozone hole, and radioactive despoliation of the environment.

Everywhere we turn, the *demands* on science, mathematics, and technology dominate our view of the future. But enhancing our scientific prowess alone is not enough; we must achieve the political wisdom to *apply* that prowess wisely and creatively. In addition to gifted scientists, we need gifted decision-makers who are scientifically literate. We need gifted journalists, editors, TV producers who are comfortable with science. (About half of the graduates of our special science schools go smoothly into all kinds of other professions.)

Joseph Berger has focused a keen light on one crucial step toward assuring the supply of young people to fulfill these many tasks. The proliferation of schools for gifted children in America is a relatively new phenomenon. But it is receiving a lot of attention as society begins to understand that social progress depends on scientific progress. The debate about special treatment of the gifted rages still: these special students have been clustered, then ignored to avoid charges of "elitism," then partially recognized for enrichment Saturday mornings at the local college. Berger explores the controversial process of finding, collecting, and nurturing superior intelligence.

The striking thing about schools for the gifted is in their application of the obvious: they expose students to the *doing* of science rather than the more sterile *study* of science. Through hard work and the creative efforts of teachers, mentors at nearby research labs, or in at least one lucky school, a resident scientist in active research, such students become scientists. As Berger notes, this technique is so successful that it is beginning to find its way into programs in ordinary schools, described as a hands-on, activity-based, discovery method.

Central to the desire to progress is the desire to discover. We must keep in mind the ennobling aspects of knowledge itself—as a deep cultural imperative. Inscribed in our genetic heritage and evident throughout recorded history is the desire to know—to know the universe's evolution, to know the biological world, to understand the convolutions of the planet and the way the human brain works.

Those of us who believe in the tremendous return on the investment in giftedness need all the arguments we can muster. This book is a valuable reference as we continue to battle for recognition of the creative child as a gift to humanity.

Acknowledgments

This book began as an article in the *New York Times* and during the book's development I wrote several other pieces for the *Times* on the undercovered subject of special science schools. So initial acknowledgments must go to the editors at the *Times* who encouraged those pieces, particularly Lawrie Mifflin, Suzanne Daley, Duayne Draffen and Gerald Boyd, and to Carolyn Lee for her generous counsel.

This book simply would not have been possible without the enthusiasm and gracious encouragement of my friend and editor at Addison-Wesley, Nancy Miller, who shared with me a childhood wonder about the young men and women who cleave to the world of science. Thanks for their fervor must also go to my agents, Michael Carlisle and Pam Bernstein. And my wife, Brenda, and daughter, Annie, gave me the quiet mornings I needed to complete this book even though it robbed them of considerable family time.

I'd like to thank all the people who let me into their schools and classrooms and chatted with me about the teaching of science: At Bronx Science, Carol Greene, Ellen Berman, Don Lamanna, and Vincent Galasso; at Stuyvesant, Richard Plass and Abraham Baumel; at Midwood, Stanley Shapiro, Jay Berman and David Kiefer; at North Carolina, Steve Warshaw, Kevin Bartkovich, John Frederick, Bill Youngblood, David Stein and Gina Norman; and so many others whose names for reasons of space I apologize for leaving out.

The folks at Westinghouse and Science Service and those long associated with these organizations were always cooperative in explaining the lore and subtleties of their contest: Carol Luszcz, Eileen Milling, Richard Gott, Dorothy Shriver, Nina Tabachnik

Schor, Jay McCaffrey, and William MacLaurin. And several scientists, particularly Leon Lederman and Glenn Seaborg, helped me understand the value of teaching research at a young age.

The deepest thanks, however, should go to the dozens of high school students, particularly Vanessa Liu, David Haile, Divya Chander, and Tamir Druz who took time out from their helter skelter days to talk with me. Their palpable passion for research not only enchanted me but goaded me on with the faith that this was a book worth doing. Their parents deserve credit for the heartfelt candor with which they described the struggles to raise their uncommon children.

The true germ of this book goes back more than 30 years ago to my student days at Bronx Science. The teachers there, some of whose names I can no longer remember, taught me a respect for evidence and proof and excellence that has served me well in a career spent largely outside of science. For that I will always be grateful.

The

Young

Scientists

Introduction

The Glittering Prizes

Every few months, American newspapers publish another dreary indicator of the country's deepening scientific ignorance. In knowledge of chemistry, a 1988 study showed, American students placed eleventh on a list of thirteen developed countries; in biology, they finished dead last. A 1990 report even found that only 45 percent of Americans are aware that the Earth revolves around the sun once a year.

These reports not only wound our pride, they show that America is losing its economic and political dominance. Such slippage would begin to eat away at the well-being of every American just as Britain's decline as an empire sapped some of the sweetness out of the lives of its people. For the vaunted American life-style depends on a powerful engine of productivity, a stalwart military arsenal, a great network of hospitals and medical providers, a genius for churning out the conveniences that give life its savor; all of these are the result of America's ability to generate scientific discoveries and harness technology to them.

"Once upon a time, American science sheltered an Einstein, went to the moon, and gave to the world the laser, electronic computer, nylons, television, the cure for polio," said Dr. Leon Lederman, the Nobel Prize–winning physicist, in 1990 as he took the helm of the American Association for the Advancement of Science, the country's largest science organization. "Today we are in the process, albeit unwittingly, of abandoning this leadership role."

The picture is bleak, but not entirely so. There are places all around the country that show us a way out of the gloom, schools that year after year teach students how to do pioneering scientific research. I learned about them by taking a close look for several years at a contest—yes, a contest—that had built a striking record for steering young men and women toward lives in science: the Westinghouse Science Talent Search, the nation's most prestigious high school academic competition.

On the ground floor of the Bronx High School of Science, a school in a New York City borough that has become virtually a synonym for ruin and desolation, there is a corridor adorned with a long row of plaques, the school's Hall of Fame. The plaques were awarded over the years by the Westinghouse Science Talent Search to honor students whose research projects it judged to be the finest in the country.

Only forty students across the country win the Westinghouse every year, and if statistical probabilities held true, Bronx Science would be lucky to have one winner every couple of decades. Instead, the school's students win virtually every year, and in most years several students win, as the corridor attests. There is one name engraved on the 1993 plaque, one on the 1991 plaque, five on the 1990 plaque, seven on 1989, three on 1988, five on 1987, three on 1986, two on 1985, four on 1984, six on 1983, stretching back like this all the way to 1962. The row of plaques might have continued in this fashion back to 1942, but the corridor ended.

Why should a school in a decaying area of New York—and there are a half dozen other schools in New York with similar programs—continue to take so many Westinghouse awards for exemplary research year after year? The reason is startlingly simple: Bronx Science teaches students how to do research. Though the school is selective, its students are not innately brighter or more capable than tens of thousands of students scattered elsewhere in the country; they are just better trained. Like the American Olympic swimmers who always seem to hail from swim clubs in California or Indiana, Bronx Science students have been given a strong edge over the competition. From the freshman year onward, they are taught how to think like scientists; they are not just swamped with facts. They are encouraged to ask questions about what they observe in the world around them, suggest possible solutions, and construct experiments that test the validity of those proposed answers. By the junior year, the most promising students are given a year to work on full-scale projects, usually under the stewardship of scientists at teaching hospitals or research institutions in the area. In the senior year, they even take an English course that teaches them how to write up their research—the course has come to be called Westinghouse English—and the papers are submitted to the Westinghouse contest.

We would hardly expect someone who began studying ballet late in college to become a principal dancer for the New York City Ballet. Ballet takes grooming at a tender age, when a body's instincts and motions are getting established, when gait and bearing and poise are being defined. Yet, when it comes to research, the American educational system operates as if scientific talent can be bred in graduate school. Very little effort is made to train high school students, let alone elementary school students, in how to think about science and do science.

Early training works. The proof is in some remarkable statistics. Five teenaged Westinghouse winners have gone on as adults to capture the Nobel Prize. (Two of them were former Bronx Science students.) Leon Cooper, a 1947 Westinghouse winner, won a Nobel in 1972 for his explanation of superconductivity, the property that allows some metals to carry extremely powerful electrical currents when they are cooled to temperatures near absolute zero. The phenomenon may one day make for lightning trains and Herculean computers. Walter Gilbert, a 1949 Westinghouse winner, won the 1980 Nobel Prize in chemistry for his work in genetic engineering—the sequencing of DNA that is creating more rugged forms of plant and animal life, some that can cure disease. Sheldon Glashow, a 1950 Westinghouse winner, won his 1979 Nobel in physics for his discovery of charms and quarks, the subatomic particles that explain how matter is put together. Ben Mottelson, a 1944 Westinghouse winner and a 1975 Nobelist in physics, demonstrated how, contrary to the dominant spherical thesis, some atomic nuclei take asymmetrical shapes. And Roald Hoffmann, a 1955 Westinghouse winner, won the 1981 Nobel in chemistry for applying quantum mechanics, the theory that explains the behavior of atoms and molecules, to predict the course of chemical reactions. His ideas were regarded by many chemists as the most important conceptual advance in chemistry in decades.

Other Westinghouse winners have taken laurels only slightly less cherished. Two have won mathematics' equivalent of the Nobel—the Fields medals—and eight have been awarded the prestigious and lucrative MacArthur Foundation fellowships. More significant still, more than 70 percent of Westinghouse winners over the years have obtained medical degrees or doctorates. In short, winning a Westinghouse as a teenager is remarkably predictive of later success in science.

This book looks at what works in science education by taking a close look at the schools and the families that nurture Westinghouse winners. The Westinghouse awards, which I studied closely in 1989 and again in 1992, have spurred improvements in science education around the country and encouraged research among the young. The Westinghouse has given prominence to schools like Bronx Science and prompted other schools to start research programs. It has encouraged many states to found their first research schools. Since 1980, a dozen states including North Carolina, Virginia, Illinois, and Texas have set up high schools that select bright students, offer them advanced courses in science, math, and the humanities, and train them in scientific research. Several of these schools draw children from remote corners of their state and, like elite boarding schools, place them in dormitories for four years. As students spend time together in class and afterwards, there is an enriching cross-pollination of ideas, energy, and enthusiasm.

Schools are only part of the secret of winning the Westinghouse. Study the backgrounds of the winning students and a number of common traits emerge that suggest who may have the best shot. Eleven of the forty winners in 1989 were foreign-born immigrants and at least two more were children of immigrants. Immigrant families have always won a disproportionate share of the prizes. In the 1940s, when the contest began, and in subsequent decades, children from immigrant Jewish families captured an unexpectedly large number of prizes. During the 1980s and early 1990s, youngsters from Taiwan, Korea, China, Japan, and India have taken a disproportionateiy large share. Most of these students were educated almost entirely in American schools, so one cannot attribute their remarkable success to a superior foreign education. Rather, these students bring with them an immigrant grit, spunk, and implacability that drives them past misguided hypotheses, botched experiments, distracted advisers, and all the other obstacles they face on the tough road to a Westinghouse. These qualities are not inbred in immigrants; they are developed, and so American parents can cultivate them in their children.

A remarkably sagacious explanation for immigrant success in the Westinghouse was offered by an Israeli-born 1989 winner, Tamir Druz of New York City. "Immigrants," he said, "understand the concept of hard work. In a sense we're more American than the Americans. We actually believe in individualism, in going out and making your own way, like the first Americans. We had a frontier too. The frontier made America what it is. Every time they felt tied down, they could become pioneers. Immigrants have a frontier. America is like our new West."

Many of the winners, of course, are children of doctors or scientists. In 1989, sixteen of the forty winners, including several of the immigrants, had one parent who was either a doctor or doctorate-holding scientist. Their dinner tables were bubbling with talk of medical exploits or laboratory shenanigans; scientific and mathematical riddles were as natural to them as jigsaw puzzles were to other kids.

"When you grow up in a household where science is the only thing," says Andrew Gerber, a 1989 winner, "it's as if you grew up in a house where your father is a soldier and you want to go to the army."

Still, when the lives of the Westinghouse students are looked at closely, the definition of genius assumes some new shadings. Genius remains an innate gift, but only to a point. Far more important, genius becomes some combination of home life and hard work, of high principles and good principals. The patterns in the Westinghouse tea leaves tell us about self-discipline and a hunger to make it, virtues that may be particularly strong in immigrants but not unique to them. They tell us about the curiosity and habits of mind that scientific parents seem to instill but that other parents can instill also. The children who win Westinghouses seem to possess a vision of the prospects that lie ahead in life and what it takes to get there, a willingness to take on rigorous challenges, to make sacrifices. Winning takes the pioneer spirit that Tamir Druz spoke of and the sense that life holds out tantalizing possibilities to those who are willing to do the getting.

When we understand such statistical patterns, the Westing-house prize no longer looms as some thoroughly implausible dream like a nine-second 100-yard dash or an eight-foot high jump that only one or two incredibly gifted mortals will ever accomplish. It becomes something that can be achieved by de-sign, by effort, by concentration and willpower. The contest can be opened up to tens of thousands of bright youngsters who are now so daunted by the seeming elusiveness of a Westinghouse they do not even apply. The spinoff for American science is immeasurable.

For those who succeed, the rewards are enormous. Winning a Westinghouse is like admission to Harvard College, one of those achievements whose power endures for a lifetime. Successful fifty-year-old chief executives still feel a twinge of intimidation and envy to learn that one of their colleagues went to Harvard. Someone who went to Harvard seems to have an inexpressible edge. Simi-larly, scientists often find themselves a little bit intimidated by a colleague who is a Westinghouse winner. The Westinghouse win-ner has the aura of someone to watch, someone possessing magical inner power. The fact that five winners have gone on to win Nobels only enhances the award's mystique.

If America wants to develop the Jonas Salks and Barbara McClintocks of the future, it must start cultivating young people and giving them work that may stimulate whatever primitive scien-tific curiosity they have. Otherwise, these potential scientists will drift to other interests and, like the homespun folk of Thomas Gray's "Elegy Written in a Country Churchyard," waste their "sweetness on the desert air."

The quest for excellence, of course, is its own reward. Divya Chander of River Vale, New Jersey, a seventeen-year-old daughter of Indian immigrants now attending Harvard, met Sen. John Glenn, the former astronaut, at one of the Westinghouse functions, and told him she wanted to be an astronaut: "I don't want to die without having had a reason to have lived, and that would be a reason."

And Vladimir Teichberg, one of the forty winners in 1989, was chosen to speak for his cowinners at the Westinghouse dinner and eloquently captured the enormous gratification achieved by students who enter the Westinghouse: "All of us have one common denominator," he said. "All experienced the excitement of doing what no man has done before."

Part I

Origins

Chapter 1

You've Got to *Do* Science

J. Richard Gott is an astrophysicist at Princeton University whose life's work has been nothing less than gaining an understanding of the universe: how it is structured and how its galaxies and voids are arrayed. In his journey to this rarefied intellectual plane, an ordinary household object—the humble sponge—has a rather special, and curious, place. The sponge has been a motif in his work. First it helped him win a Westinghouse, then it helped him explain the universe.

In 1965 Gott was a seventeen-year-old senior at Wagner High School in Louisville, Kentucky, enrolled in a program for gifted students. He undertook a study of the structure of certain metallic crystals and found that the structure, a three-dimensional network of polygons, resembled that of a marine sponge. It was composed of alternating dense and hollow areas, with the solid areas connected to each other by filaments and the hollow areas (through which seawater flows in the sponge) connected by tubes. Gott entered the project in the Westinghouse Science Talent Search. The judges thought Gott's work so original they awarded him second place among the forty winners that year.

Two decades passed, during which Gott was accepted to Harvard, graduated summa cum laude, received a Ph.D. at Princeton, forged a distinguished postdoctoral career as an astrophysicist at the California Institute of Technology and at Cambridge in England, and then returned to Princeton to teach. At the time, Princeton's astrophysicists were taking part in a rather contentious debate over the structure of the universe. Some scientists thought the universe has a meatball-like arrangement, with isolated galaxies floating freely in a void. Others thought the universe is more like Swiss cheese, with a mass of linked galaxies pocked by empty voids that have no connections to one another. Gott had a third view.

Gott is a courtly, measured man who speaks with a gentle Kentucky accent. Average in height, he has a solid build and a roundish head with a receding hairline, prominent facial features, and penetrating brown eyes. He defies the standard image of the frenzied scientist with stiff European manners and a European accent. But he is not uncompetitive and seems to take fun in knocking down shibboleths. He listened to the meatball and Swiss cheese theories and the talk somehow catapulted him back to his high school days, to his Westinghouse project on metallic crystals. He wondered if both theories were wrong and if perhaps a different model was needed to describe the universe's structure. He remembered the sponge and wondered if its structure could be applied to the arrangement of the universe.

"I happened to know that it was possible to divide space into two interlocking and divided parts," he said, with a mischievous twinkle in his eye. "We found a sponge-like topology, with a slight preference for clusters over voids."

In fact, he and several colleagues effectively set the scientific establishment on its ear. The sponge-like explanation of the universe's structure—where solid areas are connected and voids are connected—has become the dominant one in astrophysics.

Gott's experience helps explain why the Westinghouse Science Talent Search is a phenomenon worth close study. If it were just a gaudy gimmick to publicize the Westinghouse Electric Corporation, its sponsor, or make the educational establishment feel good about itself, it would not merit such national attention and respect. The Westinghouse is important because it shows us the way to turn youngsters intoxicated with science into scientists. The same habits of mind and of work that Gott had used as a boy were still valuable to him as an adult. The same habits of mind that go into a Westinghouse are those that will be required for professional scientific research. Once developed, they are not easily extinguished. A life's work in science is more like a sponge than an array of unconnected meatballs. Imperceptible filaments connect the ideas of youth with those of maturity, the habits of youth with those of the riper years. Nothing, it seems, is wasted. Somehow the Westinghouse founders understood this and created a contest that forces young people quickly to develop the outlook of a scientist.

"It's a test of qualities that are going to be required of them as scientists," Gott says. And he knows. He also happens to be the contest's chief judge.

There are a lot of nuances to the Westinghouse contest, but essentially everything is focused on identifying the students who hold the greatest promise of crafting distinguished careers in science. The contest does not just evaluate, it stimulates. Its very existence inspires and nurtures careers in science, forcing students who may have only a slight glimmer of what their life's work will be to test their potential by performing full-blown scientific research for a year or two.

"There are a lot of talented youngsters who've never had that exposure who would be good at doing research if they tried," says Gott. "We're losing them."

The Westinghouse was launched to identify young scientific talent, and it has been doing so with remarkable precision since 1941. Every year some 1,700 students from around the country polish off projects they have been working on, usually for school, and send in a report to the Westinghouse Science Talent Search.

Simply entering the Westinghouse is an impressive achievement for a high school junior. It means that the student has completed a full-scale research project requiring hundreds of hours of thought and testing and has written up the work in a form suitable for a scientific journal. Students must also send in their grades, standardized test scores, recommendations from teachers, lists of their extracurricular activities, and personal statements, all of which help the judges evaluate the students' commitment to science.

The top 300 become semifinalists—a meritorious distinction itself. Eventually judges choose the forty national winners, who receive a five-day trip to Washington, D.C., where they display their projects under the rotunda of the National Academy of Science.

To the uninitiated, the exhibit looks like a crowded merchandise show. Forty booths are spread out around a cavernous hall, each with a young salesman aggressively pitching a product to a cluster of curious spectators. At one booth at the 1989 exhibit, Jordan Ellenberg, of Potomac, Maryland, is spritzing one-liners like a Borscht Belt comedian as he explains his whimsical mathematics project, "Investigation of k-ary n-tuples of Integers." He makes the inscrutable fun. At another booth, Erica Klarreich, of Brooklyn, New York, patiently answers questions about her biology project. Many of the questions are versions of questions she has already answered a dozen times, but she never loses her poise. Around the hall, there is the hubbub of excitement that genuine novelty always seems to arouse, a feeling in the air that trails are being blazed, that something is happening that will change the way Americans do things.

Indeed, there is novelty and innovation here, and what is being merchandised may one day change the way Americans live. But the exhibitors here are teenage high school students from eighteen different states and what they are hawking is knowledge, knowledge that they have created themselves at an age when most youngsters are having trouble simply absorbing the essential lessons of the past. Each of these forty winners has spent a year or two probing a scientific question, testing a theory, and then writing a scientific paper of near-professional quality. The topics alone testify to the remarkably advanced nature of their enterprises. "Radio Frequency Ion Beam Sputtering and Rapid Thermal Anneal," by Al Avestruz of the Bronx. "A Biomechanical Methodology Evidencing Bipedalism in Pterosaurs" by Rowan Lockwood of Rockford, Illinois. Their project reports have been weighed against 1,400 other entrants and have been deemed the most original and promising. Among them, the students will divide $140,000 in college scholarship money, with the largest amounts going to the ten projects selected as the best in the ultimate round of judging. (The prize total was raised starting with the fiftieth contest in 1991 to $205,000, with the top prize doubled to $40,000.)

The people who attend the annual Westinghouse exhibit are members of Washington's scientific and academic community. They have learned that the exhibit is not only a bellwether of scientific thought but a lively show of precocious intelligence. The students displaying projects here are the best and brightest America has to offer. There is something heady about being in their presence, a sense of promise and boundless possibility. They are, says Dr. Leon Lederman, the 1988 winner of the Nobel Prize in physics, "the nation's crown jewels," the ones whose future work will determine our stature as a country.

The contest's underlying philosophy is that students discover their scientific talents and prospects for a career in the field by *working* on science. Simply sitting in classrooms listening to lectures on science will not tell them much.

"You've got to do science in order to know," says Dorothy Shriver, a lively, silver-haired woman who has been with Westinghouse almost since the beginning and has become its unofficial historian. "If someone wants to play tennis, you give them a tennis racket. You don't give them a pen-and-pencil set."

The Westinghouse had its origins in the late 1930s in a short-lived science fair for New York City high school students operated by an organization called the American Institute of the City of New York. A member of that institute was G. Edward Pendray, an executive at Westinghouse in charge of advertising and public relations who had once been a science editor at the *New York Herald Tribune*. When the fair needed funds, Pendray, who had achieved a broad reputation for his writings on the possibilities of rocket power and space flight, pressed Westinghouse to furnish annual grants. The science fair was even housed for an entire season in the Westinghouse pavilion at the fondly remembered 1939 World's Fair in New York's Flushing Meadows. That was the World's Fair that featured the trilon and perisphere and exalted the ideal of scientific progress. (It is hard, in a world being gnawed away by crack, AIDS, and homelessness, to think of a similarly ingenuous theme for a contemporary fair. But then that world managed to live through World War II and still retain much of its optimism.)

At the fair, Pendray met Watson Davis, a science writer and civil engineer who directed Science Service, a nonprofit organization started by the Scripps-Howard newspapers that was devoted to popularizing the field of science and making scientific information more accessible to the public.

Somehow in the afterglow of the World's Fair, Pendray and

Davis decided to do something to beef up the teaching of science in the country. Both men lamented the fact that there were fewer than 1,000 trained science teachers in the nation's 25,000 high schools, and both felt that a national fair modeled on that of the institute's might call attention to the problem. Westinghouse agreed to put up the prize money and finance the administrative costs, and it commissioned Science Service to run the contest.

From the start, the Westinghouse was different from a traditional science fair. Its goal was not simply to choose the best projects but to locate the best potential scientists. The distinction is an important one. The Westinghouse has a number of features that test the mettle of the student as well as the project. It is, as its name announces, a science talent search, one that explores the nimbleness and originality of the minds behind the projects and does not just reward the boldness of the project.

Neither Pendray nor Davis was acquainted with the demands of the high school calendar and curriculum, and they hired Margaret Patterson, who had run the New York science fair for the American Institute, to be the housemother of the national program. Called in as a consultant was Morris Meister, the founding principal of Bronx Science, then a new public high school for talented boys who showed potential in science. The Patterson and Meister choices were fateful ones and were to shape the later history of Westinghouse in important ways. For though Westinghouse is based in Pittsburgh, the contest has always had a strong New York accent. With Bronx Science taking the lead, there soon arose among a dozen New York high schools the kind of rivalry that basketball may engender in Indiana or high school football in the South. Year after year, New York high schools such as Stuyvesant, Forest Hills, Erasmus Hall, Midwood, Jamaica, and Brooklyn Technical found themselves sparring over who could enter more students and produce more semifinalists and winners. Bronx Science became to science prizes what the Yankees once were to the World Series.

Along the way, several of the high schools evolved science programs that would develop the talent needed to win the contest. School officials set up their freshman and sophomore classes like minor-league teams and would scout prospects for the junior and senior classes who had the intelligence, character, and stamina to win Westinghouses.

In the contest's early days, many of those top New York youngsters were children of Jewish immigrants who had come to America from the ashes of Europe. Many of these immigrant families had lost entire families in the concentration camps. Alone, frightened, desperate to gain a secure foothold in the new land, they put enormous energy into their children, hoping the children would somehow redeem their own truncated lives. The children may have heard only a faltering English spoken in their homes, but they absorbed the drive and diligence to work on a scientific project. Many won. In the 1970s, as greater numbers of Jewish families realized dreams of success and many moved to the suburbs, fewer Jewish names appeared among the New York winners. Rather, many of the new winners were Asian, children whose parents had forsaken familiar villages or neighborhoods in Taiwan, China, India, Korea, Japan, had in some cases abandoned successful careers for menial jobs here, all so their children could seize the freedom and the opportunities available in America. These parents too were alone and frightened and they put enormous energy into their children. And these children too inherited the drive and commitment necessary to devote themselves to a major piece of scientific work.

Although the present New York City school system is, by many measures, a pale shadow of the system of the 1950s and 1960s, its fervor for the Westinghouse contest has not diminished. In 1989, Carol Luszcz, then program director of the Westinghouse Science Talent Search, told me that 44 percent of the entries in that year's contest—513 of the 1,461 entries—were from New York State, and most of those were from New York City. "So just in terms of statistics, it's reasonable they do well," she said.

There is nothing in the contest's rules or procedures that gives New York an advantage. Any other muncipality in the country could do as well if it put the effort that New York puts into the contest. The New York City Chancellor's Office has a liaison officer who encourages the competition. Every year, the board of education holds a reception at the Plaza Hotel for the city's cohort of winners and their teachers and parents that Luszcz describes as "a pep rally of sorts." The city's mayor personally honors students selected as winners.

As a result of New York's aggressive posture, a dozen New York high schools have historically dominated the contest. Of the 1,960 Westinghouse winners across the country between 1942 and 1990 (the last year such figures were tallied), the following schools ranked highest in numbers of winners and total scholarship earnings: Bronx Science, New York, 118 winners, $260,200; Stuyvesant, New York, 70 winners, $199,450; Forest Hills, New York, 42 winners, $70,950; Erasmus Hall, New York, 31 winners, $9,600; Evanston Township, Evanston, Illinois, 27 winners, $25,000; Benjamin N. Cardozo, New York, 25 winners, $44,250; Midwood, New York, 24 winners, $35,850; Jamaica, New York, 19 winners, $13,750; Martin Van Buren, New York, 16 winners, $14,850; Brooklyn Technical, New York, 14 winners, $27,050. Only Evanston High cannot be seen on a clear day from the top of the Empire State Building. (The anomalies in prize money reflect the fact that schools like Erasmus were big winners in the contest's early years when the prize money was smaller, but did not fare as well in later years.)

Sadly, contest officials say, there are thousands of students in the forty-nine other states who are just as bright and as capable as New York's students, but they simply are not aware that the contest exists. Every fall, Science Service mails a brochure describing the contest to every single public and private high school in the country, but many principals and guidance counselors are apparently throwing the booklets in the trash or deciding they do not have the time or inclination to rally their students. "We get calls from somebody out in the Midwest and they'll say, 'I asked my guidance counselor about this and they didn't know about it,'" says Luszcz. Only a few private schools like Phillips Exeter Academy in Exeter, New Hampshire (eight winners), and the Ramaz School, a Manhattan yeshiva (seven winners), have made vigorous efforts over the years to have their students enter the fray.

If science teachers at a given school are not alert to the value of the contest, they will not bother to encourage a student to apply. Few students are enterprising enough to undertake a project without some adult encouragement. Indeed, teachers play a crucial role in cultivating winners. Contest officials like Luszcz can tick off the names of science teachers at high schools that win consistently: Richard Plass at Stuyvesant, Marc Bellow at Benjamin Cardozo, Mephie Ngoi and Robert Horton at Evanston.

That more students do not take advantage of the contest is a shame, because the contest has had a major impact on science and math in this country, breeding Nobel laureates and MacArthur fellows, thirty scientists honored by election to the National Academy of Science, as well as thousands of scientists whose glory is just a shade dimmer. That is a remarkable record. The Westinghouses are given to children of roughly seventeen years of age, and yet these awards are effectively predicting triumphs achieved by fifty-year-old and sixty-year-old men and women. How many other measures of youthful athletic or intellectual achievement are as prophetic?

More impressive even than the awards garnered by Westinghouse winners are the solid careers so many former winners have achieved. In 1985 Westinghouse conducted a survey of the 1,760 previous winners and managed to get 58 percent to fill out extensive questionnaires about their education, careers, families, hobbies, and the like. The results were an astonishing portrait of success, as measured by the two-thirds who had earned doctorates or medical degrees.

Topping the list of schools turning out advanced degrees held by Westinghouse winners was Harvard, which produced 16 percent of the Ph.D.s and 18 percent of the M.D.s. Other schools that claimed large proportions of Ph.D.s were Massachusetts Institute of Technology, 8 percent; Princeton University, 7 percent; California Institute of Technology, 7 percent; University of California at Berkeley, 5 percent; and Yale University, 5 percent.

Many winners remained in academic life, with 27 percent reporting that their major source of income came from university teaching and 24 percent reporting that it came from university research. An additional 23 percent worked in private industry either as researchers or managers. Nine percent were doctors. The respondents felt good about their careers. When asked what was their most important achievement, 22 percent of the former winners cited a scientific discovery or development.

The survey was particularly instructive because it underscored the practical values of winning a Westinghouse. More than half the respondents—54 percent—said that winning an award helped them get into the college of their choice. Eleven percent received their undergraduate degree from Harvard, and most of the others went to similarly prestigious colleges. Winning a Westinghouse has one key shortcoming, however. It will not make you rich. Only 17 percent of the former winners had incomes larger than $75,000 per year, and 26 percent had annual incomes of less than $25,000.

For those who believe that the the kids most likely to win Westinghouses are monastic drudges whom no one would ever marry and who spend most of their free time haunting museums, the survey was also instructive. Fifty-eight percent of the respondents—and many were recent winners barely out of their teenage years—were married, and only 6 percent were divorced or separated. Twenty-two percent had two children, 14 percent had three children, 8 percent had one child, and another 8 percent had four or more children. Most said they watched television, exercised, listened to records, or spent time with friends at least once a week. Only 9 percent acknowledged visiting a museum once a week.

Surveys miss nuances, and interviews with former Westinghouse winners like Nina Tabachnik Schor corroborate the long-lasting value of the contest. Schor, originally of Queens, is a pediatric neurologist at Children's Hospital in Pittsburgh. She is studying tumorous brain tissue in children, trying to discover some feature of the cells that would make them an effective target for chemotherapy. She has synthesized compounds that she suggests act like chemical Trojan horses. The tumorous cells absorb these compounds thinking they are the neurotransmitter dopamine, but instead the cells find that the intruders interfere with their ability to replicate.

Schor is a soft-spoken and composed young woman who was pregnant with her first child when I interviewed her. She was the first-place winner of the 1972 Westinghouse for an examination of the effect of aldehydes, or car pollutants, on chlorophyll. It was a chic topic in those early days of environmental consciousness.

She remembers that long before the names of the top-ten winners were announced, photographers kept snapping her picture. She supposed that their interest was drawn by her brightly colored exhibit. She only began to suspect something was afoot when, she remembers with a laugh, she got a call from a reporter for the *Daily Forward*, a Yiddish newspaper with a large readership in Queens, who wanted to interview her for a profile. Though the winning youngsters had been kept in the dark, word of the top-ten winners had obviously been leaked to the press. When the names of the award winners were announced, she barely heard her name. "The gentleman sitting next to me basically shoved me on stage," she recalled.

Later that evening she called home. "My parents, my sister, and the dog started screaming all at once. It sounded like Grand Central Station." In the following weeks, strangers from across the country sent her clippings from their hometown newspapers about her award. "I got a very different view of human nature," she said. "People were so nice to do it. They really took an interest."

The $10,000 award she received paid half of her tuition for four years at Yale. But more important, she said, her research experience on the Westinghouse steered her into her career.

"There was a confirmation that research was something I could do with a modicum of success," she said. "There was the encouragement it gave me. 'Yes, I can do this.' It is appreciated by people. There are people who care enough to see that things would come to fruition, that young people interested in science weren't going to fall by the wayside."

The habit of persistence was to stay with her. She enrolled in a grueling seven-year program at Cornell Medical School and Rockefeller University that led to both an M.D. and a Ph.D. in biochemistry. That kind of commitment can seem infinite to most young men and women, and even to Schor it seemed interminable. During her residence in neurology she barely had time to eat or sleep, much less do the research for her doctorate in biochemistry. But, she said, she already possessed "the knowledge that there was light at the end of the tunnel." That was the residual power of her youthful immersion in a Westinghouse project.

"Without this background, I don't think I could have done it," she said.

Other successful Westinghouse winners tell similar tales. Roald Hoffman, the Nobel Prize–winning chemist at Cornell University, spoke in a 1988 interview with *U.S. News and World Report* of the value of winning his 1955 Westinghouse. "Through the Westinghouse Talent Search, I got my first job in science, a summer job at the National Bureau of Standards that introduced me to the joys of research. In fact, I saw just how addictive research can be. The natural high of solving problems in science is so great that you must watch yourself lest you be consumed by it."

Professional stature as a scientist, scientists will tell you, depends not just on intelligence and originality, but on being in the right place at the right time, when something exciting is going on in a particular field. Not every Westinghouse winner is guaranteed a stellar career of awards and newspaper articles. But gratification will not come at all without the ability to do first-class research.

"One reason why the contest has been so successful in picking future Nobelists," said Gott, "is that kids submit research projects. They have to write a research paper. It's a test of the qualities that are going to be required of them as scientists. . . . These kids have the capacity to do exciting research."

For some, winning has other corollary values, something best articulated to me by Andrew Gerber, a student at Brooklyn's Midwood High School who had an astonishingly mature bearing for a teenager. I spoke to him minutes after he learned that he had finished ninth in the 1989 contest. We were upstairs in a hotel lounge that winners were using to place calls to their families and teachers. The phones were tied up, so I took the occasion to lob some questions at him. What did he think the contest would mean to his later life?

With a broad self-possessed smile, he looked around the room and at the other winners with whom he had just spent five intense and often intimate days and said, "These are the future chairmen of physics departments and math departments around this country."

Although one could lament the fact that Gerber should be networking in so calculating a manner at so tender an age, wiser adults would have to concede that he was being shrewdly realistic.

Part II

The Schools: New York

Chapter Two

A Winning System

The Westinghouse is woven into Bronx Science legend the way that football is embedded into the lore of Ole Miss.

Students gossip about the prospects of classmates who are working on Westinghouse projects the way that students at other schools might gossip about the football team's chances next Saturday. They know who has made it to the top 300, who has cracked through to the top forty and won a trip to Washington, and who has put it all together to claim one of the ten top money prizes. They know how Science stacked up against Stuyvesant High School in Manhattan or Brooklyn Technical High School in Brooklyn. When I went back to Bronx Science's Bauhaus-spare building on a recent visit and saw, among the long rows of Westinghouse plaques, the plaque for 1962, my graduating year, the names Sheila Grinnell and Robert Strom were instantly familiar. I doubt I ever took a class with either of them or even spoke to them between classes. But yes, I remembered, they were the ones who won my year. I remembered that Sheila Grinnell was a tall, pretty, and remarkably poised girl. And I remembered that Robert Strom had not only won the Westinghouse but had several years before won big money on the television quiz show "The $64,000 Question." They were the football heroes of our school.

Bronx Science does as well as it does—120 winners through 1993, 50 percent more than any other school in the country—not because of the school spirit that can flourish in such a competitive atmosphere but because, like the top colleges in football, it has evolved a superb and winning system. That system selects some of the best students in New York, then teaches them to think scientifically and to perform high-quality research. In the freshman year, students are already enrolled in biology or chemistry, rather than earth science. By the sophomore year, the top achievers are taking honors biology or chemistry courses. By the junior year, the best students are spending the equivalent of a course working on research projects either at the school, or more likely, at a laboratory in one of the many teaching hospitals or universities in the city. Almost everyone who takes the junior-year research course submits a project to the Westinghouse Science Talent Search.

At the heart of the Bronx Science system is teaching and a philosophy of self-discovery that underlies it. While other schools fill their students with scientific facts, Bronx Science students are taught to think like scientists.

In a discussion over a lunch of tuna fish salad in the Bronx Science teachers' cafeteria, Carol Greene, director of biology projects, talked to me about the school's approach.

"Everything we do here for gifted students should be done for every kid because we emphasize the process of science, not the facts of science. In order for a student to understand the process, you have to do experimentation, and you have to encourage and nurture a questioning attitude. I've taken workshops with teachers from other parts of the country. Very often they are most interested in covering the curriculum. They will tell you, 'What you do is a good idea, but I can't do it while covering the curriculum.' Perhaps the higher-ups at those schools have to say, 'We won't hold you to the curriculum, we'd rather do other things.' "

Sit in on Don Lamanna's honors physics class and the Bronx Science approach becomes palpable.

Lamanna is in his mid-forties and looks and talks like Robert Duvall. Indeed, a thread of the street punk runs through his nasalized explanations of the elegant laws of physics; when a student gives a particularly discerning answer, he is likely to praise him by saying, "Beautiful!"

He has sharp eagle features and is balding at the forehead. One leg is longer than the other, giving him a pronounced limp, but he paces the classroom back and forth with the intensity of a Talmudic scholar mumbling paradoxes, breaking his stride only to catapult his arm up and scribble something on the board. What students see is a man who enjoys telling other people about the circuitous, whimsical, and clever pathways a scientist's mind may take.

On the day I visited, Lamanna, wearing brown suspenders and a green tie, was standing at the front of an upward-sloping lecture room before a tall laboratory desk, on the countertop of which sat three ordinary brown bags.

"Here are three lunch bags that I collected during the break," he said, his smile apologizing for the mundane illustration he was starting off with. "For the purposes of this lesson you can pretend we have 100 lunch bags. Now, there are a few things we know about these lunch bags. You cannot touch them, you cannot see through them. You can only weigh them. Each one has a certain number of marbles randomly put in. All the marbles are identical. Can you devise an experiment using only a triple beam balance to find the mass of one marble?"

"Weigh all the bags," a student promptly suggests.

"You read ahead," Lamanna jibes back.

In fact, the student has figured that by weighing each of the bags, common denominators will emerge that can reveal the weight of a single marble. And the data Lamanna provides—39 grams for one bag, 24 for a second, 13 for a third, 5 for a fourth, and so on—reveal that the only reasonable common denominator, assuming the identical marbles had been randomly thrown into the bags, is 1. If a single marble's weight were .5 grams, he points out, there would probably have been some odd decimal-place numbers in the data.

"If this is the data you get for 100 bags, you can be reasonably sure of the weight of one marble even though you have not seen one marble."

Of course, Lamanna is not teaching this class how to weigh marbles. "What's the purpose of this experiment?" he asks. "It's to show you the thinking process used by a famous American physicist, Robert Millikan."

Millikan, who lived from 1868 to 1953, won the 1923 Nobel Prize for his measurement of the charge of an electron. What made Millikan's discovery in his laboratory at the University of Chicago similar to the students' discovery of the mass of a single marble is that electrons are as invisible as the marbles in the brown paper bag. Yet Millikan was able indirectly to derive their charge in a manner similar to the way the students deduced the weight of a single marble. He measured the charge of hundreds of oil drops and found a formula that was a common denominator.

Another teacher might have simply laid out the history of Millikan's famous oil-drop experiment, drawing Millikan's special box with its electrodes, its oil-drop atomizer, its eyepiece. Lamanna is doing that, but he is also trying to show students how Millikan thought, or better still, have them think through the problem of an electron's charge in the same way that Millikan did.

He asks them about the various forces acting on Millikan's oil drop and elicits the formulas for those forces. He points out that Millikan finally noticed that all his measurements of oil drops were a multiple of 1.6×10^{-19} coulombs. (A coulomb is a unit of electric charge.) That figure, then, also the common denominator, was the charge of a single electron. The class has come full circle, and as if on cue, the bell rings. A perfect lesson, all the more perfect because the students, with considerable guidance from Lamanna, have figured out Millikan's experiment as if they were Millikan working in his Chicago lab. They have learned science by solving a problem in science.

Carol Greene uses a similar approach in teaching a freshman class about the nervous system in vertebrates, how it functions as two distinct systems, one automatic and involuntary and one subject to willful control. The talk is heavy with words like cytons, neurons, synapses, dendrites. Greene, with a maternal smile, calls a handsome boy with a punk haircut up to the front of the room, has him sit on a table, and taps his knee, demonstrating his knee-jerk reflex. She traces the path of a sensory neuron—from the dendrites to the cyton—by skimming her fingers along the boy's leg to his back. The impulses, she says, are not only going from the spinal cord to the leg muscles; they are also traveling from the spinal cord to the brain. The boy, after all, is mentally aware that his knee is being touched.

"How can we demonstrate that the reflex is not dependent on the brain?" she asks.

"We can separate the spinal cord from the brain," a young girl volunteers.

"Yes, and that can be done using a frog." She shows a picture of a headless frog hanging from a bar. "This was done before animal-rights groups," she jokes. "It's called a spinal frog. It has no intact brain but it does have a spinal cord. If a little bit of acid is scrubbed on its torso, the frog makes a scratching motion. But it's got no brain. How is that possible? Describe what must be happening."

Several arms quickly shoot up (inadvertently demonstrating the lightning speed of the students' own nervous systems).

"The motor neuron transmits an impulse down to the leg muscle and when the impulse arrives at the leg muscle it contracts," a student answers. The answer is correct, but Greene politely suggests that one step has been missed. Before the leg muscle can be told to contract, the sensory neuron in the skin must alert the spinal cord to the acid's presence.

Greene has revealed important details about the experiment's design—the use of a spinal frog, the acid on the torso—but she has gotten the students to propose the experiment's fundamental strategy—the separation of the brain from the spinal cord—and she has gotten the students to explain how the process works. In other words, she has asked them to approach the problem the way it might have been approached by the scientists who proved that the two nervous systems are separate. She has gotten the students to think like scientists.

The sensibilities and habits that are picked up through the Lamanna and Greene teaching methods endure for a lifetime, become a mental discipline that helps students tackle the world. This distinctive Bronx Science approach did not simply evolve willy-nilly. The school has always enticed the city's finest teachers, some of whom instinctively understood the most effective approaches to teaching science. But in the 1970s, these approaches were systematically shared with the entire science faculty. In the post-Sputnik angst over how badly America was trailing the Soviet Union in science, the school was given a federal grant of $40,000 a year for three years. The money paid for the school's teachers to meet regularly and discuss their goals in teaching science and the methods they could use to best accomplish their aims. The sessions continued after the grant ran out, persisting for ten years even through a New York City fiscal crisis that cut high school budgets by 11 percent. With many inadequately paid teachers taking second jobs after school, the sessions were eventually abandoned. There is some fear that after the current generation of teachers retires, the approaches that evolved may wither. Nevertheless, they are still deeply embedded throughout the school and can be seen in a range of classes.

"At some point," explains Vincent Galasso, the school's principal and a former chairman of the biology department, "we made a conscious decision that students would go into independent research. Then we asked ourselves what can we do to create that." The approach that evolved, he said, is "more open-ended." It forces students to do some "brainstorming" within the lesson.

"It's not just looking at a slide and examining different kinds of tissue, or looking at an example of vegetative repoduction where once it's done, you're not looking to find out anything more about it. Our approach promotes further activity. We don't spoon-feed. We have kids devise as much of the experiment as possible. The student has a say in what's going on. There's more decision making and the more involved he or she is, the higher-level learning that's taking place."

Problems are thrown out and students are asked to solve them, to explore questions raised by a set of facts, to wonder and inquire. They are asked to look at a situation from a variety of perspectives. Each suggestion is valued. The learning is active, not passive. Children discover for themselves the workings of biology by looking at the quantitative data they come up with in the laboratory; the data, not the teacher, yield a solution to a problem. What is the metabolism rate in a germinating pea? Place the pea in a corked vial attached to a pipette filled with water. Measure the volume of water that is displacing the air the pea takes in. "That will be an assay to the amount of oxygen used," says Galasso, using a fancy word for measure.

"You could put it on the board in one sentence," he says. "But having students do it and do the thinking involved, that's where we're ahead of other schools. We're more willing to take chances. Maybe there's not one right answer."

Even at many good schools, teachers have fallen into set ways of doing things. No one has come along to convince them that another way may be better. Moreover, many schools may not have the luxury of choosing among approaches. With a shortage of science teachers, science and math are often being taught by licensed English and social studies teachers.

Bronx Science's commitment to excellence is not just evident in the science research program, but it can be found throughout the school, in ways large and small.

A small example came at a class I encountered at lunchtime. As they do every day, a dozen students were gathered together with teacher Robert Saenger and were eating their lunch out of brown paper bags while working on a math problem scrawled on the board.

"If the integer K is added to each of the numbers 36, 300, 596, one obtains the square of three consecutive terms of an arithmetic sequence. Find K."

These students, among the school's most talented in math, would rather spend their lunchtime playing with numbers than gossiping in the cafeteria about teachers or classmates. The school not only lets them use their lunch to work on math, but it even provides a teacher to help them.

The school offers college-credit courses in English, American history, and art history. In languages, the school not only offers French and Spanish, but Japanese, Chinese, and Latin. Japanese has been taught at the school by Keiko Hirano since 1982, some time before the American obsession with the Japanese economic rise. She has sixty-five students, and one of them has a precocious understanding of why she has elected to study the language. "I want to go into business," says Giselle Davila. "The Japanese are dominating business and so I feel I could compete with them."

Still, Bronx Science's most impressive offerings are in science: advanced courses in biology, chemistry, physics, calculus. They make Bronx Science what it is. The school does not just offer these courses; it offers them in the Bronx Science way, requiring students to immerse themselves in the laboratory. Students perform experiments that have tiny tolerances for error so that precise, careful measurements are essential. They learn to make statistical adjustments by calculating the standard deviations and they can determine whether errors, anomalies, or disparities are due to their technique or to random variation.

"We teach them how you tell whether it's random or something I'm doing wrong," said Greene. "If it's random it's not as important and can be minimized by doing averages. That's why scientists are always averaging results."

They work on basic pieces of equipment like the hemocytometer—a device for measuring the number of cells in a sample of blood. In biology, they work on such common test populations as yeast, bacteria, and slime molds. They do a bioassay, a process that measures quantities of a chemical by its effect on a biological process. (A minuscule and elusive amount of hormone, for example, can be measured by its impact on the rate of growth of a plant.) They learn how to count cells. What the school calls "hands-on lab experience" mirrors real scientific experience, procedurally and intellectually.

Finally, students are given some realistic philosophical approaches to their work. "We try to breed in a certain amount of skepticism," said Greene. "We show them how you can play with numbers. It makes them alert to the fact that it can be done."

Greene's springtime class in how to conduct a bioassay offers a quick sense of why Bronx Science churns out so many scientists and Westinghouse winners. It is the morning's first class and eleven students straggle in, with several yawning away the patina of sleepiness. Greene begins by showing the class a small plant and asking why its leaves will grow toward the window.

"It receives more light from photosynthesis," answers a girl named Cheryl.

"You're not the first people to have noticed this," Greene responds. "Charles Darwin and his son, Francis, did." And she writes the lesson's aim on the board: "How does the plant grow toward the source of the light?"

Darwin, curious about the mechanism that caused plants to grow toward light, cut off the tip of an oat coleoptile—the young shoot of the germinating grass seed. The remaining plant did not grow toward the light, leading him to conclude that the tip had something to do with the light.

"But someone might say you mangled that poor coleoptile," she teases. How then can a more solid connection be made between light and the growth of the coleoptile tip?

"Put a little cover of tinfoil on the tip!" suggests one student.

"Seth, that's a good idea, but Darwin thought of it first."

Through questioning like this, the class discovers that the tip is essential to a plant's growth toward the light and that it is the tip that interacts with the light. Greene moves on to the 1911 experiments of the Danish plant physiologist Peter Boysen-Jensen, who proved that a chemical messenger was involved in growth toward the light. He was able to do this by putting pieces of gelatin between one set of tips and their shoots and putting pieces of mica between another set of tips and their shoots. The gelatin permitted the chemical to pass; the mica did not. Where precisely the mica was placed was also important. Mica inserted on the shady side blocked growth toward the light, indicating that the chemical was active on the shady side.

Eventually, students discover that a growth hormone, an auxin, is involved in the coleoptile's growth, and that light has an inhibiting effect on the auxin. The tip of the plant releases auxin to the side opposite the light and that side grows faster than the side facing the light.

Everything the students have learned so far has been geared toward understanding why plant growth can be used to measure quantities of a chemical, in this case an auxin formally called indole-acetic acid, or IAA. In the following week, students will be given a dark-brown bottle with a solution containing an unknown quantity of IAA and asked to find the concentration. They can do that by measuring the effect the solution has on the growth of tipless coleoptiles and compare that growth to the effect of a known concentration of IAA on coleoptiles. The amount of plant growth is directly related to the amount of IAA.

"You remember in the San Francisco gold rush, prospectors would run into the assay office." Greene says. "What were they doing there?" A student replies that they were measuring the amount of gold they had mined. Well, Mrs. Greene suggests, the

experiment they will be doing is a bioassay, a measuring of a substance through its biological impact. The lesson has come to an
elegant close.

For an elite group of students, lessons such as the one on the
bioassay are all designed to converge on what will be the apex of
their Bronx Science experience—the junior-year project. Actually,
the students start in the sophomore year by selecting a project and
continue into the senior year when they submit a research paper
to the Westinghouse contest.

Even in selecting a project, the students get help. Teachers
are aware that even the most avid aspiring scientists need to be
carefully steered away from wild and unrealistic flights of the imagination and toward a subject worth spending perhaps two years on.
The biology department produces a "Guide for Selecting a Biology
Project." It states very early: "Finding a problem which can be
answered is sometimes the hardest part of the experiment. The
best problems are those which come from your own interests." It
suggests that students think about features of their own lives: aller-
gies or inherited traits like color blindness that might stimulate a
research idea. It suggests conversations with professional scientists, urges that students be alert to unanswered questions that
develop in class, and points out that organizations like the National
Science Teachers Association and Science Service publish lists of
titles of already completed projects that can inspire worthwhile
spinoffs.

Given the caliber of students at Bronx Science, the problems
the school often deals with are not ones of indolence but of over-
arching ambition and perfectionism. Those are traits that can defeat
good research as readily as laziness. So the school finds itself training students to accept mistakes.

"We don't want them to know too much," said Greene. "We
want them to make mistakes because that's part of the process.
Kids have to recognize that there doesn't have to be a right answer,
because if you feel there's got to be a right answer you're going
to be narrow in how you approach things. It's much freer, more
open. You have to be more willing to take risks. If you think an

existing idea is the only idea, then knowledge would never progress."

After picking an idea, students elect a junior-year projects class. Classes are small—no more than fifteen students. The school tries to run the program with a light touch. Its teachers are aware that students who are pushed into the rigors of scientific research will recoil.

"We've institutionalized that in our program," said Greene. "We tell them this is really a no-risk proposition. They can sign up for a bio project and start out the junior year and if they see there's going to be a problem, they don't have to stick with it."

Increasingly, students are doing their projects outside the school, at laboratories and hospitals. In fact, in recent years, few, if any, biology projects have been done within the confines of the school. Bronx Science may be one of the best-equipped science schools in the country, but even its equipment is simply too constricting for the complexity of projects students are now undertaking. Many are on the cutting edge of contemporary research.

Teachers at Bronx Science have long lists of hospitals, universities, and mentors who have worked with their students in the past. However, the school encourages its students to find mentors and laboratories on their own. Greene believes the search process tests the students' commitment and persistence and quickly determines if a student is really serious about spending a full year on a single project.

"Having kids look for a placement weeds out those who won't stay with it," she said. Those students who "can be turned away by ten or twelve people and keep going" are the students who will keep going at a project when a month's work is wiped out by the sudden death of a bacteria culture or when early results appear to defy a working hypothesis.

Laura McEneaney, sixteen, of Rego Park, Queens, chose the topic of her junior-year project out of a desire to cure the ailment that has plagued her mother. Her mother suffers from Crohn's disease, a chronic inflammation of the bowel that produces nausea, diarrhea, and severe and constant pain. There is a belief that Crohn's disease is an autoimmune response in which the body produces antibodies against its own cells.

"I heard about the Westinghouse, and I wanted to do something to help Mom at the same time," said Laura, a quiet, deliberate girl.

Laura started her search for a mentor with a tip from her mother, who read that Dr. Daniel Present was an expert on Crohn's disease. "Call him up," her mother urged. Present urged her to speak to Dr. Daniel Mayer of Mt. Sinai Medical Center, who has been working with multiple sclerosis, also an autoimmune disease. Mayer agreed to take Laura on, and in her junior year, Laura was using antibodies to stain epithelial cells taken from Mt. Sinai patients. She was trying to understand what mechanism in the cells allowed them to recognize foreign proteins. It was only a tiny part of the battle to cure her mother's disease, but it is through the accumulation of such small bits of research that most cures have been found.

Julie Tsai, seventeen, of the Bayside section of Queens, decided, after a summer course in molecular biology, that she wanted to work on the frontiers of DNA research. An article about DNA research mentioned Rockefeller University prominently, so she called up Rockefeller and, pretending she was applying, asked a worker to send her a catalogue of the school's research programs. The harmless ruse yielded a list of the names of scientists who were working in the specific area that intrigued her—the regulation of certain genes by other genes. The chairman of Rockefeller's molecular biology department gave her the names of three scientists who might be willing to take on a high school student. The first one she spoke with called her in for an interview and was so impressed that he enlisted her in his research.

In his junior year, Jeff Haspel, seventeen, of Park Slope in Brooklyn, worked on the twentieth floor of Mt. Sinai Medical Center with transgenic mice—mice that have had a foreign gene transplanted into a set of their own chromosomes. The technique was less than a decade old and Jeff worked with one of the top scientists in this new field. When we met, Jeff's talk was full of such up-to-the-minute neologisms as cloning vector, lower band plasmic DNA, genetic mapping, microinjection. Jeff, however, did not get to the transgenic mice lab through the hospital's familiar route for students, the volunteer office. Instead, he decided to take an elevator straight to the hospital's reproductive science department on the twentieth floor. There he found a scientist and explained his quest.

"Have I got a guy for you," he recalls she told him.

The guy was Dr. John Gordon, producer of the first transgenic mouse and a man who, Jeff says, needed an extra pair of hands in his lab.

Joseph Kubler, sixteen, of Whitestone, Queens, found his adviser on a field trip to the Museum of Natural History. Dr. Peter Moller, of the museum's ichthyology department, was working with momara fish, a species that emits an electric charge and has an uncanny ability to respond to electrical fields in the water. Working Saturdays in Moller's laboratory, Joseph exposed the fish to a magnetic field and tried to teach the fish to swim north and south, all the while using a computer to keep track of the momara's electrical discharges. While he worked on his own project, Joseph also pitched in on such chores as cleaning the fish tank and taking dead fish out. Moller, Joseph says, decided "I'd work for him and he'd help me."

It took enormous courage for Julie Tsai and Jeff Haspel and Joseph Kubler to take on institutions as daunting as Rockefeller and Mt. Sinai. After all, they are in their teenage years—that awkward period of murky identity. To get themselves seen and heard and finally placed inside also required some old-fashioned chutzpah, a trait that increasingly seems to go along with success in science.

Mentoring them was not an easy proposition. Mentoring takes time. Mentors have to acquaint students with their laboratories, show them how to perform the often delicate operations central to that laboratory's experiments. They may have to talk through the student's project, pointing out weaknesses in logic or overly ambitious designs. They have to trust the students with the keys to the laboratory, with expensive equipment and chemicals. (A single drop of the enzyme that Julie Tsai was working with costs $55.) Every few weeks, the mentor has to fill out an evaluation form that charts the student's progress.

Why do the mentors do it? Some mentors take on students as a way of paying their field back for the help they received when they were on the way up. There is also a benefit in having a fresh, unspoiled, unjaded eye look at their projects.

"Sometimes your ignorance leads you to ask questions that they have not seen," said Greene. "You're not hampered by all the things you're supposed to know."

The institutions also encourage mentoring, she said, because they're concerned about the decline in young people entering pure research.

To undertake their projects, the students have to take crash courses in the fields they are researching. For her project on Crohn's disease, Laura McEneaney had to read a textbook on immunology and attended classes on immunology at Mt. Sinai's Medical School. During the summer, she took a course in the laboratory methods used in immunology. She learned how to count cells, how to culture cells.

"Immunology is a new science," she said. "They know almost nothing about it."

The students also have to learn the politics of the science establishment, about the need to publish and renew grants. At the same time, they also have to play politics within their own school and cope with English and French teachers upset about overdue homework. Most important, they have to learn how to handle their own frustrations, of test animals dying in the laboratory, of results that don't live up to predictions.

"They call it character-building experience," said Jeff Haspel. "I had a month where nothing worked out." But Jeff and the other students say they like the feeling of being part of the adult world of research. "We're giving the impression that we can be something better than a candy striper volunteer in a hospital where the expectation is that it's all over their heads," he said. "Here you can be an individual and ask questions and do just about anything."

Jeff, whose mother is a microbiologist and who grew up around microbiologists, was fascinated to discover how researchers seem to plan their day around the one indulgence of lunch, however long their working hours.

Eventually, the students who undertake projects have to move from the laboratory to the typewriter or word processor. The classic research paper starts with an "Introduction" that reviews the relevant literature and offers a rationale for the project. The paper then details the "Methods and Materials" used. It describes the "Results" of the experiment, with charts of the data collected. It concludes with a "Discussion" of the significance of the findings and how they firm up or invalidate the experiment's hypothesis. For the junior-year-project students, a preliminary paper is due sometime in June, and the final paper in September of the senior year.

"No paper is written without many drafts," Greene says. She encourages the students to discuss their projects with her. "If they can't communicate it to me, then they don't understand it."

It should be noted that the basic form for a research paper is also the basic form for a doctoral dissertation. If students can confidently leap this hurdle as high school teenagers, it seems a fair bet that they will have far less trouble leaping this hurdle a second time in their late twenties or early thirties as doctoral students.

The Westinghouse entry, which is roughly 2,000 words, is usually an adaption of the projects class research paper. It is a measure of the passion and frenzy at Bronx Science about the Westinghouse that, in 1993, thirty-seven of the thirty-nine students working on biology projects entered the Westinghouse. (The school as a whole had eighty entries in the 1993 contest.)

Greene, who is in charge of biology projects, has turned out an average of one Westinghouse winner every year since 1979. In 1990, Julie Tsai and Jeff Haspel and Laura McEneaney did not win, but their classmate in Greene's projects class, Johannes Sebastian Schlondorff, was named a winner for the research he did on cell motility at the Albert Einstein College of Medicine. But Greene is not the kind of teacher who is an unalloyed cheerleader. She has given much thought to what she is doing in sponsoring Westinghouse researchers, and while choosing to support the program, she has some gnawing misgivings.

She has tried in recent years to tell students that projects are performed for their own value, not for the Westinghouse. The Bronx Science program is a research program, not a Westinghouse program, she emphasizes. Greene even likes to tell students that "the Westinghouse application is so daunting a process that if you even enter the Westinghouse that's an accomplishment." She encourages the juniors just starting their projects to throw a party for the seniors before the year's Westinghouse winners are announced. The point is to let the seniors know that the Westinghouse will not be the only reward for their efforts. Greene even thinks the school should change the name of the "Westinghouse English" class to "Research Writing."

"This program is a research program," she said. "It's not a training camp for Westinghouse winners."

Still, it is obvious that she struggles with the tensions implicit in her view. The school, after all, is aware that the Westinghouse contest is a nationally known arena that wins the acclaim needed to draw the interest of scientists and the money that enriches Bronx Science's programs. It is those programs that continue to attract the city's best students. The challenge for the school is striking the proper balance between emphasizing the pure pleasure of research and the glory of the Westinghouse.

"We involuntarily fell into a trap," Greene said in her candid lunchtime interview. "We had kids who are ambitious and motivated and they won Westinghouse awards, but that was never the intention. That's my pet peeve. If they are in a project class, I tell them, 'If you are here just to do a Westinghouse, you shouldn't be here. You have to feel you want to do research. We are not a Westinghouse mill. You're doing research, not doing the Westinghouse.' "

"It is not a training camp for Westinghouse winners," she continued. "It would exacerbate a situation. What happens to the kids who don't win? It's as if they invested time for nothing."

Students, Greene feels, should want to do research for the pleasures and satisfactions of research. Material reward is not a sufficient spur for scientific research because, in the real world, the rewards are small, and in a system often dependent on government and foundation grants, scientists are always struggling simply to support themselves.

"There are kids who will say, 'I'm not going into science because of the grant problem. I don't want to be fending for my pay every two or three years.' If kids are pushed into it and the motivation is not there, they can be turned off."

"The Westinghouse is well known," Greene continued. "If the

school scores well, its good for P.R. We've produced this winner, therefore we must have a good science program. There's a competition among schools who want to retain gifted kids, and in science, if you're providing a program that will give kids research opportunities, there's only one way to demonstrate credibility and that's by turning out winners.

"But there's a negative side. I sometimes wonder if we're not walking a tightrope between providing something beneficial to kids and exploiting them."

She told of a student, one of the school's brightest, "who happens not to be interested in doing a Westinghouse next year, but his parents feel he should" and believe he should enroll in a junior projects class.

She does not want to exploit him just for the school's glory, and she explains what the dangers are. A student who wants to undertake a research project must have a single-mindedness that will enable him or her to work on the same project day after day for much of two years. The student must be willing to turn down the seductions of television or friends or a neighborhood stickball game, must be able to cope with the frustration of seeing the project's rats or insects perish before the results are in, must be able to start from scratch if necessary. Until a student is mature enough to do this, she believes, pushing that student into research is counterproductive.

"If I were really manipulative," she said, "I could get the kid to take that class, but he's not ready to do it. He may become a research scientist, but if I take him too young, I might ruin it for him."

Chapter 3

A Tree Grows in Brooklyn

David Kiefer conducts his class like an orchestra. Taut, controlled, his burly shoulders rising in an agony of anticipation, he squeezes information from his students as if he were drawing a poignant adagio from a violin section. If a response is slightly off-key, his face seems anguished. There is a sense that any graver error might unravel him. But when a student hits just the right note, just the right sharpness of phrasing, he smiles and lets out an exhalation of deep relief.

Kiefer is a master teacher and his relish in his craft is almost palpable. He came to love his work during a three-year stint in the Peace Corps teaching math to Kenyan children, and the satisfaction was so great that he relinquished a budding career as a chemical engineer so he could teach in the New York City public school system.

"I enjoy the skills of putting things as simply and as systematically as possible," he says. "No matter what it is in my life, I enjoy communicating to people in a simple and systematic way."

Kiefer has now been a teacher for almost a quarter century, and the course he is now teaching is among the most gratifying of his career. He teaches a ninth-grade class in research. Not biology, not chemistry, but research. His high school, Midwood High School in Brooklyn, New York, is one of a small but growing number of schools around the country that have been focusing many of their traditional science courses on laboratory techniques. Midwood, however, is distinctive even in this rarefied world for offering this freshman course devoted entirely to the stringencies and skills of scientific investigation. The course helps explain why Midwood, a school that would ring few bells of recognition even in New York City, produced forty-three semifinalists and six finalists in the five Westinghouse contests between 1989 and 1993. Still, all such programs ultimately come down to what happens between a teacher and the students in a classroom. And what happens between Kiefer and his students could serve as a model for most of the nation's classrooms, and not just those in science.

The class I observe one morning is learning about the pendulum. The thirty or so fourteen- and fifteen-year-olds squeezed into a front quarter of the lab have spent an earlier period timing the swings of the pendulum while changing variables like the weight of the bob, the length of the string, and the angle of the swing's arc. They have come up with certain data and are reporting that data to Kiefer.

But this class is something of a ruse. Kiefer does not really care whether the students learn the precise mechanics of the pendulum. He wants his students to learn how to conduct research.

"Whenever we do a lab," he explains to me later, "my interest is not in the pendulum. We try to milk it for all we can—controlled experiments, writing hypotheses, analysis of data, graphing. These are very important skills that are often rushed over. We expect a Regents teacher to squeeze it in and it's not possible." (Regents is an informal name for the more exacting curricula prescribed in a variety of subjects by the New York State Board of Regents, the state's chief educational body. Knowledge of this content is tested in a semiannual rite of passage known as the Regents exams, and too many teachers spend too much of their time teaching to the test, leaving little time for such luxuries as controlled experimentation.)

Kiefer, in his late forties, has the build of a police officer. Wide-shouldered, barrel-chested, he has gray hair that is thinning at the top, a florid complexion with prominent rosy cheeks and alert blue eyes. He begins by asking the students, most of whom are fourteen years old, to list ways that data can be analyzed. The simplest method, a student suggests, is casually inspecting the data and looking for a revealing pattern. A second method is graphing the data and looking for a telling shape in the graph—a flat line indicating constancy of effect, a rising line indicating that one factor increases with the growth of another.

"When a scientist looks at a graph it's not just pretty," Kiefer says. "It contains links, connections."

A third method suggested by a student is an analysis that uncovers a mathematical relationship. If, when x is 1, y equals 6, and when x is 34, y equals 204, then y is 6 times x. Such mathematical relationships, Kiefer notes, produce formulas, and scientists, he confides, love formulas. "If scientists can have a formula that gives a general result, they jump for joy," he says.

Kiefer asks students to gaze at the data they have gathered and come up with a reasonable hypothesis. He demands that they state their hunch clearly and thoroughly yet without excess verbiage, so, as he puts it, "If your grandmother saw this, what would she say?" The grandmother test is his rough gauge for clarity and simplicity, and he gently corrects several hypotheses offered by students as being too general or too narrow, wordy, or imprecise. The students finally reach a consensus on the wording of one proposition: "If the length of the string is increased then the number of swings in a given length of time will decrease."

They begin a more meticulous analysis of their data. They realize, for example, that changing the arc did not have an effect on the duration of the swing. When they increased the angle that the pendulum covered from 10 degrees to 30 degrees to 50 degrees, the number of swings in 55 seconds remained at roughly 43.5, and the length of time of each swing, or the period, stayed constant at 1.3 seconds. The students graph their data, where x is the angle and y is the period—the number of seconds per swing—and they come up with a flat line, again indicating that the period remains constant, no matter how the angle changes. They conclude, in these two methods of analyzing data, that "the angle does not affect the period."

But in doing that graph students pick up some fundamental scientific tools. They learn that the angle is the independent variable on the graph, and the period the dependent variable, dependent, that is, on alterations of the angle. That is an important lesson that transcends pendulums and applies to graphs the students will be doing throughout their careers at Midwood and, for a few, throughout their professional lives in science. They also learn about choosing a meaningful scale for a graph, and how many decimal places would yield significant information. Again, that lesson transcends pendulums.

Finally, they begin to learn how to articulate a scientific finding clearly. They study data one student collected on what happens when the length of the pendulum string increases.

Length (centimeters)	9	10	20	30	40	60	80	90
Period (seconds per swing)	0.64	0.67	0.96	1.1	1.3	1.5	1.8	1.9

Changing the string's length does influence the number of seconds per swing, the period. But how does one state the nature of that influence mathematically? The students realize from the data that doubling the length of the pendulum does not double the period of a swing, and tripling the length does not triple the period of the swing. With Kiefer prodding, the students struggle to define what is going on in the relationship between length and period, but they come to realize that the relationship is more complex mathematically than they first imagined. Kiefer wants them to be as precise as possible in their definition and he even teases them: "You can't go around saying, 'Grandma, if you make it twice as long, it doesn't take twice as long.'"

There is a long pause while students think, but time has run out. "Something deeper is going on inside the data and you'll have to wait until Monday to know what the secret link is," Kiefer says just before the bell rings, providing a teasing coda to a masterfully conducted lesson.

Kiefer's class is not a class many American college-bound high school students are likely to take. But Midwood regards scientific research as so important it is willing to structure an entire academic program around it. Midwood offers the class to 300 out of its 600 entering ninth-grade students. They take the five-period class in addition to a "regular" honors biology course of six periods a week, which means that as freshmen they are taking an extraordinary eleven periods of science a week.

These are the students in Midwood's medical science magnet

program, which started sixteen years ago and has been the key to its survival as a top-flight school in the heart of inner-city Brooklyn. Students from all over Brooklyn, and some from other boroughs, apply to attend this selective program. (Midwood also has a similar magnet program in the humanities, and perhaps a third of Midwood's enrollment is made up of students for whom Midwood is the neighborhood school.) The program's mission is fundamentally educational. Midwood's teachers and administrators, like their counterparts at the Bronx High School of Science, believe that early training in the methods, philosophy, and ethics of research is likely to produce scientists or, at least, people who appreciate the culture of science. The habits of mind students take away from Midwood will serve them well through college, graduate school, and even in their professional work.

But it would be Pollyannaish not to say that the research portion of the medical science program also has a baldly expedient, even self-serving goal. It is calculated to win the school a few Westinghouses every year. In its way, Midwood's research program resembles the vaunted sports program in East Germany before the collapse of that country's Communist regime. East Germany regularly earned far more Olympic medals than might be expected from a country of its size and economic power. It did so largely by exposing as many of its citizens as possible to the athletic skills that were being tested in competition, then focusing inordinate training time and money on those who showed the greatest promise. Indeed, in New York, the race for the Westinghouse has all the feel of an Olympic competition. Principals at top academic high schools measure each other by how many Westinghouses they produce.

Why would a contest sponsored by a private company be taken so seriously? For one thing, in the rather small club of hard-driving academic high schools, the Westinghouses are a rather compact gauge of excellence. Comparing numbers of students with averages above ninety may tell more about lenient grading practices than about teaching. Comparing numbers of students scoring over 1400 on their Scholastic Aptitude Tests (SATs) says more about the quality of students admitted than the performance of the staff. But winning Westinghouses is testimony to the quality of a research program a principal has put together for his or her school's brightest students.

Midwood, which is fifty years old, is located in the Flatbush section of Brooklyn right outside the campus of Brooklyn College. It is housed in a plain five-story brick building whose only distinguishing touch is a belvedere. The blocks surrounding the school are middle- and working-class, with many single-family houses and some co-op apartments filled with Jewish, Italian, and black families, including those of a number of Brooklyn College professors. But the school's zone reaches far beyond these prim blocks and takes in large stretches of rundown housing filled with poor black and Hispanic families.

Had Midwood chosen to draw its students strictly from its geographical zone, it would have started out with a student body that was 80 percent black and Hispanic. If the experience of most other Brooklyn high schools held true, the minority of whites and Asians would have vanished within a few years. Instead, Midwood draws its students from all over the borough through the "magnet" of its medical science program, and it has retained a stable population that in the 1988–89 school year was 44.3 percent white, 37.6 percent black, 9.4 percent Hispanic, and 8.7 percent Asian.

Unlike students chosen for Bronx Science or Stuyvesant High School, Midwood's medical science students are not selected through an entrance exam. They are picked on the basis of their marks in junior high school, their reading scores, and other indicators of achievement. Bright students whose behavior or attendance is erratic are screened out; the school does not have time to bother. Administrators also seek a healthy racial mix. Midwood gets many students who pass the entrance exam for Stuyvesant or Brooklyn Technical High School, two selective schools a modest subway ride away. But these students decide they would just as soon stay in the neighborhood if they can have an education on par with that offered at the selective schools.

In the first half of the freshman year, the 300 students in the medical science program meet five periods a week for "Science Research Methods," the course Dave Kiefer was teaching when I visited. A look at Kiefer's course outline (with a few explanatory additions on my part) gives a flavor of how many skills and concepts fundamental to research the course covers.

Orientation
Frequency tables [how frequently objects, phenomena, etc., occur]
Frequency graphs, bar and line
Systems of measurement
Length
Errors in measurement
Scale reading
Precision, reliability
Significant digits [to what decimal places measurements
    should be taken]
Rules for rounding off
Accuracy, percent error
Solid-volume measurement
Triple-beam balance
Lab report format
Solid-density lab
Report #1 due
Writing a scientific paper
Density
Liquid-density lab [measuring density of liquids]
Analysis of data
Graphical analysis
Report #2 due
Gas density [measuring density of gases]
Scientific method
How to write a hypothesis
Introduction to the pendulum
Pendulum lab
Advanced methods of data analysis
Report #3 due
Mean, median, mode, range
Average deviation, standard deviation
Interpreting statistics
Micrometer; beads, percent occupied [measuring the empty
    space in a cylinder by knowing the volume of beads—a

useful technique for measuring empty space within an
atom]
Bead lab [finding volume of a small object]
Correlation
Correlation report
Orders of magnitude
Orders of magnitude project
Oleic acid experiment
Estimating sand grains [Guessing the grains of sand on Coney
Island's beach teaches students to work with big numbers.]
Search for solutions

One motif in the course is "correlation." In Kiefer's class, students may chart such whimsical correlations as hat size to shoe
size, the numbers of teenagers at home to the size of the monthly
telephone bill, science grades to math grades, elevation of cities to
their average temperature. The rationale is that so much of science
involves connections between phenomena—the impact of light on
growth, the impact of pendulum length on the duration of the
swing.

Indeed, much of the course is done in a spirit of fun—the
sheer delight boys and girls have in watching chemicals or machines magically collide. In the gas-density lab, students learn how
to measure the weight of a gas using Alka-Seltzer tablets. They
weigh the tablets and drop them into a graduated cylinder filled
with water whose weight they have also measured. When the tablets have fizzed, they weigh the water-filled cylinder again and compare the result to their first set of measurements. The difference
reveals the weight of the carbon dioxide dissipated in the air. If
they set up an apparatus to collect the released carbon dioxide in
water, they can also measure the gas's density. The volume of the
water displaced by carbon dioxide will disclose the volume of the
gas. And density equals mass (or weight) over volume.

These techniques are basic to all sorts of laboratory research.
But most high school students learn only a handful. As Kiefer
suggested, biology and chemistry teachers, anxious to cover state-
prescribed curricula, never tell students about such matters as the

limits for error in measurement and the significant digits a number used in a scientific experiment should contain.

"I can't do these kind of experiments in chemistry because I have a syllabus to teach," says Stanley Shapiro, a chemistry teacher who is the school's research coordinator. "If I spend a week on a problem like this, I can't teach what I need to teach in chemistry. That's why we need research classes. In regular classes, kids don't have time to think. They have to study for the Regents. Here they learn to think. They become independent workers. They become scientists."

To train students to write like scientists, the research methods classes also demand regular laboratory reports. Shapiro, who teaches sections of the course, requires four reports, about one a month, of ten to twelve pages each. Kiefer insists on seven shorter reports. Grammar and style—such points as the scientific community's distaste for use of first-person pronouns—are graded. "By the time they finish, they virtually have a Westinghouse paper on a trivial topic," Shapiro says.

They have also developed what Kiefer says is "a hell of a base" for the research projects they will do for the rest of their high school careers. For the research class is merely a prelude to the scientific sonatas and symphonies that follow.

In February, after the freshman fall term, the first winnowing takes place in Midwood's four-year program of cultivating scientists. The top 60 of the 300 freshmen in the medical science program are skimmed off into two classes that take a course called "Research Biology," which meets ten periods a week and is a continuation of the six-period honors biology course that all 300 freshmen have been taking since September. The stress here, however, is blatantly on laboratory experimentation and techniques. The students reproduce classical experiments and they design their own.

Finding ideas for the students to work on is not difficult. High school teachers have realized over the years that there are a number of living things that are simple and inexpensive to experiment with: pond organisms, drosophila (fruit flies), and planaria. (Many schools and, significantly, most high-school-level competitions outlaw experiments with live vertebrates, though tests on vertebrate tissue samples are permissible.) One group may examine the effect of temperature on the ability of planaria to regenerate. Another may teach planaria to go through a maze. There are also scores of experiments that can test the reaction of germinating seeds to light, cold, heat, darkness, gravity. In recent years, students have learned to make homegrown solutions of acid rain and test their impact on plants.

The students learn how to take care of their organisms and what variables can best be tested on those organisms. They write reports and research papers. They discuss ethical problems arising from their research—the complex issues centering around experiments on live animals or fetal tissue, for example.

When the school year is over, those two classes are encouraged to spend the summer at Midwood taking additional training in research. The topics covered during the summer include the selection of a research topic; the use of a research library; chemistry lab techniques such as spectrometry, acid-base strength, organic synthesis, and stoichiometry (the determination of the proportions and weight relations in which chemical elements combine in any chemical reaction); biology lab techniques such as culturing, soil analysis, and genetic fingerprints (the unique identifying characteristics of genes); and computer skills such as word processing, spreadsheets, graph plotting, and data base management.

The process of selecting researchers continues into the sophomore year, resembling the weeding process of baseball's spring training or Wimbledon. Of the sixty research biology freshmen, the top thirty to forty, based on grades and teacher recommendations, end up in a single sophomore "Research Projects" class. The rest end up, with some consolation, in honors chemistry classes.

"We bring a lot of horses to the trough," says Shapiro, "and there are a few thirsty kids who will beg to get in. By the time they're sophomores, we're dealing with kids with 95–96 averages, the really top kids in the school. We've gone from 300 to 35 in one year."

In making the selections for the research track, the program's administrators say they will pass over students who have a quirky brilliance only in science and math for those who have good grades in all subjects. "They are the kids who work harder," said Shapiro, of those with the highest averages. "They may not be the smartest, but they have *zitsfleisch* [a Yiddish term that mingles patience and diligence] and the work ethic and they are the ones we know who do the job." Shapiro, it happens, has also discovered through trial and error that the Westinghouse prize administrators weigh class ranking heavily in choosing the semifinalists. "Over half were valedictorians," he said. "It's not just a science fair. It's a rare kid who gets in on a project alone."

The research-track students receive a kind of individual grooming they would not get in most public schools and even some selective public and private schools. They are assigned three teachers to guide them through any projects they may do in school. Each student meets with Shapiro, Jay Berman—the assistant principal who stitched together the Midwood program—or a third teacher, Jay Touger, for one hour a week and is helped to focus the research and get the papers out. As compensation, the teachers are given five fewer hours of classroom teaching. It doesn't take a Westinghouse mathematician to figure out that the teachers are volunteering five hours for which they are not paid.

"We push them," Shapiro told me as we sat at his desk, one of more than half a dozen cramped into an antediluvian science faculty room filled with antique oak cabinets and dusty displays. "Some kids love it, and some find it very boring. It's the kids who love it we want."

The selected students spend every day of the sophomore year working on biology or chemistry projects in school. Some projects are the students' own ideas, some are the teachers' ideas, but much of the work is aimed at national and state contests. There are a host of these run by Duracell, the National Aeronautics and Space Administration (NASA), Du Pont, and New York State. At first glance, the Midwood program sounds baldly commercial, emphasizing glory and profit as the goals of scientific pursuit, a lesson that one might think schools should avoid. But Shapiro contends that the program's results more than justify its worth. Most children who enter the program, he says, are "terrified." They have been enrolled by parents intent on making their kids "the success I never was." But through the program, the students achieve verifiable successes that burnish their own self-confidence. Students learn to write proposals, build displays, give oral reports on their work. Eventually, they sum up their work with ten-page papers that follow the classic model of a scientific paper.

"They learn through the year that they can have an idea, gather the data, design questionnaires, come up with solutions," Shapiro said. "They make every possible mistake. The simplest project is frustrating. But they end up achieving. The reason I feel this is a great program is the kids take a hard project, put themselves at risk, and then succeed. That gives them confidence. These kids try for tougher schools. They say to themselves, 'I had this stupid project and I see how out there few people are much better than I am.' "

In 1989, Midwood students won $500 grants from New York State for a wide assortment of energy-related projects: a study of home heating from compost, a comparison of rubber and copper for solar heating, the extraction of oil from shale. Projects submitted to other contests compared self-esteem among achieving and nonachieving students and examined the effect of varying sound frequencies on seed germination. All these projects bolster the Westinghouse applications that most students eventually turn in. The students, says Jay Berman, are "building their records as scientists."

"What Westinghouse is looking for is potential scientists," he said. "You have to build a record that shows your potential. All of my research kids, for example, have to join a science club, like the Junior Academy of Science. They start thinking of themselves as scientists at an early age."

As part of Midwood's biomedical program, the research-track students also take chemistry during this year, but in their classes the emphasis is more openly on research. They also take a half-year course in biomedical ethics, and another summer enrichment course.

The students are being immersed in science. The nation's high schools think nothing of this kind of consuming bath, this devotion of time and passion, when it comes to the school yearbook, the school play, the football team. But asking students to expend their bottomless energy on science is regarded as overly taxing. Students cannot take it, adults say; but the truth is too many adults cannot take it. They too readily project onto youngsters their own myths about the cryptic nature of science. Midwood proves that there are far more students than we imagine who are fascinated by the seemingly magical, but often eminently explicable, workings of life and the universe.

At Midwood, all the separate streams of knowledge—the biological processes and chemical equations the students have learned, the research skills they have mastered, the organizing savvy they have picked up by conceiving and executing projects—converge in the junior year. That is when the small coterie of projects-track students turn their attention to the Westinghouse. Almost everyone is placed in a hospital or university lab and paired with a mentor whose research is in the student's area of interest. For five periods a week during that year, they are freed from classes to work on their projects outside of school, though most work far more hours than that.

Favorite locales for projects are Brooklyn College, right across the street, with its gold mine of departments in chemistry, math, physics, biology, psychology, sociology, and geology; Downstate Medical Center, a state university medical school that is a ten-minute subway ride away; Brooklyn Polytechnic Institute; and Maimonides Medical Center, another borough institution. Other settings include industrial, forensic, and public-health labs, the Coney Island Aquarium, the Brooklyn Museum and other city museums, and local environmental protection agencies.

Midwood students are encouraged to find their own mentors, but Midwood's teachers have already forged alliances—a cynic might say they have made deals—on which students capitalize. Some of these deals required considerable self-sacrifice. Berman, for example, agreed to do Maimonides Medical Center a "favor" by serving on its "animal-care-and-use committee," a panel required of all research hospitals by an irksome state regulation. In return, Maimonides's doctors and scientists supervised four Midwood students in 1989.

"The first year of the program," said Berman, "I made a lot of phone calls, a lot of visits, and I did a lot of begging. I visited all the professors at Brooklyn College. A lot of them said no, they're not interested. By the second year, they said Midwood students are great. By the third year, I had a kid working with every member of the biology department."

Berman will call a professor at Brooklyn or a doctor at Downstate working in, say, cell membrane transport and ask if he or she is interested in taking on a student. If the researcher is agreeable, an interview is set up. Six of the nine Westinghouse semifinalists at Midwood in one recent year worked with Brooklyn College professors. "They put up newspaper clippings about the Westinghouse," Berman said. "Now everyone wants a kid."

One of those Brooklyn College students was Erica Klarreich, a dark-haired and somewhat bashful scholar who at the age of fifteen crafted an experiment that studied phagocytosis, the immunological process by which white blood cells engulf bacteria. Only she used amoeba, rather than white blood cells, and yeast cells rather than bacteria, and investigated the effect of the drug trifluoperazine on inhibiting the ingestive process involved in phagocytosis. Brooklyn College was a very congenial spot for her junior-year Westinghouse work because it is only a few blocks from her home. Her mother, a math teacher at the Yeshiva of Flatbush, also happens to be an alumna, and her older sister is a math major there. Indeed, Erica ultimately chose to attend Brooklyn College as an undergraduate even though, as a Westinghouse finalist, she could have virtually had her pick of the nation's colleges.

In working on a project, a student may choose to zero in on a small portion of the mentor's inquiry or undertake a project only generally related to the mentor's. Mentors who use students as lab assistants are frowned upon. Most mentors, Berman speculates, agree to oversee projects because of a debt they feel toward their own profession. Someone helped them when they were young.

One durable mentor is Donald Gerber. He was a Westinghouse semifinalist as a teenager. Now he shepherds Westinghouse aspirants while doing his own research on arthritis at Downstate Medical Center. His teenage son, Andrew, finished ninth in the 1989 Westinghouse competition, studying the relationship between certain drugs and iodine in forming charge-transfer complexes that alter the brain's electronic properties. Gerber coached several of Andrew's classmates but stayed away from Andrew, who worked with a mentor elsewhere in Brooklyn. The family wisely sought to avoid the emotional tangles of what might have been seen as a father-son Westinghouse submission.

The students, it should be noted, complete their daunting projects while taking somewhat more conventional classes in advanced placement chemistry, biology, or physics, for which they will receive college credit, and the necessary run of English, math, and social studies classes. The advanced placement classes alone meet ten times a week. The load, Shapiro says, is such that in May, when projects need to be completed and studying begins for finals, "everything falls apart. The kids get kind of crazy. You don't see them for days."

The Westinghouse students spend the fall of the senior year writing and polishing their reports and composing the personal essays the competition requires. They do much of their work in a course bluntly called "Westinghouse Research." The class, of course, works on principles applicable to all research papers, but it does not shy away from the nitty-gritty peculiar to the Westinghouse: what essay elements the Westinghouse readers are looking for, how a Westinghouse paper differs from an article in a scientific journal, what kinds of questions are likely to be asked by judges. Students learn, for example, that the Westinghouse paper has to be more comprehensive than a journal article, that it must assume the reader is not familiar with the subject and must explain basic concepts that a journal writer would assume his scientific audience already grasps. Every week students meet with a teacher for an hour or two so they can refine the submissions.

Midwood's students did not grow up in a hothouse for geniuses. Most were raised in working-class Brooklyn, not in Silicon Valley or Princeton where research scientists are as prevalent as postal carriers. Yet, nine Midwood teenagers were among the 300 semifinalists in the 1993 Westinghouse and they produced an array of research topics, including a few in the social sciences, whose titles impress even as they may baffle:

1. Does Attending Religiously Oriented High Schools Alienate Students from Their Religion?

2. Role Modeling and Norm Change in Adolescent Male-Female Interaction: An Experiment in Understanding and Changing Communication Style

3. Lectin Histochemical Study of Main Olfactory and Vomeronasal Systems of Developing and Adult Opossums, *Monodelphis domestica*

4. Interaction Between Hydralazine and Hypochlorite as Measured by Effect on Colloidal Suspension of Fat and Protein

5. Discovery and Functional Analysis of a New Protein Kinase C Isoenzyme in Human Platelets

6. Effect of Flicker-Rate on Color Vision

7. Novel Method of Estimating Human Cell Proliferation and Interphase Subdivision Using Human Genome Painting

8. Investigation to Find Neurophysiologic Factor Most Significantly Predictive of Intellectual Developmental Delay in Premature ELBW Infants

9. Responses of Urban and Suburban Children to Violence in a Hypothetical Situation

While most American high school graduates are happy grasping a few fundamental concepts of science and math, these Brooklyn teenagers were voyaging in an intellectual stratosphere few adults brave. And experiment number 5, the study of a new protein's effect on blood platelets, won Zachary Zisha Freyberg, a child of Russian immigrants, tenth place in the 1993 Westinghouse and $10,000.

Stanley Shapiro, Midwood's research coordinator, worked for many years as a scientist in a commercial laboratory and, after he began teaching, quickly understood that there was little connection between the classroom and the lab. "Our feeling was that you're not going to get a scientist from anything that goes on in the classroom," he says, relaxing in the fossil of a lab Midwood has given him.

In most American science classes, students learn scientific concepts and facts that they feed back on tests. They do not learn methods of research and they do not perform any research. Expecting students trained in such a system to become scientists, Shapiro observes, is like expecting teenagers to become professional basketball players by only taking classes on the rules and dynamics of basketball.

"How great would it be just getting lectures in basketball?" he asks. "You gotta play the game."

That is what American schools need to learn by studying places like Midwood. If students do not come out of Midwood with a gut pleasure in research, then research is truly not for them. Their rejection is backed with the confidence that comes from an authentic exposure, not just hypothetical musing. They have played the game. But for those who savor research, who respond with verve and even passion, Midwood has performed perhaps the greatest service education has to offer. It has allowed students to discover the kernel of identity, of self-definition, so crucial in constructing a life. They will probably not end up as mute inglorious Miltons in a country churchyard, their scientific muse never having been detected.

Shapiro is a small, compactly built man in his late forties with a ready smile that visibly registers his delight in what he does. He believes schools do not demand enough of students, do not stretch them as far as they can be stretched. That failing, he says, is a residue of the 1960s, when teachers fresh out of education schools bearing the dogmas fashionable at the time were often discouraged from burdening students with tests and homework. Shapiro says teaching has taught him a different lesson.

"I learned achievement in life means doing a lot of boring things, doing tedious tasks."

In a standard lecture he gives to audiences of science teachers, he puts his message across in this fashion:

"Science is an active verb. To science is to discover how the world works. Scientists hypothesize, analyze, synthesize, and explore. He constructs, collects, and records. She experiments, searches, and computes. They discuss, read, write, dismantle, clean, and repair. This is science."

Shapiro likes to point out that of the twenty-seven Midwood students who submitted Westinghouse projects in one recent year there were eighteen "losers" whose work received no recognition. Yet, every one of those losers, he says, is glad to have gone through the four-year regimen. They have gained a wealth of skills that will serve them in good stead no matter what paths they follow.

"This shows they've done college-level work, independent work," he said. "The students know how to use instruments, know how to perform a statistical evaluation, show a high level of writing ability, of library skills. They have demonstrated analytical, judg-mental skills."

Indeed, Shapiro points out, students attach their Westinghouse project reports to their college applications and often find that, win or lose, the project reports leave a far stronger impression on admission officers than such titles as president of the drama club.

"We found at Midwood that if you compare kids who do the project and kids who don't who have the same SATs and grades, our kids get accepted hands down because colleges see they've accomplished at a high level. I also feel that for many of these kids this could be the most interesting thing they ever do, the only time in their lives that they do something original."

Midwood's research program started three years ago out of some very pragmatic—cynics might say crass—aims. It was de-vised as an intentional three-year plan to capture a slew of Westing-houses, just as owners of baseball teams set their sights on building a pennant team. Before 1989, Midwood had not had a Westing-house finalist for nine years. It wasn't the dry spell that bothered school officials. It was what the dry spell said about Midwood. Midwood was not producing students dedicated to careers in science.

True, the medical science program that started around 1975 had reversed Midwood's slide, had averted its becoming what some Midwood teachers call another Erasmus, a Brooklyn neighborhood high school that had won dozens of awards over the years, then saw its brightest students leave for schools with more attractive academic programs like John Dewey and Edward R. Murrow High Schools. Midwood had eluded that fate, but it still lacked the cachet that made it the talk of educators. It was not winning Westinghouses.

Jay Berman was a graduate of Erasmus and he could remember when Erasmus was snatching as many Westinghouses as Bronx Science. As a teenager, Berman in fact had been in a special Erasmus class where twenty-three of the twenty-five students were Westinghouse semifinalists. He remembered that figure so well because he was one of the unlucky two. Still, he realized that the secret to Erasmus's success was Dr. Thomas Lawrence, the biology chairman at Erasmus in the early 1960s, who had organized a research program and scoured the school for twenty-five bright minds to go through it. "When you were selected to be in his class, the whole school would look up to you," Berman recalls.

The program both turned out science researchers and captured Westinghouses for glory. "Westinghouse is a very big force in New York City," explains Berman. "It identifies schools who are able to take the most talented kids and develop them to a point where they are nationally recognized. If you're at an educators meeting and you're not getting top winners, people will say, 'What happened?' "

"Any school can have one or two winners," adds Shapiro. "But five or six would indicate the school."

In 1986, Midwood's principal asked Berman to set up a science program. Berman had started science programs at two other Brooklyn high schools, Grover Cleveland and Abraham Lincoln, but the programs fell far short of his hopes because there were no teachers with professional experience as researchers. Midwood did have a critical mass of students that could benefit from a research program, but Berman realized he would also need trained teachers. "People have to have a research background," he argues, in a view that is not shared by all his colleagues. "They need to know what goes on in an investigation. Lots of teachers have ed courses."

Berman, who was given the title of assistant principal, was fortunate to find Shapiro. Shapiro had worked for many years as a biochemist at the Gillette Research Institute. He had a master's degree in organic chemistry from New York University. In the mid-1970s, Shapiro had also worked as a science curriculum specialist at New York City Community College. By the mid-1980s, he was teaching at James Madison High School in Brooklyn and was producing a Westinghouse semifinalist every year. Berman lured Shapiro to Midwood and made him coordinator of student research.

In cobbling together the program, Berman began with a list of the school's best kids and went to each one asking him or her to enroll. It was not an easy sell. He was peddling a patently grueling idea that would deprive youngsters of their evenings, weekends, and summers. Every student in the program would have to take an extra class every term for three years. Most would have to sign aboard for at least one summer of work and perhaps two. During the junior year, they would have to spend at least four hours a week in after-school research.

"I had to go begging," Berman says. "Most of the kids refused. But once the program was set up it became something desirable. Now there are kids who have applied to the program and get very upset if they don't get in. I get in-house publicity. Older kids are talking to younger kids."

Berman not only got the staff he wanted, but he persuaded the principal to offer the project students ten periods of science a week, rather than the typical six. That cost money, Berman notes, in the form of paid teaching time, but the principal came through.

As Berman chats animatedly about his program, we hear the hubbub of students changing classes in the hallways outside and Berman realizes it is almost time to teach a class. Before he leaves, though, there is one thing he wants to show me. He searches his cluttered office and pulls out a file that lists the program's students and the colleges to which they have been accepted. Jorge Garcia, a Colombian immigrant, can choose between Columbia, Cornell, Boston University, and the University of Rochester. He has won a $10,000 Urban League scholarship and a $40,000 Pulitzer scholarship. Thomas Westcott, a Westinghouse finalist, has been accepted by MIT, Cornell, and Johns Hopkins and has been offered scholarships of $40,000 and $20,000. And so it goes for many of the other students.

"Jorge would not have gotten into any of these with a 93 average," Berman tells me. The difference, he says, is that Garcia had a Midwood-quality science project to his credit.

"To me the Westinghouse is icing on the cake," Berman says, walking out the door. "The important thing is learning science." But, he acknowledges, in 1989, when his school had nine semifinalists and three finalists after years of drought, "I was a hero."

Chapter Four

A Teacher and His Creatures

Richard Plass of Stuyvesant High School in Manhattan has never done research more sophisticated than raising guppies with his sons. Yet he has turned out 202 Westinghouse semifinalists, nurturing more successful research projects than probably any other teacher in the United States.

It is not a mastery of biology that accounts for this extraordinary record. Even his comments on papers that are being readied for the Westinghouse betray a lack of any exceptional expertise. "Go, go, go," says the spidery scrawl on the title page of one paper. "I couldn't find anything to critique," says another.

"The kids in Stuyvesant are beyond me," he confesses. "I'm a biology teacher, not a biologist."

Plass's secret is an age-old one. He simply loves teaching, loves working with kids. "I'm a plain old guy," he told me, as we spoke in his crowded cubby of an office in the winter of 1992 while he munched on an apple—his lunch for that day. "I like being with lots of kids, doing lots of different things. All a kid has to say is I want to do research, period. We don't ask them what their grades are, what their backgrounds are. You want to do it, you got it."

Plass is both an impassioned teacher and something of a salesman, a Willy Loman who pitches salvation through science projects on a smile and a shoeshine. The more customers he can win over the merrier he is. While other teachers will take a handful of projects or even a dozen, Plass will take sixty, seventy, eighty. He can't say no, and whenever a student will come asking to do a project he will agree to play the angel, no matter how late in the game. Then, once the projects get off the ground, Plass makes himself available to a seemingly inexhaustible stream of students who come knocking at his office door, asking factual questions, requesting the use of his phone, offering him drafts to read, pleading that he intervene with a parent upset over late nights at the lab.

In a selective school like Stuyvesant—9,445 students took an admission test for 501 places in the September 1993 freshmen class—Plass's obsession can translate into a trove of prizes. And Plass is not the only ardent promoter of science research at Stuyvesant. Arnold Bellush and Albert Tarendash in the physical sciences and Richard Rothenberg in mathematics, along with an inspirational principal, Abraham Baumel, all help explain why Stuyvesant had four of the nation's forty winners in the 1992 Westinghouse and similar showings in many of the years prior.

Plass is a gray-haired man of forty-eight with glasses, a small Chaplinesque mustache, and a physique that shows no evidence of exercise. He is homespun enough to have chosen Queens College for a graduate degree so he could have dinner with his mother. He talks in a rapid-fire staccato that allows his listeners few opportunities for distraction. Describing him as busy is like describing Everest as tall.

Plass is not only a biology teacher, an assistant principal who chairs the biology department, a shepherd of three dozen or more Westinghouse submissions in any given year, but also periodically an executive of the New York City Biology Teachers Association. And he runs a summer camp for gifted students on Long Island, heads a summer research program for high school students in Pennsylvania, runs a business that sends American teachers to study and live in Russia, is a vice president of the Long Island University Alumni Association, and is the father of two sons. And in his spare time he just completed a doctorate in educational administration and supervision at St. John's University. His thesis: The role of the department chairman as the functional leader in a school.

He is thus an uncommon role model for students who seem to thrive on work the way normal human beings thrive on oxygen. His example as a maelstrom of energy may partially explain why students such as Valerie Liu, a 1992 Westinghouse winner, have interests ranging from ice skating to piano playing and do them all so well.

"Powerful people do lots and lots of things," Plass says.

Plass's assignment to Stuyvesant is no small factor in his achievement. The school has the cream of New York City's 270,000 public high school students; many educators contend that its student body is now superior to that of Bronx Science. That may be because Stuyvesant, in lower Manhattan, is more accessible to students in Brooklyn and Queens than Bronx Science, on the northern edge of the Bronx. The Bronx, poorer and more rundown than it was twenty years ago with far more poor blacks and Hispanic immigrants, does not have the wealth of academically minded students it once had. Of course, Stuyvesant has had its own shortcomings. Until recently, when it acquired a new building in Manhattan's Battery Park City, Stuyvesant was housed in a moldering Victorian fortress that had only one working biology laboratory. Its oak desks and storage cabinets were an antique collector's dream, but it had no sophisticated equipment of any kind other than a dusty autoclave for sterilizing test tubes and an aged incubator that was used mostly for warming bagels.

But what Stuyvesant has always had is its proximity to two dozen of the nation's finest scientific and medical research centers, and access to a subway system that can easily transport students to those labs daily.

"Think of kids from L.A. going from School A to Lab B," principal Baumel said. "It's impossible within one day."

More important, Stuyvesant has an ambience that treasures academic prowess. John Abraham, a 1992 winner, says the "mentality at other schools is to do average." At Stuyvesant, 60 percent of the students have more than a 90 academic average.

"At other schools you get classified as a geek or a nerd," said Zachary Gozali, a 1992 winner who transferred from private and prestigious Fieldston School to attend Stuyvesant. "Stuyvesant saved my life. It turned me into what I am today."

Still, until Plass came, Stuyvesant was a perennial silver medalist in the Westinghouse to Bronx Science's gold. Plass gave Stuyvesant a shot in the arm: he imported an award-winning system from another New York public high school, Grover Cleveland High School in Queens, where as a science teacher he had also churned out Westinghouse semifinalists. The simple secret of the system is immersion of students in research at a tender age. And the form it takes is a gimmick called "Creature Features."

Seventy students in two classes of freshman research biology take four periods of research lab a week in addition to the normal complement of six classes of biology (two of which also bring students into a lab). Creature Features gives them some experiments to play with through the beginning of the year and some ideas for the year's dominant project.

Plass's objective is to show students how simple, inventive, and serendipitous research can be. Students start the year tinkering with a number of "creatures" from a list he has compiled of harmless and easily cultivated living things: paramecia, brine shrimp, the cyclops crustaceans, drosophila (fruit flies), *Tenebrio molitor* (meal worms), planaria (flat worms), slime molds, the easily observable red bacteria known as *Serratia marcescens*, beans, and pixie tomatoes. They learn about these organisms and their life cycles, they watch the creatures grow and, in some cases, metamorphose, and they perform some simple experiments. Then toward the middle of the year they pick a feature whose effects on the organism they will test. The feature can be a substance such as vitamin C, vitamin B_{12}, saccharin, caffeine, sugar, amino acids, aspirin, monosodium glutamate, acetaminophen, or antibiotics. Or it can be a physical phenomenon such as temperature, light, ultraviolet radiation, magnetism, spin, pH, or electricity. The students design an experiment testing the effect of almost any substance or physical phenomenon on the list on almost any of the organisms. In principle, it's no more difficult than mix and match, as this list of projects indicates:

The Effect of Insecticide on the Reproduction Rate of Cyclops
The Effect of Acid Rain on the Reproduction of *Paramecium bursaria*
The Effect of Iodine on the Metamorphosis of the *Drosophila melanogaster*
The Effects of Caffeine on the *Tenebrio molitor*

The Effect of Saccharin on *Paramecium bursaria*
The Effect of Penicillin on *Drosophila melanogaster*
The Effect of Ultra-Violet Light on the Growth of the Slime
  Mold

Over the years, Plass has determined which experiments will produce engaging results. That is why he likes the red bacteria *Serratia marcescens*. "Because it's red, you can follow it and see what it does," he said. "It turns white if you do this to it. It turns pink if you do that to it. It turns redder if you do that to it. You could put in a chemical. You put it into hot or cold. Anything you want to it. And it does something when you do something to it. So it's a nice tool for experimentation."

Fairly soon, the students in the research class are working on lengthy and distinctive experiments, studies in genetics or bacteriology for which regular biology students simply do not have time. Students must follow classic scientific form. There has to be a control group and a well-formed hypothesis. "We don't just want to throw in a chemical in a shotgun approach and see what can happen," he said. "You need to have a rationale. Because scientists have a rationale for what they do. They don't just do experiments. There are reasons why they do experiments."

The students do not work on their experiments entirely in isolation. The program Plass has designed and that other teachers also endorse immerses students in committees—paramecia committees, drosophila committees, psychology committees—where students trade their laboratory experiences.

All of this Plass does with a cheery enthusiasm that might fatigue more tranquil temperaments. Plass has a deep, if visceral, understanding of the allure and pleasures of research. In a booklet, predictably called "Creature Features," that he published in 1980 that has been bought by science teachers around the country, he offers one of the most succinct descriptions of why research classes and programs such as the Westinghouse are so seductive to students:

> You will find variations in reproductive patterns, mutations, growth, and many times life and death itself. You

will witness binary fission, color changes, bursting cell membranes, conjugations, mitosis, ameboid movement, colony formation, root hair growth, mating fruit flies, two headed worms, size and shape abnormalities, metamorphosis, antibiosis, and other serendipities beyond your imagination.

You will learn how to make solutions; culture and feed many diverse creatures; use dozens of laboratory devices; do statistical analysis; gain access to large research libraries; write to and speak to famous research scientists; attend meetings and lectures at colleges; organize term papers; and present yourself and your project to peers and adults.

You will be the mother and father to organisms that might depend upon you and only you for their very lives. That is an awesome responsibility even though they might be very small and not very consequential in the greater scheme of things.

You will learn about yourself and your ability to do independent work out of the classroom. You will get sudden flashes of insight, invent shortcuts, design new techniques, and most exciting of all, perhaps be the only person in the entire world to ever observe some peculiar event happening on your microscope slide. This always happens, by the way, when the lab is empty and there is no one about to share the experience with. It will be the most brilliant, self-satisfying, and mature experience that will ever happen to you. You will walk through your school proud of yourself, with a secret you cannot explain to "ordinary" students because you are not sure they could really understand or appreciate the extraordinary concentration, dedication, and determination you have undergone.

Your student science research instructor, though, will break out into a gigantic Cheshire cat grin, and simply say, "Where do we go from here?"

Following Plass's blueprint, students finish off the second term by composing a report on their experiments, complete with an abstract, a review of the prior literature, a hypothesis, results, graphs and photographs, and conclusions. Students also give oral presentations of five to six minutes, combined with a graphic or a slide show. These techniques prepare students for the presentations they will have to make in the Westinghouse and, for those contemplating professional careers, at scientific conferences.

Because psychology experiments have become increasingly popular at science fairs—and with the Westinghouse—Plass also has students in the spring work on a host of experiments involving relatively simple matters such as facial expressions, eye contact, and word memorization.

The sophomore year offers a similar honors research program in chemistry. Then in the junior year, students choose a "Junior Research Class," sometimes called the Westinghouse class, which pairs them with professional scientists in working laboratories. Plass offers a class in biology, and there are also junior research classes in physics and chemistry, mathematics and psychology. Not surprisingly, there is a lively competition by teachers for the best students.

As at Bronx Science, students under Plass's guidance are asked, as a test of their maturity, to find their own mentors in the host of hospitals and universities with which New York City is blessed—at labs in Mt. Sinai Medical Center, Sloan Kettering Institute for Cancer Research, Cornell Medical Center, New York University Medical Center, Rockefeller University, Beth Israel Medical Center, the Public Health Research Institute, St. John's University, and others. Plass advises the students only on how to start the process rolling, how to dress for the initial interview, how to bypass a departmental secretary. (The solution to the last challenge: call the school's graduate admission office and, without explicitly posing as an applicant, ask for names and personal telephone numbers of professors working in an area of interest.) The name Stuyvesant opens up a lot of doors, and many institutions welcome the chance to cultivate future scientists who may end up one day coming to work for them. A recent Rockefeller University publication contained a feature on the high school students it guided that was entitled "Combatting the Scientific Brain Drain," and that offered this rationale for the program:

Attracting the best and the brightest youngsters into careers in science has become a high priority for the nation, faced with declining numbers of scientists graduating from our universities. It is also a concern for many universities, confronted by rising numbers of faculty vacancies created by retirements and the "brain drain" of scientists flocking to more lucrative industry jobs.

Some schools in New York, however, are notorious for not welcoming high school students, and Plass discourages students from even knocking on their doors. "The reputation of the school is dependent on how they treat people who walk into it," he says. "If you don't treat someone nice when they walk in, then they walk out saying that place is not nice.... Kids are wonderful that way. Kids read your face as you mechanically move your lips and read every emotion you have as an adult. If you give them a crinkly eye or a sigh, they know you're in trouble. I have moods. And the kids since they know me so well they can tell when I'm uptight or busy in my head or something's bothering me ... so when they walk into a university, they know they're not being treated nicely."

Plass will break his rule and make a connection for those who after six weeks fail to hook up with a laboratory. He has compiled a notebook of personal telephone extensions of helpful professors, just in case. He also tries to make sure students end up working on topics they enjoy, not just ones for which a researcher is available. He urges students to focus on a broad topic area that engages them—genetics, AIDS, molecular chemistry—and tells them to leave the narrow research topic to the mentor. "I don't want someone to do chemistry for two years and not like chemistry," he said.

The junior research classes are open to anyone, even students who were not trained in research as freshmen. "I take on as many kids as I can handle," Plass says. "Sometimes it gets overwhelming. But I can't say no to a kid. I feel it has to be done."

In 1992, Plass started out with sixty students, but the publicity about the four Stuyvesant winners led thirty more students to plead with him to take them on as well. And he did. He cannot say no, particularly to those who started with him in freshman biology, the ones he calls his "babies." He also handles an additional sixty seniors who are finishing up their Westinghouses and writing papers. And he continues to teach a single section of research biology. "I need to be with children in a classroom setting," he said. "That's my personal need to be a teacher." His total load, he says, is typical of teachers like Bellush, Rothenberg, and Tarendash. All, Plass says, are regularly at school by 7 A.M.

The junior research class meets formally only once a week, as a seminar. But soon students are spending roughly six hours a week at hospital and university laboratories. Plass makes it seem that the secret to Stuyvesant's success is really the much-maligned New York City subway.

"We're in a unique situation," Plass said. "A kid in Huntington [on Long Island] who wants to go out to Brookhaven [National Laboratory] or Cold Spring Harbor [the famed genetics laboratory] or Adelphi or Hofstra—you can't get there from here without a car, without someone in the afternoon driving."

For four periods a week, Plass sits in his office waiting for students to ask him questions. "And they show up," he says, a statement proven by the dozen or so students who knock at his door during our two-hour interview. "They come in, use the phone, call the professor, read my paper, da-da-da-da, all day long."

Plass tells his students at the start that no one can fail, but if they want a grade in the course, they must submit not only a final Westinghouse paper, but a progress report in the fall and a more thorough one in the spring, which he will read during the summer and mail back. Three-quarters of the students who start the program in September will start work toward their Westinghouse paper by January. Others manage to start as late as the spring, but about an eighth, he says, "realize they can't do it."

"They must spend two or three days after school, that's six hours a week. That keeps them away from their homework. If they're at Mt. Sinai [in upper Manhattan] and they live in Queens, it's tough. They get home in the dark, late at night. They can't join some of the clubs. They're really dedicating a lot of time and effort on one project."

Those who persist into the senior year spend one afternoon a week after school meeting with Plass and honing the paper. "I don't teach kids how to do research," he says. "I teach them how to write a paper. I'm as anal as I could possibly be on paper-writing. I want an absolutely perfect paper." While he may not fully comprehend the arcane area under investigation, he can, he says, "speak the language."

"I can tell by looking at the gestalt if a kid is heading in the right direction," he says.

Along the way he gets to know the students "very, very personally. It would be rare that I didn't know a kid and their parents and what they do and their parents do. This kid Jerry brings me Chinese food 'cause his father owns a restaurant in Long Island. This girl Wendy lives on Staten Island and travels for an hour by ferry boat. I just get to know the kids. I'm here at 6:30 in the morning."

While the Westinghouse competition is intimately woven into the fabric of the Stuyvesant research program—the warp to its woof—the program's purpose is not to win Westinghouses. Plass speaks with great fervor about why more of America's high schools must start programs like the research classes at Stuyvesant. "These kids are learning how to work at a world-class facility," Plass says. "These are scientists. These are kids who want science as a career. Chalk-and-talk is no good. Go out and do what science is. Science is doing things in an experimental form. We can't do that here. So we put them out there to do it instead. They are learning how to be a young adult. Being mature, being responsible, dealing with brilliant adults. Keeping things alive. Using thousands of dollars of equipment and being responsible for that. Learning library skills. Writing skills. Kids whose goal is to be a scientist, they're writing scientific papers right now, at seventeen years old. They have a skill built in as an ability that you'd have to wait until graduate school to be taught."

Still, Plass says, it's important for students to enter contests like the Westinghouse because competition is an inherent part of science. Scientists compete for publication in academic journals, Plass points out. "They don't get published they might lose a job, they might not get promoted, they might not get recognition, they won't have a following either in the literature or in the university. Those things are hard for scientists to have, very very difficult in any financial climate. So these kids are entering their papers in contests, looking for recognition themselves."

If Plass intuitively appreciates the desire of New York City children for recognition, for something that will distinguish them from the swarms of other urbanized children around them, it is perhaps because he lived a rather unremarkable New York City childhood. Plass was born in 1944 in the southeast Bronx, a few blocks from the Hunts Point market. His father was a quality-control engineer in the electrical industry and his mother an administrator at Metropolitan Life Insurance. When he was eight years old, Plass and his family moved to the then somewhat more rustic spaces of Flushing, settling into the Electchester Houses in Queens, a high-rise development sponosored by the electrical unions. Young Plass went to the public schools there.

Although he passed the test for Brooklyn Technical High School, one of the three selective science-oriented public high schools in New York City, he decided to attend Jamaica High School in his Queens neighborhood.

"I had a girlfriend whom I met at Campbell Junior High School who was also interested in science and we became very fast friends and leaving her was a situation that even as a ninth-grader I could not tolerate. And that's what happened. I didn't go to Tech. I went to Jamaica. Then that year Jamaica was very crowded and they split the boys off from the girls and put us in Thomas Edison High School for a year. So I didn't get to see her at all. We met like on a bus. That's cruel and unusual punishment to do to a boy who made Brooklyn Tech. We dated for a long long time. We didn't marry, but we dated for seven years or so. We went to college and I met my wife on the boardwalk at Rockaway one summer. We fell in love, and we've been married twenty-six years, but that's a whole other story."

His wife, Mickey, is a math teacher at Louis Armstrong Intermediate School, also known as I.S. 227, a school in Queens under the direct jurisdiction of the citywide schools chancellor rather than one of the thirty-two community school boards, and one where teachers receive training from professors at Queens College. "A lot of her students wind up coming to me," Plass says. "We went to a dermatologist a few weeks ago on Bell Boulevard. There's a young lady behind the nursing tables and she says, 'Hi, Mr. and Mrs. Plass.' The girl, Mindy, had my wife for math and me for bio here." The Plasses have two sons: David, a graduate of MIT, who in 1993, at age twenty-four, was a computer science engineer; and Robert, who at twenty-two was studying for two doctorates at the New York College of Optometry.

Plass knew in the eighth grade at Junior High School 218 that he wanted to be a teacher. "I had a couple of really truly inspiring science teachers," he said. "They were wonderful, warm, time-giving teachers that were role models for me. I wanted to be a person like that. I wanted to be a teacher. So it was easy for me. Once you know you want to be a writer, you just write. Once you know you want to be a teacher, that's your goal and you don't have to worry about other things that bother you in your life. I never changed my mind. I never regretted it, not a day of it."

After graduating Long Island University's Brooklyn campus and receiving a master's degree in science education at City College—his wife was there getting her degree—he found a job in 1966 at Grover Cleveland High School. He taught at the school, which is in a working-class section of Queens known as Ridgewood, for sixteen years. For most of that time his was more the career of a restless pedagogue than a man destined to be a mentor of scientists. He taught chemistry for nine years, biology for four years, and worked as the school's dean for discipline, supervising the teachers patrolling the halls between classes and tracking and penalizing students who cut classes. "I get bored real quick doing things for a long time," he says.

He was even asked to coordinate the program for gifted students. " 'Your job," he remembers principal Myron Liebrader telling him, " 'is to prevent kids from going to Stuyvesant High School.' And I did that for a long time."

In 1976, a new biology chairman came in with some experience in teaching research, and he and Plass discussed the idea of starting an honors biology program for ninth- and tenth-graders where students would get double periods of science to work on laboratory experiments. "The rationale was the school had some gifted kids whose parents didn't want them to travel outside the Ridgewood area to Manhattan, and we were losing kids to parochial schools,"

Plass said. The principal leaped at the idea as a way of getting the school some limelight.

"You could enter kids into poetry contests, no one cares," Plass says. "A speech contest, no one cares. Enter them into an essay contest, a spelling bee. But put them in a science fair, people like it. The *New York Times* shows up. I don't know why that is. But if you're doing science you're doing the top stuff. It may not be true but everyone perceives it that way."

Plass carefully selected the best junior high school students entering Grover Cleveland and assembled a group of comparatively easy experiments they could start on. Later, students began working on their own experiments—all inside the school's labs. One year, he asked the seniors to write papers on how they went about doing research in their particular areas. Using some of their ideas and experiments, he composed "Creature Features" over a summer. He also started an in-school science fair that got students' competitive feet wet. Once the research freshmen moved into the senior year they began entering the Westinghouse. In his last four years at Cleveland, Plass's fledgling research program produced twenty Westinghouse semifinalists and a finalist.

Plass's impact at Grover Cleveland was sweetly captured in a letter he received in 1990 from Joanne Neglia, a student of his between 1979 and 1982 who had read a wire-service article about him, complete with a photograph, in the *Orlando Sentinel* in Florida. At Cleveland, she had done a project on the impact of acid rain on euglena, a green protozoan with a characteristic red pigment spot. It had qualified her as a semifinalist. She was now, she told him in her letter, an assistant to the manager of a Paine Webber branch in Orlando and was working on a novel. She enclosed a wedding picture of herself and her husband in the back seat of a limousine.

"Who would ever think that this Sunday's *Orlando Sentinel* would have an article that would take me back to the fondest memories of high school?" she wrote. "Mr. Plass, Westinghouse, our research papers and all of it. (By the way, you look wonderful.) I'm glad to see you're still inspiring others! Since students are too young to realize this, I'll tell you now nine years later, Thank you for making us write such awesome papers. Thank you for making us compete, thank you for all the extra hours we needed to spend in the lab. It taught me that nothing is impossible, that we're all creative and commitment + sacrifice = productive successful results!"

Although he revolutionized Cleveland's science program, the restless Plass says he realized he "wasn't doing enough for kids" as a plain teacher and so got a two-year degree in administration at night at Queens College, which then cost only $75 a credit. Armed with the administration degree, he looked around for a job as an assistant principal. There just happened to be a rare opening at Stuyvesant, and Plass had the right credentials.

"I got real lucky, quite frankly, when this came up," he said. "I was the right age, and the right experience and the right time and the right background and the right publications."

He was hired by the then-principal, Gaspar Fabricante, specifically to invigorate the school's effort in research. "I was charged to do that. 'When you come here, I want you to start a research program. I want to see awards. I want to see recognition.' He told me that privately and personally in his office after I was appointed here. Bronx Science was flying and we were doing nothing here. So when I got that charge it was wonderful. I was like a pig in mud."

He began the biology research program with eleven kids in 1982. Now he is up to ninety, and the whole school has caught research fever. In the 1992 Westinghouse competition, Stuyvesant's students submitted 170 entries, a figure that was sure to net some winners. Indeed, twenty-nine semifinalists and four winners were caught. (That was not as good as 1991, when Stuyvesant had six winners, but it proved better than 1993, when Stuyvesant's trove was to dip to two.) As a result, the school's fame has spread far beyond the city. Mikhail Leyb Sunitsky, who as a recent immigrant from Russia was a 1992 winner for a mathematics project, recalled that his mother heard about Stuyvesant in the Soviet Union. She made sure her son applied for Stuyvesant as soon as they reached these shores. Once ensconced in Stuyvesant in 1991, Mikhail led a U.S. team competing in the International Olympiad in Mathematics in Sweden. It turned out to be something of a reunion for him.

"Most of the people on the Soviet team were my old friends," he said.

Such tales, and the yearly tide of students lapping at Stuyvesant's shores, have made Baumel, the school's principal, and teachers at the school against-the-grain optimists about the future of science in America. Baumel feels that the United States is still preeminent in science research. That is why students from across the world still come here to do research, he says. America has an open system that prizes intellectual inquiry and confrontation while systems such as Japan's tend to be more rigid and narrow. Baumel caps his argument by pointing out that much-vaunted Japan has won only a handful of Nobels. Yet he and some teachers also despair that Americans still prize football heroics over scientific strides. "The United States has been very uncomfortable with intellectual achievement," said Albert Tarendash, a physics teacher who is a Stuyvesant graduate himself. "People are coming to the realization that it's a necessity to have this kind of school."

Plass has no time for this debate. Like a beaver setting up a home for his young, he keeps piling up logs and branches and twigs so his students, his babies, can do their scientific projects. He works every spare moment at school tracking the progress of each project on a computer disk, then moves his disk to an identical computer at home and works every spare moment there. His triumphs are mostly vicarious ones. "These kids are doing biology with me as if I was with them in the lab," he says. But he savors it nonetheless. "It's a lot of time and a lot of patience. A lot of things happening at the same time. I like a lot of things happening at the same time. I'm a kid myself."

"This is the best job in the country," he says. "I'm really doing what I want to do. They always say that in a teacher's lifetime if you reach one kid, that's good. That's baloney. I want to reach hundreds and hundreds of kids. I got hundreds and hundreds of the best kids in the country."

Part III

The Schools:
The Heartland

Chapter Five

Healing a Nation at Risk

During the 1980s, the landscape of science education in America began blossoming with breathtaking colors. One state after another opened high schools whose provocative mission was to turn out scientists and mathematicians at an early age. For publicly financed institutions, many of these schools were revolutionary. They came with college-style dormitories that allowed students from the far reaches of the state—its backwaters as well as its big cities—to live at the schools while studying. They boasted teachers who had actually worked as scientists. They handpicked their students.

State governments had historically supported residential schools for juvenile delinquents and handicapped children. But never before had they set up such costly quarters for their brightest youngsters. If the structure was bold, so was the thinking behind it: Bring the cleverest, most inventive young minds together in a cocoon equipped with up-to-date equipment and the most sophisticated teachers and let them bounce ideas off each other.

North Carolina established the first boarding school in 1980, and it was followed by Louisiana, Illinois, Texas, Mississippi, South Carolina, Indiana, Oklahoma, and Alabama. At least ten other states opened "regional" schools. These were not residential, but drew their students from a cluster of neighboring school districts and kept them together for much of the day exploring science and mathematics.

The phenomenon arose from an abundance of concerns: America's anemic performance in developing new technology, the inability to attract enough young people into science careers, the widespread impression that American students were not up to their peers in Europe and Japan, a general suspicion that the United States had passed its peak and was on a gentle but inexorable downward slope. The country that had long been the world's leading inventor was repeatedly trying to catch up along trails blazed by other countries. Japan, and even Germany, the two nations the United States had defeated in World War II and on whom it had spent billions of dollars for reconstruction, were now building the world's cars, cameras, and videocassette recorders. As Richard Barnet, a strategy analyst, wrote in a long reflection in the January 1, 1990, issue of *The New Yorker*:

> The world awoke not so long ago to the realization that Japan, long famous in the West for producing junk, had become the master of advanced technology, and now the Japanese are handing the world another surprise: not only is Japan the third-largest military power in the world, as measured by military budget, but it has become evident in recent years that Japan's edge in such civilian technologies as semiconductors, data processing and telecommunications has important military implications.

As Barnet was writing, various reports lamented the scientific ignorance of American children. The 1988 "Nation's Report Card," an annual survey of achievement sponsored by the U.S. Department of Education and administered by the Educational Testing Service of Princeton, New Jersey, found that just 7 percent of America's seventeen-year-old students were prepared for college-level work in science.

"These results have serious implications for students' adult lives—including how they will be able to participate in society as informed voters and decision makers, perform everyday tasks, express intelligent points of view, and contribute to the nation's economic future," the study said.

More ominous still were comparisons of American students with those of other industrialized countries. In a 1992 ranking of students from fifteen countries in math and science, American students at all grades consistently scored below those of South Korea, Hungary, Israel, and other nations.

Statistics are, of course, misleading. Although its high school students may have an intellectual edge, Japan steers a far smaller proportion of them into college. American universities still attract the cream of the Third World's young adults into their doctoral programs. Japan is better at adapting scientific ideas than originating them; its scientists have won only five Nobels compared to nearly 200 for the United States.

Still, American business could read the handwriting on the wall. Its vitality was threatened by the decline in the literacy and competence of the American worker and a shortage of students animated by science and mathematics. More than ever in this century, foreign competitors were turning out the young engineers and scientists who were creating the inventions and concepts that would shape life in the twenty-first century. Even at American universities, foreign students were earning a growing share of the doctorates. Of the 861 math doctorates awarded in 1990, only 45 percent went to Americans. Of 15,478 doctorates in science and engineering, about 40 percent went to foreign students. Companies that were confident of competing with foreign firms worried nonetheless whether the American consumer was scientifically literate enough to take advantage of the products they were generating.

The more refined spheres of science were just as anxious. In January 1990, Dr. Leon Lederman, winner of the Nobel Prize in physics in 1988, warned that the nation was losing its leadership role in research. He was about to take over the presidency of the American Association for the Advancement of Science, an organization with 130,000 members, and was making a not-so-subtle pitch to Congress and the president for more research dollars. Still, what he said in a report entitled "Science: End of the Frontier" was worrying. Lederman had questioned 250 researchers and 50 universities and found that their responses "paint a picture of an academic research community beset by flagging morale, diminishing expectations, and constricting horizons."

"Once upon a time, American science sheltered an Einstein, went to the moon, and gave the world the laser, the electronic computer, nylon, television, the cure for polio," the report said.

"Today we are in the process, albeit, unwittingly, of abandoning this leadership role."

Lederman recommended doubling the $7.8 billion spent by the federal government on basic and applied research at the nation's universities, but since he is the founder of a special science high school in Illinois, his message set off alarm bells in high school science education as well.

There was another cause for the spread of science-minded high schools. Southern states such as Louisiana and Mississippi were waking out of a historic backwardness, reconciling themselves to a new era of broadened civil rights for people of every color and searching for a more powerful economic role for themselves. They too wanted gleaming office towers and glittering shopping malls like those rising elsewhere. That would take economic development, and economic development required bright young engineers and scientists. If these states could not turn out young men and women capable of filling the more skilled jobs demanded by modern industry, companies would pack up and move to other states. Alabama, for example, lost out to Tennessee in 1992 in the competition for a new Saturn automobile plant because the state's residents were seen as too ill-educated to assure the kind of work force needed in an increasingly technological society. Indeed, private corporations have often taken the lead in starting the state science high schools and have donated laboratories and expensive equipment. Many have encouraged, even paid, their scientists to mentor students in research projects.

The special science schools have not been universally welcomed. They have been opposed by associations of principals who fear the schools will skim off their best students. In 1987 and again in 1988, Gov. Mario Cuomo of New York could not persuade the state legislature to support a state-sponsored high school for Long Island whose students would have been drawn from a cluster of school districts. Resistance from the state's high school administrators was too firm. Long Island eventually settled for putting together a consortium of schools whose students sign up for guidance and training at campuses such as the State University at Stony Brook. That venture produced a trove of Westinghouses in 1992. When Massachusetts Gov. William Weld announced plans to start a commuter science high school that would be based at Worcester Polytechnic Institute, there were more than a few dissenting voices. John Polidori, a spokesman for the Massachusetts Teachers Association, said, "Math and science education deserve priority attention, but for all children, not an elite few."

It is also hard to sell the public on the expense of special science schools. The yearly cost of educating one student at the Illinois school was $16,000 in 1989, more than twice the per-student cost at most public high schools and roughly the price of tuition at some of the nation's most prestigious colleges. There have also been legal hurdles. Education laws have had to be rewritten so schools could hire teachers who may lack the credentials and teaching experience to qualify them for standard teaching licenses but who have spent their careers doing laboratory research.

By 1993, the United States had a roster of at least twenty-three specialized science high schools, many of them residential. I was able to put together a list from information provided by the congressional committee on technology and from other sources. If classic magnet schools such as Midwood High School in Brooklyn were added, the list would grow larger. I have marked residential schools with an R.

Alabama School of Mathematics and Science (R)	Mobile, Alabama
The Bronx High School of Science	Bronx, New York
Brooklyn Technical High School	Brooklyn, New York
Central Virginia Magnet School	Lynchburg, Virginia
Eastern Guilford School of Science	Gibsonville, North Carolina
Eleanor Roosevelt High School	Greenbelt, Maryland
Illinois Mathematics and Science Academy (R)	Aurora, Illinois
Indiana Academy for Science, Mathematics and Humanities (R)	Muncie, Indiana
Kalamazoo Area Math and Science Center	Kalamazoo, Michigan
Louisiana School for Math, Science and the Arts, at Northwestern State University (R)	Natchitoches, Louisiana

Massachusetts Academy of Mathematics and Science	Worcester, Massachusetts
Mississippi School for Mathematics and Science (R)	Columbus, Mississippi
New Horizons Governor's School	Hampton, Virginia
North Carolina School of Science and Mathematics (R)	Durham, North Carolina
Oklahoma School of Science and Mathematics	Oklahoma City, Oklahoma
Pennsylvania Governor's School for the Sciences, at Carnegie-Mellon University	Pittsburgh, Pennsylvania
Roanoke Valley Governor's School	Roanoke, Virginia
Science Academy of Austin at LBJ High School	Austin, Texas
South Carolina Governor's School for Science and Mathematics	Hartsville, South Carolina
Southwest Virginia Governor's School	Dublin, Virginia
Stuyvesant High School	New York, New York
Texas Academy of Mathematics and Science (R)	Denton, Texas
Thomas Jefferson High School for Science and Technology	Fairfax, Virginia

The state schools have already begun to justify their existence. In 1989, seventeen of the forty Westinghouse winners came from science high schools or magnet schools with special science programs. A majority came from perennial winners such as Bronx Science and Stuyvesant. But three came from schools that had been established in the 1980s: J. David Rosen from the Thomas Jefferson High School for Science and Technology in Virginia, S. Celeste Posey from the North Carolina School of Science and Mathematics, and Rowan Lockwood from the Illinois Mathematics and Science Academy. In 1991, Ashley Reiter, a seventeen-year-old senior at North Carolina, snatched first place and a $40,000 scholarship for a mathematics project. In 1993, Elizabeth Michele Pine of Chicago, a seventeen-year-old student at the Illinois Academy, won the $40,000 first-place award for a project that used DNA sequencing to demonstrate links between two species of mushrooms.

Prizes are only a minor pretext for these schools. Lederman points out that bright students often feel isolated at traditional neighborhood schools. "They react, become superaggressive or retired or draw in or become discipline problems or bored," he says. The most fragile ones abandon science for other enthusiasms. By contrast, he says, those who go to specialized schools find that suddenly "everyone is like them, they don't have to hide and they start to flower."

Milton Kopelman, the former principal of Bronx Science, puts it another way. The students, he says, begin to stretch one another in ways they could not if they were working in isolation in conventional neighborhood schools. "The sum," he says, "is greater than the parts."

Chapter Six

Like Going to Camp All Year Long

In Kevin Bartkovich's high school class in North Carolina, the students are not just learning mathematics, they are discovering and, at the outer limits, inventing it.

The air is thick with locutions such as bifurcation trees, He'non maps, and iterations. Anyone who studied mathematics only ten years ago would be lost in the fog of an unencountered language. For a visitor with a workaday grasp of science and math, the experience is something like dropping down on a street in Budapest and trying to discern the talk of the town. Impressions are all one can come away with, and my chief impression is that the young people here are spellbound, obsessed with what they are talking about, whatever it is they are talking about. Just before the class formally starts, six boys and a girl are huddled around a computer screen mounted on Bartkovich's desk examining what looks like a warped series of elliptical orbits.

"Going here there are x-values, going out there, that's the y-values," enthuses Jason Martin of Morganton, the student who has generated the images.

"That's cool!" sighs one awestruck friend.

Later, when the lights are put out and a projector flashes another computer-driven image on a film screen hanging behind the desk, something intelligible emerges. It looks like a gingerbread man. On closer inspection the gingerbread man is a construction of hundreds of points plotted on a graph that have been generated by a mathematical exercise that has been repeated over and over again. The formula is relatively complicated, but the fundamental concept is the same as a simple geometric paradigm. Take an equilateral triangle and out of the middle section of each side grow a similar, but smaller equilateral triangle. A Star of David emerges. Repeat the exercise again and again, with ever smaller triangles growing out of ever smaller sides and an intricate snowflake emerges. The details grow infinitely smaller and finer, yet the scope is bounded by the dimensions of the original triangle. The gingerbread man also grows ever finer in detail, but the basic shape remains the same. The students in Bartkovich's class actually talk about the gingerbread man's limbs and ears. Through the wizardry of the computer, they are taking what seem to be blowups of small sections of the gingerbread man and examining them closely, trying to identify the "boundaries" and pinpoint the moment when further iterations will break down into chaos—where the repetitions produce no discernible pattern. As questions buzz across the room, there is a feeling that the students are moving into regions of knowledge that have not been explored before. There is a feeling of having moved beyond the edge, perhaps into chaos itself.

Bartkovich, a handsome, sinewy native of Maryland whose scholarly spectacles give him the image of a mild Clark Kent working hard to disguise Superman, teaches a class in fractals. It is probably one of only a handful of such high school classes in the United States. The term *fractals* did not exist until 1975. It was spawned by the mathematician Benoit Mandelbrot as a way of understanding the infinite geometry of clouds, mountain ranges, lung tissue, blood vessel systems, even for regularizing the irregularities of economics and weather. It is a way of imposing order on chaos.

A simple Mandelbrot example, mentioned by James Gleick in his book *Chaos: Making a New Science*, is the answer to the question "How long is the coast of Britain?" The answer is that it depends on the yardstick. If someone were to use a mile-long ruler the standard measurement would emerge. If the ruler was 100 yards long, the coastline would grow far longer because of the jagged twists and turns of coves and small capes that would have to be added to the measurement. And if the ruler was only a yard long, the loops and wiggles of pools of water and outcroppings of sand and rock would be included in the measure and the length would grow far longer. A small enough ruler measuring pebbles and sand grains and ripples of seawater would theoretically force the measurement toward infinity. Yet on first impression the length of the coast had seemed quite finite and quantifiable. That is the paradox of fractals.

Fractal mathematicians realized that the traditional geometry most people learn, with its sharply defined shapes and its three dimensions, is a poor way of explaining many, if not most, natural phenomena. They opened up a whole world of understanding, and not just with measurements but with patterns of growth and formation. DNA, for example, cannot instruct our body to produce something of a determined shape and size called lungs, but it can generate in cells a process of division and repetition and "self-similarity" that produces the clustering of microscopic air sacs that ultimately grow into lungs.

The students in Bartkovich's class are being given a whole way of looking at life at an age when most of life is still ahead of them.

"It's not as though there's this well-defined theory we can learn," Bartkovich told me when we spoke outside class. "People are still figuring out what this is all about."

On this day before Memorial Day, he is dressed in Bermuda shorts and polo shirt, a wry counterpoint to the gravity of the convoluted mathematics he is teaching. He is a fitting guide into these unknown realms. He lets the students navigate on their own, alerting them only to turns that may be wrong or intellectually perilous.

"In fractals I saw the chance to get to the frontier without having to do semesters of preparation," he told me. "We could never get to the frontier going through another route. There are too many things you have to do first. With fractals there's not a high overhead. There are low math prerequisites, yet you can do amazing things, creative things. It's not that necessarily you're going to come up with something no one has done, but it's not nicely packaged, so there's a lot of room for exploration."

Many teachers would argue that, with students of such tender age, it should be Bartkovich's job to supply them with the fundamental mathematical knowledge that they can use for research later on. But Bartkovich disagrees.

"Should students do research or just learn facts?" he asks rhetorically. "I believe they can do research. They need to be involved in the creative process. Textbooks are static. They tell you things after it's all been figured out. They don't tell you how it was discovered. Nobel laureates and people considered true geniuses did many creative things at a very young age, and we shouldn't say to our students you can't do anything creative until you're twenty-five."

"I'm not afraid to have the students get ahead of me. I try to know enough and give them the basic grounding, and then they go and explore things I don't understand and they come and explain it to me, and we all learn from each other that way."

His choice of approach pleases his students. Susan Bramley, a senior from Greenville, finds standard advanced courses like calculus quite unexciting by comparison. "You just memorize and do the same type of problems," she said. "You're doing the same type of thing that people have done since Newton."

When the class nears its end, Bartkovich decides to leave one tantalizingly complicated question about the gingerbread man hanging in the air and teasingly suggests that students try to solve that mystery while watching the Indianapolis 500 car race that is on television that weekend. One student's response suggests how much more exciting racing against fractals has been.

"Watch cars go round and round?" whispers Jason Martin to a friend. "What a dumb thing to do."

That this class should be taking place in a high school is surprising in itself. But that it should be taking place in North Carolina is almost stunning. For decades, North Carolina ranked near the bottom on almost every measure of American education— proportion of high school graduates, SAT scores, per capita spending, percentage of pupils going on to college. The state still ranks low, but there is a feeling among its people that a turnaround has begun, and some date the shift to just around September 1980 when the North Carolina School of Science and Mathematics

opened as the first publicly financed residential high school in the
United States.

The school, a southern-fried Bronx High School of Science
with dormitories, was started at the initiation of the state's governor
at the time, James Hunt, a more visionary politician than most
governors and one who faced a policymaker's catch-22. He realized
that if the state wanted to pump up its economy by expanding its
fledgling base of high-tech and pharmaceutical industries, it needed
a first-class educational system. Yet a state whose economy was
still largely tied to the agricultural and blue-collar occupations of
tobacco, furniture, and textiles would never have a strong enough
tax base to pay for a first-class educational system.

"You can get a ninth-grade education and work in a cigarette
factory for the rest of your life" is the way William Youngblood, an
administrator at the school, explains Hunt's thinking. "You can't
get a ninth-grade education and work in a pharmaceutical company.
You're frozen out of the twenty-first century."

North Carolina's dilemma was compounded by its being a
largely rural state with no world-class cities—65 percent of its
schools are in bucolic districts—and areas so backward that homes
still have no electricity. An education in the state's biggest city of
Charlotte, which has 400,000 people, is quite different from one on
the Outer Banks or on the Cape Fear coast or in the rugged Blue
Ridge and Great Smoky mountains. Many rural schools cannot find
teachers for such basic subjects as physics and chemistry, let alone
for advanced placement courses, and have to rely on untrained
teachers to fill the voids. Even if they could find trained teachers,
it is by no means clear they could summon a critical mass of
students capable and ardent enough to want to take advanced science. John Kolena, a physics teacher, points out that outside the
cities most high schools may have perhaps two or three students
who would even want to take calculus, making it impractical to hire
a qualified teacher.

There was no way, says Youngblood, that the state legislature
could come up with the money to upgrade hundreds of schools,
but it could set up one strategically located school that could polish
the scientific talents of bright youngsters from every corner of the
state. And that school could serve as a laboratory of new teaching

techniques that could be widely disseminated. The ambitions were noble. "We dream of an aristocracy of achievement rising out of a democracy of opportunity," Youngblood says, quoting Thomas Jefferson.

But to create such a school would require one practical feature that no other publicly financed high school in the United States had ever dared ask for: dormitories. Wealthy people had long sent their children away to private boarding schools, but would the public finance such an extravagance?

The school was strongly encouraged by the high-technology companies and three major universities hidden away among the dense pines of the Durham, Raleigh, and Chapel Hill region, an area that has become known as the Research Triangle. So eager were these companies and universities to cultivate their own young scientists and researchers that they were willing to help pay for many of the startup construction costs and help subsidize its free tuition and its room and board. In the first four years of the school's operation, research-based companies and other private sources pumped in $7 million of the $26 million that was needed to run it.

The school offers a banquet of unaccustomed academic delights. Its biology courses include genetics, anatomy and physiology, immunology, and biophysics (which deals with such topics as the elasticity of muscle, the fluid properties of blood, magnetism in the navigation of birds). The school offers organic chemistry, environmental chemistry, polymer chemistry, astrophysics, and an advanced physics course that studies atomic particles and quantum mechanics. For mathematicians, there are, in addition to the "fractals and chaos" class, courses in finite mathematics, number theory, and algorithms. The school offers two years of language not only in French and Spanish, but in German, Latin, and Russian. Its humanities program, which the science students confide is the school's unsung treasure, includes courses in world religion and philosophy and one class intriguingly entitled "Wisdom, Revelation, Reason, and Doubt." Of course, there are things the school does not offer. It does not have driver education or typing.

The school is in Durham, a sleepy and quite ramshackle town of 119,000 that prospered after the Civil War on a tobacco business founded by farmer Washington Duke. Victorious northern soldiers relished the taste of the local brightleaf and, within a few years, the marketing imagination of Duke and his family began giving America its nicotine habit. By the twentieth century, the Duke family business virtually monopolized the industry, embracing divisions that were eventually spun off into R. J. Reynolds, Liggett Myers, and Philip Morris. The family fortune helped create such philanthropic ventures as Duke University, one of the nation's finest schools, but it also gave Americans lung cancer and emphysema. So it is a point of historical irony that Durham now styles itself as the "City of Medicine," boasting a number of research hospitals and health facilities, including Duke University Medical Center, that employ one-fourth of the city's work force. The results of that irony helped make Durham a preferred location for the science high school, and the choice was sealed when founders considered that within a few miles lies Research Triangle Park, whose fifty companies scattered among an eight-mile deep pine forest include such research giants as IBM, Burroughs Wellcome, and Glaxo.

The school itself is situated in what was the campus of a decaying county hospital—Watts Hospital—and its school of nursing. Indeed, there are students who were born at Watts, and legend has it that one or two have actually dormed in the rooms in which their mothers gave birth to them. There were sixteen buildings on the hospital's twenty-seven acres, most of them graceful turn-of-the-century stucco structures with Spanish-style roofs that qualified them for listing on the National Register of Historic Places. But their innards were antiquated and had to be turned into classrooms and bedrooms. Operating theaters became chemistry laboratories. Chills run down some students' spines when they realize they are taking a class in what was once the hospital's morgue. The school also added a new four-story dormitory and a gym building.

The school has its own observatory and greenhouse and a room studded with personal computers that more adventurous students can, virtually around the clock, link up telephonically with a Cray supercomputer. It has a library that is open seven days a week. With a $50,000 grant from Glaxo Inc., the pharmaceutical manufacturer, the school opened a laboratory outfitted for cutting-edge research on DNA. Student Celeste Posey used the lab in her fifth-place Westinghouse project in 1989. The laboratory contains microfuges that separate out particulates from solutions, a shaking bath to cultivate bacteria, transilluminators for photographing DNA, and mini-gel boxes for tracking the migration of DNA through an electrical field. Obviously, Glaxo wouldn't mind if the laboratory happened also to germinate some researchers for its own firm. But that wish squares wonderfully with the school's own needs.

The staff of fifty-eight—there is one teacher for every ten students—is as exceptional as the courses and the equipment, and reminds me of the scene in *Citizen Kane* where Orson Welles, having just started a newspaper, glances in the window of the established *New York Chronicle* and sees a group portrait of its nine stellar reporters and editors. He is, he says, like a kid looking through the window of a candy store. Eight years later, he got his candy. The film shows the nine reporters reassembled now for a group photo, but at Welles' newspaper. At the North Carolina School, half the teachers came not from other high schools but from colleges, government, or private industry. More than 40 percent hold doctorates, a rate far higher than that of conventional high schools, and all have master's degrees. Donald Houpe, the head of the foreign languages department and the Russian and Spanish instructor, has a Ph.D. in linguistics and speaks Cherokee, Arabic, and Swahili in addition to a batch of romance languages. Kevin Bartkovich, the fractals instructor, has a Ph.D. in mathematics education from Duke. Sarah Allen, Ph.D., was once a chemist for Celanese.

They come to the North Carolina School not for the salaries, which at $23,000 to $43,000 are just on par with the rest of the state, but mostly for the chance to work with its scintillating students. "The kids are incredibly motivated and motivating and they do it to us," says Allen. "We have a bunch of seniors getting ready to leave and I don't know who's more distressed." Myra Halpin, Ph.D., a chemistry instructor, says she gets "a great deal of pleasure listening to students you work with ask intelligent questions, showing a lot of intuition into a problem, looking at a problem a lot of ways."

To even begin attracting such a talented staff, the school had to persuade the state to exempt its teachers from the requirements for certification that demand education courses many accomplished people simply do not want to take. This exemption required a legal contortion or, some might say, a gimmick: the school is technically governed by the University of North Carolina system, not by the state public school system. The teachers may never have taught high school before, but they bring to their jobs an unmatched firsthand grasp of their fields.

Steven Warshaw, Ph.D., a lanky Texan with thinning blond hair and an understated though genial manner, came to North Carolina after a career as a water-quality expert for the Texas Department of Water Resources. I saw how effective such professional training can be in the classroom when I accompanied him and his ecology class on a field trip to Eno River State Park.

On a muggy spring day, the class packs into the school's two vans and we head out on the road for about twenty minutes, rumbling the last mile on a dirt path into the park. There, with Warshaw donning a rakishly angled safari hat, we hike through the sun-specked pines for a quarter mile until we reach the Eno. The stream gurgles and shimmers over a bed of rocks and boulders, and in a clearing we see ranger Scott Hartley standing in front of a table that has been set up as an al fresco laboratory complete with two microscopes. Hartley tells us the river has been surviving against enormous development pressures—from builders who want to raise more houses for the Research Triangle's growing job market and from state officials who want to build a reservoir by damming the Eno and flooding the valley. One of the most sensitive ways of monitoring the Eno's biological viability, far more revealing than merely taking chemical readings, is to sample the variety of insects that continue to live out their life cycles in the valiant Eno. If the species of insect life drop off and only the hardiest kinds remain, that would be a telltale marker that the Eno is perishing.

Hartley puts on knee-high rubber boots and invites several of Warshaw's students to do the same, though one, Dawn O'Brien, just slogs in with her hightop sneakers. She and Hartley push large, rigidly framed "kick nets" into the stream, jogging loose some rocks, and letting what comes loose wash into the net. The students dredge up a mother lode of aquatic insects—insects that spend part of their life cycle underwater surviving on dissolved oxygen—and crustaceans as well, and they collect them in a large white pail.

Among the creatures that the river has always nurtured, we are told, are stone flies, taddis flies, crayfish, hellgrammites (the larvae of the dobsonfly), and mussels, and it is our job to identify which ones are still around. This is harder than it seems because many of the specimens are in larval or other immature stages and look deceptively alike. To make the fine discriminations, students examine the insects closely against a chart that breaks them down according to a cascading list of features: wormlike or beetlelike, then hairlike tail or nonhairlike tail, and the like. By a process of deduction, they pinpoint the species they have trapped.

Student Michelle Prysby of Greensboro turns her specimen over and over, nudging the body parts with her fingers, as Warshaw coaches from the side.

"That's not a hairlike tail, so what are we left with?" he asks. "Is this our guy? I think we need to look under a microscope."

Michelle starts to do exactly that. "I think a little water would be a good idea," he coaches her again.

"Look!" intervenes Katie Fielder, sixteen, of Elk Park. "There's two hooks at the end of each leg. That's a stone fly nymph."

And so it is. The presence of this immature metamorphosis stage of the stone fly is one piece of small testimony to the persistent health of the Eno. More testimony could still be gathered, but it is time to go. The vans are needed back at the school to ferry the baseball team. The lesson is somewhat rushed, but it is valuable nonetheless and what makes it distinctive, why such a lesson is given almost no place else in the United States, is that Warshaw has brought a wealth of practical experience from his training as a water-quality scientist that allowed him to set up the lesson with the park ranger. His students learn ecology through the direct experience of seeing insects that survive under the rocks of a shimmering, fragile stream.

As we trek back through the pines to the van, I ask Julie Bass, seventeen, whether she could have duplicated such a class at her home high school in Asheville, the birthplace of Thomas Wolfe.

"First of all," she says, "we wouldn't have ecology. Second of all we wouldn't have a field trip. In that school everything is from a textbook."

*   *   *

The North Carolina School is only for juniors and seniors, and in 1990 it enrolled 550 of them. The school's founders decided that sophomores, particularly those hailing from remote rural areas, would find it hard to tackle both a tough academic regimen and the adjustments of living on their own. Several of the state residential schools have come to the same conclusion, though others, like the one in Illinois, have successfully enrolled sophomores. Here's how North Carolina's students get in. Teachers and administrators across North Carolina nominate standout tenth-graders. A twenty-four member statewide selection committee—which is racially representative and includes at least one person from each congressional district—selects students on the basis of high school grades, test scores, essays, and interviews. Roughly one out of every six applicants gets in.

There is a conscious, even aggressive, effort to maintain balances of race, gender, and geography. When I talked with the school's executive director, Dr. John Friedrick, he spent considerable energy describing the school's affirmative-action program and suggested that some state science schools that have not been broadly representative have not been able to sustain political support. The North Carolina School, after all, is a political creation and its founders have felt its survival depends on maintaining the backing of all groupings within the state. For a welter of reasons, simply relying on word-of-mouth applications will not produce enough black students. So, Friedrick said, in a state where one-fourth the population is black, the school actively makes sure black students know about its existence. It recruits students not just by contacting black high schools but by pitching the school's virtues in black churches as well. To prepare potential minority candidates for the tough courses they will meet at Durham, the school also arranges summer enrichment programs as early as the seventh and eighth grades.

In 1992, 47 percent of those enrolled at Durham were female and 23 percent were black, 1 percent Hispanic, 10 percent Asian, and 2 percent native American. Ninety-four of the state's 100 counties were represented. The school's contingent of black students felt comfortable enough in its place at Durham to raise the thorny issues that flowed from the California jury's verdict in the police beating of motorist Rodney King and from the subsequent Los Angeles riots.

The school has provided a haven for young people who might have felt like misfits in conventional high schools back home. That feeling of finally finding a place seems almost universal among the students. Mike Ling, who works for a local environmental consulting firm, was one of a half dozen alumni who had dinner with me in a Greek restaurant. With just a whisper of anguish, Mike, a graduate of the class of 1988, told me how he came from Gastonia, a textile town in the south central part of the state where less than half the students were college bound. Mike, whose father was an industrial relations executive and whose mother was a social worker, had unorthodox ambitions. "I definitely stood out," he said. "I would like to read and see an interesting film. I didn't just want to go to the mall. That set me apart." Gina Norman, who now works in the school's public relations office, recalled how back home "I learned not to use more than two syllables. I'd get fussed at and I learned not to use it." Julie Woosley, a slender, effervescent research chemist at the Research Triangle Institute, contrasted her two years at Durham with the sophomore year she spent at her hometown high school in Cullowhee. "We had a physics teacher who was a month ahead of the class," she said. The chemistry teacher was also not well trained: she could tell because her father was a chemistry professor at Western Carolina University in Cullowhee.

"We did not have chalk or paper, but the football team had a VCR and a wide-screen TV so they could see tapes of how they played," she said. "When I got to Science and Math the thing that impressed me the most was that there were people who were curious about current events, religion, you name it."

The school has unearthed scientists in quite unlikely places. Todd Rose is a sturdily built eighteen-year-old senior with a square jaw and strongly chiseled face who speaks with a molasses-thick drawl. He comes from Nashville, North Carolina, a small town of 1,300 people in the eastern part of the state where tobacco and soybeans are farmed. But Todd discovered a scientific muse from a stepfather who was a volunteer paramedic on the local ambulance squad. Had he stayed in Nashville he could have taken the shop classes in plowing and welding that the local high school offered but no science courses to speak of.

"My whole family was farmers and the only way I could see getting out of it was through science," he told me.

He heard about the Durham school from a friend, applied, and was accepted. Once at Durham, his exposure to medicine and caring doctors firmed up his determination not only to become a doctor, but very specifically to become a neurosurgeon. In the North Carolina School's mentorship program, he spent six to eight hours trailing cardiologists and neurosurgeons into the operating room, even observing open-heart surgery.

"That just blew my mind that I was setting here at seventeen looking at a person on a table while a doctor is explaining to me everything that's going on," he said. "It made me think this is something I want to do. Saving someone's life. It blew my mind that they could take someone and put them on a machine for six hours. Someone's putting their life in your hands. I had a feeling that I wanted to be a surgeon, but I had no idea that I wanted to be right in the thick of things, right in the operating room. I like the power and intensity of that situation."

He particularly remembers seeing a toddler who suffered from a terminal brain defect and her hopeful response whenever she saw the doctor caring for her. "It was basically a grim diagnosis, but he took the care even though she probably wouldn't live to the age of three," Todd recalled. "That little girl, her face lit up when the doctor walked into the room, and you can't put a price on that."

The schedule at the North Carolina School is far more taxing than at conventional high schools. In the fall of 1991, Kristine Johnson, a senior from Winston-Salem, was taking British literature, art, calculus, a seminar in European history, a course in embryology and evolution, and supplementing that mouthful with German and flute lessons at Duke University. In the spring, she again took history and calculus, but added ecology and polymer chemistry and the course in "Wisdom, Revelation, Reason, and Doubt." For three hours a week, she also did a mentorship in pediatric neurology at the University of North Carolina at Chapel Hill. Like Todd, she followed doctors as they went about their rounds, though the patients she saw suffered from such disorders as spina bifida. Medicine, it turned out, was not a field for which she pined.

Despite the rigors of her schedule, Kristine seemed like a very spirited eighteen-year-old as she moved briskly through the school in her Bermuda shorts and sneakers. She spoke about everything she did with a breathless fervor. When I encountered her, she was sitting in a small room filled with computer monitors and a rich variety of audiovisual consoles and was working on a project for her polymer chemistry class. She was trying to shape computerized images of chemical reactions into a kind of abstract art. She began by throwing salts like aluminum chloride into a beaker containing sodium silicate acid and videotaping the reactions. Then she digitized the video images so they could be transferred onto a color computer. With that computer, she could enhance the colors of the dissolving salt crystals or change the colors entirely, picking whatever hues she wanted off the computer's palette. She could oscillate the colors from red to blue to red again until she seized on the effect she wanted. The tableaus she liked best would be matted and hung for display.

"I was interested in linking chemistry and art," she told me. "There's so much color in a chemical reaction."

The payoff of this crowded schedule is precisely what the school and the state's leaders would have wanted. At this young age, Kristine had scuttled such earlier ambitions as journalism and already knew she wanted to be a chemist, with plans to study the field at the University of North Carolina at nearby Chapel Hill.

"It's orderly, systematic," she said of chemistry. "There are exceptions to the rules, but you learn to explain those exceptions."

Listening to Kristine it was hard to believe that she could ever have been a disenchanted student. But that's how she described herself when she spoke about her school years in Winston-Salem.

"In middle school there were only a few classes that I found to be challenging," she said. "The really interesting teachers were very rare. I was unhappy in my old high school, Mount Tabor. Students didn't like me because I liked to learn, because I did my homework. My peers didn't care about classes I was in."

For the genuinely science prone, the most compelling courses are those in research. Yet the fact that the school is only for juniors and seniors sharply condenses the seasoning interested students can get. Ultimately it is that fact that explains why the school has not won the larger trove of Westinghouses that one might have expected from such a select student body at such a well-endowed place.

In ways that do not quite mirror the more extensive experience at Bronx Science and Midwood, students learn basic research methods and laboratory techniques, then design their own projects. The courses are offered to forty or fifty students chosen on the basis of psychological tests and interviews that gauge their abilities to work autonomously.

"It's not something all of the students are ready for, even as juniors," said Warshaw, then the school's science chairman.

The students are divided among three biology sections and a single chemistry section. One of the three biology classes focuses on the genetics of microbes like bacteria and yeast and on recombinant DNA, the second on pathogens in plants, and the third on the behavior and physiology of invertebrates. These narrow topics have been chosen because the school has the equipment and the teachers to support such research. Some years ago, for example, several of the school's teachers took a workshop in recombinant DNA at the Cold Spring Harbor Laboratory in New York. The emphasis on plant pathogens was the serendipitous result of a greenhouse that was built with a gift from a seed company.

"If a kid wants to do marine biology, we can't support that," Warshaw said. "The emphasis in the course is not that they get to research their favorite topic. The emphasis is that they find out what it's like to do research."

The school has to put its research students through a more compressed and accelerated boot camp than do places like Bronx Science. At Bronx Science, students are already starting on their projects in September of their junior year. At North Carolina they are just getting acquainted with the school and with advanced science. Many have never taken chemistry. As Warshaw admits, "It's a very rapid development we're expecting of them."

The teachers start by taking students over to the Duke University library—which houses a far more sophisticated collection than that of the high school—and showing them how to plow through research journals.

"We have them pick out a paper they can read—and they have to spend some time finding one—and we talk with them about what they understood," says Warshaw. "It's very difficult for them in the beginning. There are several vocabularies. We home in on some narrow areas so they don't have to be responsible for so many words. It enables them to read with a fair amount of understanding. Some procedures are so technical they don't understand. But they are very good at understanding the concepts."

In class, the students learn how to grow bacteria in sterile fashion so that there is no infection from other strains. They learn how to distinguish different varieties of bacteria and yeast, how to inject pathogens into tobacco plants, how to keep plants alive. They learn such cutting-edge techniques as gel electrophoresis, which separates different strands of DNA migrating through a gelatinous agar and allows the students to identify genes on the chromosomes.

Once students are ready to tackle a project, the North Carolina School offers them two precious commodities they could not get in most high schools: space and time. The school has laboratories such as the Glaxo DNA lab that is reserved for research and not open to general science classes trooping in several times a day. That means that research students can be pretty sure their beakers and agar plates and fishtanks and seltzer-bottle terrariums will be safe from tampering hands. "That's a real luxury," Warshaw says. And the research students can work on their projects in the lab not only during their free periods but also after classes and late into the night.

When I visited the school just before graduation day in 1992, Ryan Bookout of Elon College, a young man with round wire-rimmed glasses, was studying the effects of home-brewed acid rain on the embryos of Japanese medaka fish, using the decrease in their heart rate as a measure of their viability. Before he came to Durham, Ryan had exhausted the science courses at his local high school and would have had to scratch around to invent his own science program for his junior and senior years. At Durham, he not only had all the school's facilities but could use the electron microscope at Duke University to get a detailed look at his embryos' hearts. And he could take humanities courses that he also prized, particularly a class in international relations that exposed him to the subtle contours of the Arab-Israeli conflict.

"A biologist who can't speak to the normal person is useless to the real world," he told me with teenage portentousness.

Laell Robbins of Fremont had exposed *E. coli* bacteria to a carcinogenic bromide and was studying the damage to the bacteria's DNA with all the Glaxo lab's state-of-the-art equipment. "One thing I learned is to think critically," he said, "to map out what you can do and what you can't do and to know there's a fine line between those."

Elizabeth Smith, seventeen, of Ayden was investigating the impact of nitrogen deficiency on one-leaf plants. Every evening, she slipped down to the greenhouse to make sure her plants had enough water and measured the leaves to see how much they had grown. "At home, we don't have the chemicals I need, we don't have a greenhouse, we don't have the money for vermiculite or pebbles," she said. "Before I came here I was thinking about being an architect. Now I'm thinking about botany. I had found something I like and I enjoy and I want to keep at it."

Celeste Posey, the 1989 Westinghouse winner, is a tall, slender young woman with dark eyes and wheat-colored hair that falls below her shoulders. She comes from Cary, a town next door to Raleigh and twenty miles southeast of the high school. Her father, Hollis, is a senior programming manager at an IBM office nearby.

Like so many Westinghouse students, Celeste had many talents. She was a straight-A student who scored 1510 out of a possible 1600 on her SAT. She was president of the school's Latin club, editor of the yearbook, a member of the girl's soccer team, and she put together a first-rate research project. She worked with viral DNA and developed a distinctive method of mapping what are known as restriction sites, the points where the DNA can be broken with the use of enzymes. She started her experiment by purchasing a virus from the U.S. Biochemical Corporation that was not supposed to have any restriction sites. When she discovered that indeed the virus did have a restriction, she realized that she possessed a mutant strain.

"She called the supplier and said she had found this restriction," Warshaw, Celeste's science teacher, told interviewers at the time. "They went into their labs and sure enough, all of their cultures had this change, which is called a mutation."

When Celeste's award was announced, her mother, Cay Posey, a deeply religious woman, told interviewers that Celeste "is under God's care."

"I don't worry about her," Mrs. Posey said. "She has been a good steward of her talent. Her faith and hard work have been affirmed."

But in fact, the program at the North Carolina School was fundamental to Celeste's achievement, and Celeste said so. "Here you're in a rarefied atmosphere because everybody is good in science and math," she said. "We have equipment coming out of our ears and time to use it." Celeste planned to use her $10,000 Westinghouse scholarship to do undergraduate work in microbiology either at Duke University or Wake Forest, both, incidentally, within the state.

With inventive students such as Celeste Posey, whose knowledge in their area of study soon surpasses the teacher's, the teacher's role is more of a shepherd than an instructor. "At some point you mainly have to stay out of their way and make sure when they need something you work with them to provide for their need," Warshaw said. Still Warshaw wants his students to cultivate a robust respect for data—"Data are the hard currency of science, what sets it apart from other endeavors," he says—and understand that science is increasingly a cooperative effort, not work for a lone hero.

Warshaw came to North Carolina when he was forty years old. After leaving his water-quality job in Texas, he was teaching at a small rural school when he visited his sister in Durham and learned of the North Carolina School's existence. "It was total luck," he recalled. "My sister lived down the street from the school and she said, 'There's a school down the street that specializes in teaching science and math to the gifted. Why don't you go out and check it out.'" School was closed that day and the only people Warshaw could talk with were the tennis coach and one forlorn student. But on his next visit to Durham in 1985, he learned of an opening and applied.

"The kids here are an absolute joy," he said. "They are what makes teaching in this school. The principal here says that he feels like he died and had gone to heaven."

By the late fall, Warshaw gently weans his research juniors away from their dependence on the school and pairs them with scientists in the Durham area so they can work on their independent projects. Matching students with mentors is not always simple. "The mentors kind of burn out after a couple of years," Warshaw says. "We have to match up personalities, make sure the kids are not being used as dishwashers but are doing meaningful work."

Needless to say, the research students are encouraged to compete in regional and national contests, including the Westinghouse. It is not done just for the glory of the school, though that is not a negligible factor. The school's educators believe that research projects tested in the fever of competition tend to be sharper, bolder. They force the students to reach more deeply into themselves. Success in a contest also sets off unanticipated ripples. News articles about the Westinghouse winners at North Carolina have sparked interest throughout the state in scientific competition. In 1992, Warshaw points out, the state had five semifinalists, though only two were from his school, while in earlier years his school was more dominant.

North Carolina also has the separate mentorship program for those students who want a less-demanding exposure to professional research. The program encourages students to spend three to five hours per week for a year assisting scientific professionals and, along the way, gaining a more tangible sense of what a career in science is all about. Students usually do their research at Duke University in Durham, the University of North Carolina in Chapel Hill, North Carolina State University in Raleigh, or the firms at Research Triangle Park. At the end, students submit papers based on the research they have observed. Eighteen-year-old senior Kristen Boyles, for example, did a year-long mentorship at Duke's South Hospital, compiling data on chronic pain patients for a psychiatrist. She spent one afternoon a week at the hospital, kept a journal, and wrote a paper distilling her experience.

"Here at school it's kind of artificial," said Warshaw. "There they do work in labs with the latest equipment. The advantage to them is they get to learn some cutting-edge procedures and they make contacts."

Each year, the school cancels classes for a week and students plunge into short-term projects. Kristen Boyles spent the "special projects week" with seven classmates and an instructor holed up in a campus cottage speaking, reading, and dining only in German. Nicholas Lee of Winston-Salem and Spence Allen of Washington, North Carolina, invented a kind of skateboard that sails on a cushion of blown air, using no wheels. A hair-dryer-like blower forces air into a plastic lining underneath the board, creating pressure that lifts the board, with Nicholas or Spence on it, off the ground while at the same time driving it slowly forward. I saw them take a slow slide through the physics department corridor while teachers and classmates marveled at this absurd but scientifically clever machine. Science, it was clear, can be just plain fun.

"It's like turning on a car instead of walking," Spence told me, explaining why he built such a whimsical vehicle. "We wanted to prove we could walk."

Sending children, even teenagers, away to boarding school is not without controversy. Many relatives and friends look with scorn upon parents who make such a choice. Yet it seems apparent that at the North Carolina School many students thrive in the residential atmosphere.

"It's kind of like going away to camp all year long," said Beth Glenn, a seventeen-year-old from Kernersville whose prominent braces did not restrain a dry sense of humor.

Students wander into each other's room to work through a baffling math problem, gossip about a teacher, or just seek some relief from the homesickness many feel. The dorm rooms are as typically unkempt as their college counterparts, except that the objects scattered about are closer to childhood than adulthood—a Winnie-the-Pooh bear, a Happy Birthday balloon, a bottle-cap collection, teenage cosmetics. One girl plastered a wall with rejection letters she had received from colleges. Another hung Monet and Botticelli prints. In the boy's rooms, portraits of Einstein alternated with posters of Arnold Schwarzenegger as Terminator.

As he showed me his room, Bimal Shah, a seventeen-year-old

junior of Indian heritage from Winston-Salem, said that he liked learning "how to live, how to grow up, how to deal with your environment," particularly in a school where the other students and the teachers were a challenge.

"In the old school you're surrounded by kids who don't care about learning," he said, with boyish earnestness. "Here you're around the smartest people in the state. At my old school everybody came to me with their homework. And if I didn't know it, that was a problem."

Kristine Johnson seemed to appreciate studying together in the evenings with students as passionate about learning as she was. "Studying is a lonely task," she said. "Here you have a study group in math or history. That makes it more fun."

Still, it cannot be easy for a fifteen-year-old to leave home for two years and live at a high school, and a highly competitive one at that. On the field trip to the Eno River, Dawn O'Brien, a junior from Wilmington, told me she hungered for her friends back home and worried that her two years in Durham might break the emotional connections. At the same time, she was ever-conscious of how much her mother worried about her. Dawn had been sick once at school and the mother was aware that her little girl spent much of the day lying in a dormitory bed by herself. Dawn was aware that her mother was aware. There had been a mugging in the school's neighborhood and that added another anxiety to the mother's list. Dawn also bridled under rules that set an 8 P.M. curfew for students who left the campus for town.

Officials of the school say about 10 percent of the 280 juniors who start return to hometown schools. "Most of them have difficulty in making the adjustment or they go home because they're homesick and not ready or, rarely, for disciplinary problems," said Warshaw. "Many of these kids have made nothing but 98s and 99s. When they come here and get a C on their first test, they realize they're not at the top of the heap anymore and that's a big adjustment. And then they have to live with someone in a dormitory, keeping the place clean at a very young age."

One thing that seems to nourish students through those two tough years is their encounters with teachers who begin to transform their lives. When I spoke with the half-dozen alumni at the

Greek restaurant, the talk flamed to life when they relived the memories of their teachers. Everyone seemed to savor recollections of two physics teachers, John "Doc" Kolena and Andres Manring, who always came into class carrying some whimsical object that turned out to be basic to an elemental law of physics. These teachers would ask them why, when they showered that morning, the shower curtains fluttered toward their bodies (the answer has something to do with Bernoulli's principle explaining the dynamics of gases and liquids, recalled Gina Norman) or why water goes down a drain clockwise in the southern hemisphere and counterclockwise in the northern hemisphere. Kolena, they remembered, once rolled an aquarium filled with water into the classroom, dumped in a pint of milk, and shone a flashlight through the mixture that created a blue glow. Why, he then asked, would he have "ruined a perfectly good aquarium"? The demonstration, the alumni remembered, showed that blue and other short waves of light bend more than longer waves when they're refracted off an object, a principle that helps explain why the sky is blue.

"It's seven years later and I remember it," said Gina.

Bruce Lee remembered how Bill Youngblood, his chemistry teacher then, taught him "to do really quality work, to really be proud of what you've done" beyond simply getting A's. And Gina spoke of how Jon Miller, an English instructor, taught her not just to write, but how to think. He never cared how farfetched a student's opinion was, she said, as long as the student could support the statement.

It is the chance to work with such talented teachers that keeps students coming to North Carolina and working hard while there. Indeed, academic outcomes seem to reflect the verve of most students. In 1989's junior-year class, 37.9 percent of the final grades were A's. The class of 1992 had a mean of 584 on the verbal portion of the SAT and a mean of 659 on the math portion. Through 1989, for four years in a row, the school produced more semifinalists in the prestigious National Merit Scholarship competition than any other high school in the country. In 1992, it finished second with seventy-nine Merit semifinalists to ninety-one for another special school, the Thomas Jefferson High School for Science and Technology, in Virginia. In the 1992 graduating class, three students were accepted to Brown, four to Harvard, three to Princeton, four to MIT, three to the California Institute of Technology and one to Stanford.

Still, two-thirds of the graduates chose to go to colleges within the state, such as the University of North Carolina at Chapel Hill or Duke University. That fact vindicated the chauvinistic officials and businessmen who started the school and gave them ammunition against critics who predicted that the school would inspire a mass exodus of the state's elite to northeastern schools.

"We tell students they are here as the seedcorn of North Carolina's future," said Dr. John Friedrick, the executive director of the school. "The money that North Carolina has invested in them needs to be returned for the benefit of those who couldn't afford to attend this school."

Even the prediction that the school would skim off the cream of local high schools, depleting them of their brainpower, has not turned out to be true, school officials say. In fact, Warshaw says, the school has taken only one or two students from the best high schools in cities such as Raleigh and Charlotte, and its skimming has been even spottier elsewhere.

To further justify its rarefied existence to the state's taxpayers, the North Carolina School spends a lot of its energy on programs for all the state's teachers and students. More than 3,000 teachers have passed through the school's summer workshops to learn experiments they can do in their classes back home. Warshaw may show them how to splice genes. Loren Winters, a physics teacher, may demonstrate how to use high-speed photography to explain the physics of a racquetball bouncing off a wall. "Most science teachers teach science, but don't know science," said Bill Youngblood, the director of "outreach." "We teach them how to teach good experimentation. That's how you turn kids on."

The school's math department has written a precalculus textbook that is used around the state, and other textbook projects are planned by other departments. Such programs have turned the volume of criticism down to a whisper.

It is still too early to know how well the school is succeeding in its prime mission of steering young people into scientific careers. Many of the first alumni are still in graduate school. However, of the 1,494 students who graduated between 1982 and 1989, 80 percent went on to major in science and engineering.

The North Carolina School does not come cheap. By 1992, a single student's education cost the state about $12,000 a year, roughly four times the expense at conventional high schools. Kolena, the physics teacher, admits, "We're certainly taking money from someone's education," though he adds, "I'd like to think we're returning it." But a rousing justification for that expense came in 1989 when Celeste Posey won fifth place and $10,000 in the Westinghouse and two other seniors finished in the Westinghouse honors group of 300. Until 1989, the state had not had a Westinghouse winner in ten years, and had only had five winners in the entire history of the contest.

"I see this as the beginning of our coming of age," trumpeted Youngblood, the principal at the time.

In 1990, the school claimed two more semifinalists. And in 1991, the school produced the first-place winner for the entire nation, Ashley Melia Reiter, a blooming mathematician from Charlotte.

Her project was on fractals.

Chapter Seven

Different Strokes

Communities often react to new science schools the way neighbors might react to the kid down the block who buys a set of drums. Still, Leon Lederman likes to tell people how easy it was to sell the state on the Illinois Mathematics and Science Academy. Lederman is the genial former director of the Fermi National Accelerator Laboratory. If this Nobel laureate had not made it big on the scientific stage he could have earned a pretty good living working the Catskills. He quips that in his campaign for an Illinois science school he went to see Gov. James Thompson and said, "How about a James Thompson School for Gifted Kids?" and the governor replied, "Gee, that's a good idea."

Actually the battle plan rivaled Desert Storm's in its political and financial convolutions. A nonprofit corporation was set up to raise funds and juggle planning. Northern Illinois University took a formal look at the quality of math and science instruction in the region. The state board of education investigated the practicality of establishing a residential school. A conference was convened to develop a curriculum and a mission statement. Governor Thompson, legislative leaders, corporate chief executives, educators, and scientists were enlisted in the cause, and a board of trustees was recruited. Lederman, the school's major founder and its guardian angel, raised hundreds of thousands of dollars on his own, eating a lot of rubber chicken and wearing out a lot of jokes. In 1986, five years after the start of the North Carolina School, the Illinois academy opened its doors in Aurora, a town forty miles west of Chicago.

"They came with their footlockers, their bass fiddles and bongo drums," Lederman recalls.

A three-year school, in contrast to North Carolina's two-year program, it now has 630 students and an $11 million annual budget. It offers courses in advanced algebra, analytic geometry, computer languages, number theory, multivariable calculus, discrete mathematics, astrophysics, microbiology, thermodynamics, and organic chemistry. And it does not scrimp on the humanities. The school offers advanced placement classes in economics and European history, electives in six languages, including Russian and Japanese, and a philosophical course that struggles with the timeless conflict between science and religion and other intellectual and ethical dilemmas.

Stephanie Marshall, the academy's executive director, believes that students learn far more from examining research, talking to experts, talking to each other, than they do by simply mastering textbooks. "Yes, students need to learn to read and write and add and subtract, but more importantly, they need to learn to think and adapt and anticipate consequences," she says. Marshall is something of an iconoclast who believes in unconventional approaches. She invented a teaching cycle of six days rather than the standard five because it provides large blocks of time for in-depth research. The academy may be the only high school in the nation with a full-time resident scientist on its staff. Ronald Pine, a former research curator at the Smithsonian Institution, does not teach classes and gets paid to conduct his own mammalian research, which students have affectionately labeled "bats, rats, and possums." But he works with teams of students on research projects and helps students prepare their work for publication.

The Illinois school is called an academy rather than a high school because, though it is state-sponsored, it is spared from the strictures of the state education code. As with the North Carolina school, teachers there do not have to meet the state's certification requirements and the school has been able to hire a faculty loaded with doctorates: 25 percent have Ph.Ds, and all teachers have master's degrees. The school scours the state for bright kids, selecting them on the basis of course grades and teacher recommendations. The merit approach is not strictly followed, however. This is, after all, the 1990s, and the school, like Harvard and Berkeley and Exeter, is concerned about its racial, geographical, and gender diversity and works hard to make sure the student body is reflective of the state. The academy sponsors programs for minority students in Chicago, East St. Louis, and Joliet to prepare candidates who can qualify for admission.

For those who doubted the wisdom of gathering bright students in one place and teaching them how to think and work like scientists, a major rebuttal came in 1993 when Elizabeth Pine of Chicago (no relation to the in-house scientist) won first place in the nation in the Westinghouse. She used DNA sequencing to demonstrate the close relationship between two fungi that had been thought to be dissimilar.

Lederman is one of the school's chief salesmen and most aggressive money raisers. He does not fit the conventionally sober picture of a Nobelist. Indeed, when Lederman is delivering one-liners he sounds like Mel Brooks. Lederman grew up in the East Bronx with a brother who, he says, was the real genius. He attended James Monroe High School during the Depression years, when the school had what he remembers as phenomenal teachers.

He tours the state like a vaudeville act, giving scores of talks to parents' associations and citizens' groups in the hopes both of extracting donations and recruiting students. The latter, if you think about it, is the tougher sell. Many parents are reluctant to send a son or daughter away to school in the tender years of high school. It is not so much that they worry about the dangers or enticements that lurk. It is simply hard to say good-bye to a child you have not finished raising. In the last three years, Lederman, who is now vice president of the board of directors, has personally won donations of $4.5 million.

He is proud of the atmosphere that has been created at Illinois Academy. The students, he says, are brimming with enthusiasm and energy, and at Illinois Academy they are no longer isolated freaks. They are among kids who speak the same language and share the same passions, and they flourish. "These kids have been up all night talking to one another," he says. "Anything you throw at them they absorb. Differential equations, monolinear math, they'll absorb." He believes that the collision between such students and superb teaching will yield a potent intellectual product.

"You're nurturing the Fort Knox of the country, the most precious thing we have," he says. "One of them is going to cure senility and I need it fast."

The school costs the state $17,000 per youngster, more than double the average per-student cost of a high school education, but Lederman argues the expense is more than worth it. "If one of these kids makes a breakthrough like James Watson, you pay for the school for a hundred years."

On the other hand, he says, failing to take such educational risks may nip some potential James Watsons in the bud. "A lot of these kids would probably be O.K.," he says. "Some of them are so connected with their brilliance, they will take care of themselves. But some are very vulnerable. When I was in City College there were bright guys who ended up sitting in their rooms with their mother leaving a plate outside the door, or others went off to join a commune. So no question these kids are vulnerable."

When Lyndon Johnson was president of the United States, Emmette Redford was president of the American Political Science Association; both hailed from Johnson City, Texas. Struck by the coincidence, reporters asked Redford how a little town like Johnson City could have bred two people who had achieved so much in the art of government. Redford replied, "Well, there wasn't anything in town except three churches and a courthouse, and although Lyndon and I gave some attention to what was going on in the churches, we were more interested in what happened at the courthouse."

In fact, the town had a superb high school instructor in civics, Scott Klett, who inspired enormous interest in the workings of government. Because the town was the county seat, some of those workings could be seen firsthand, particularly when trials were in session. "I doubt whether there ever has been a group of kids with more intense interest in politics than the group that went through school with Lyndon," Redford said. Of course, he added, hardly anyone in town became a scientist because the local school had no laboratories and no instructors who could cultivate an interest in science.

The anecdote, related in Robert Dallek's 1991 biography of Johnson, *Lone Star Rising: Lyndon Johnson and His Times*

1908–1960, illustrates how a particular culture and ambience can breed particular offspring. It is a lesson that is the basis of the science schools sprouting around the country, and it is a lesson that has finally been learned by Texas itself.

In 1988, the state legislature, concerned about the state's ability to compete in a science-driven world, opened the Texas Academy of Mathematics and Science. It is not so much a high school as a college program for high school students. It is thus a striking wrinkle on the concept of selective science schools and bears a closer look by states that cannot afford to lavish money or political capital on setting up independent science high schools. Massachusetts, in fact, announced plans in 1992 to copy the Texas model, on a commuter and not on a residential basis, at the Worcester Polytechnic Institute.

The Texas Academy is located on the campus of the University of North Texas in Denton, a city forty miles north of the Dallas–Ft. Worth nexus. The academy's students are juniors and seniors in high school, and in the fall of 1992, 337 mathematics and science students were enrolled. They are put up in North Texas dormitories and allowed to earn credits toward their first two years of college while simultaneously speeding through their final two years of high school.

"We're hoping to give these students a jump by pushing and challenging them," William Brady, director of the academy, told *The Chronicle of Higher Education* in 1989. "We want to turn them on to math and science even more than they already are."

The students effectively become science and math majors in college, taking university courses with regular university faculty. They are also offered a few courses in the humanities. Tuition is free, but students pay $4,000 a year for room and board. At the end of two years, they can stay on at North Texas or opt to attend a college elsewhere in the country. One student, Sherri Webb, told *The Chronicle* that she had always planned to attend MIT, yet enrolled in the academy because she felt the program would allow her to get a head start on her high school classmates.

The academy's toughest challenge is treating high school kids as, well, high school kids. Unlike the regular college students, the academy students must be in their dormitory by 11 P.M. and cannot leave the campus without approval. They need parental permission to date college students. The date can only come up to the dormitory room on weekends, and even then the door must be kept open. Students can join the marching band and most other clubs, but fraternities and sororities and sports teams are forbidden. An effort is made to make up for some of the high school rituals that students miss; the academy, for example, sponsors a dance. But generally the directors count on the students' maturity to see them through what they miss of a traditional high school life. Indeed, the admission staff will turn down a student who has high marks and SAT scores if they feel the applicant lacks the independent personality to thrive among older college students.

The college campus school is a more economical prototype for specialized science schools, but it is not cheap. The state had to give the academy a total of $2.1 million for the 1989–90 and 1990–91 academic years. It also turned over to the academy the $1,270 per pupil in state aid that would have been sent to the students' home districts. The state's aim is to get the students to stay in Texas, and the state's colleges conspire in that aim. They sponsor an all-day recruiting fair for the academy's students.

In the academy's first year, which ended in the spring of 1989, the academy's students chalked up a 2.9 grade point average, slightly higher than the average of regular freshmen at the university and quite impressive given the students' age. However, according to *The Chronicle*, sixteen of the eighty-eight students who started the program did not come back, a suggestion that many found the regimen too grueling or were too young to handle a college environment. College mathematics courses seemed to pose the greatest difficulties. Most of the students, after all, had skipped high school math courses and lacked a strong foundation. Many did not do as well as their college classmates.

Still, Julian Stanley, a professor of psychology at Johns Hopkins University who serves on the Texas Academy's board, told *The Chronicle* that the academy is a cheap alternative to the country's other special science schools. It creates an instant advanced high school by capitalizing on a university's courses, faculty, buildings, and laboratories.

"The common factor is the exhilaration these students have being with each other," he said.

Still another variation on the theme can be found in Kalamazoo, Michigan, the town forever memorialized by the Glenn Miller song. The Kalamazoo Area Mathematics and Science Center avoids the anxieties that dormitory life stirs for some parents. It is a regional rather than a residential school. It draws students from fourteen different public and church-sponsored high schools in the Kalamazoo area, but the students don't live at the school. They are driven there by their parents or ferried by their home school's bus system. The selected students attend the center for half of each school day, taking science and math courses, then spend the other half day at their home schools, taking English, social studies, art, and extracurricular activities.

What science and math courses they take at Kalamazoo! There are electives in organic chemistry, science writing, anatomy, physiology, advanced mathematical problem solving, and one complex computer programming course called Pascal. There are accelerated, honors-level courses in chemistry, physics, and computer studies. Every member of the faculty has at least a master's degree.

Research skills are emphasized. There is a mentorship program that allows students to work on projects with professional or academic scientists from the area's four colleges and universities and from private research firms. To make research possible right on campus, the center has an electron microscope, several visible spectrophotometers, oscilloscopes, twenty-five medical-school-quality binocular compound microscopes, and classrooms equipped with Apple and Macintosh computers.

"While the state-wide programs such as North Carolina, Illinois, Mississippi, etc., will continue to draw a large amount of attention," the center's director, Jon Thompson, wrote me, "the regional programs such as the Kalamazoo Area Mathematics and Science Center will ultimately have a greater impact on students because a greater number of students can become involved. We do not have to take students away from their family life and their peers."

Kalamazoo is a public school, but it was started with a $2 million grant from The Upjohn Company, the 100-year-old pharmaceutical manufacturer whose headquarters are in Kalamazoo. Upjohn is the company that created such popular over-the-counter products as Kaopectate, Cheracol, and Unicap, and such prescription drugs as the anti-inflammatory agent Motrin. It established the Kalamazoo science center as a centennial gift to the community, but there is little doubt that it wanted to make sure it continued to have a strong pool of scientifically trained residents in the Kalamazoo area. A 1987 Science Center brochure practically spelled that goal out. It said that the science center "is a way of meeting our problems— the decline of scientific literacy, the shortage of technical man- power, dwindling federal support of education. All communities large and small face them. They are national problems, but their force is localized, communal. So must be their treatment. The intent of KAMSC is to educate the scientific and technical leaders of tomorrow."

The school opened in August 1986 with a class of 75 ninth- graders and by 1989 it had 300 freshmen, sophomores, juniors, and seniors. Students are nominated for the center in the eighth grade and selection is based on an entrance examination, a writing sam- ple, grades, and national test scores. About 200 of those nominated actually apply, and 75 are accepted. The students are superior aca- demically to the average Michigan youngster. In 1988, for example, the mean scores of the center's juniors on the verbal portion of the Preliminary Scholastic Aptitude Test (PSAT) was 54.9 com- pared with a statewide mean of 39.6.

To fertilize interest in science for those youngsters who don't qualify for admission, the center runs a summer school for elemen- tary, middle, and high school students and it sponsors Saturday- morning science seminars. It has held workshops that have trained more than 1,000 teachers in science safety and in the use of an electron microscope.

The number of science schools has grown so rapidly that, with the the characteristic American affection for fellowship and camaraderie, they formed an association in April 1988. The National Consortium for Specialized Schools of Mathematics, Science and Technology has the rather lofty, some might say quixotic, aim of stimulating interest in the teaching of high-quality science. It also has the practical objective of representing the so-called science-intensive schools before Congress, state legislatures, foundations, and private industry in the competition for education dollars.

Stephanie Marshall, of the Illinois Academy, was a key founder of the association, and at its first convention in 1988, twenty-seven schools and associations were represented by roughly 100 teachers. There has been a convention every year since. Teachers exchange experiences, talk about curricular issues, map strategies for increasing minority enrollment, mull the wisdom of national competitions.

The group also hosts an annual conference for students. At the first one, held at the Thomas Jefferson High School for Science and Technology in Virginia, Carl Sagan told the 118 delegates, "At a time of dangerous decline in science training and science literacy in America, the consortium is making a valuable effort to reverse the trend." At a second conference in October 1989 at the North Carolina School in Durham, Dr. Heinz-Otto Peltgen of the University of Bremen, West Germany, lectured about fractals and chaos. For diversion, there was a dance and a cookout dinner where students savored southern pork barbecue and fried chicken.

The science schools have often been called elitist and charged with fostering exclusive groups who will feel superior to some hypothetical mass of others. This is simply a lie. American society has been built on the notion that excellence should percolate out of the grinds. What are Harvard and Yale but selective schools? What are IBM and the *New York Times* and the New York Yankees but selective institutions. Protecting children from selectivity will not prepare them for the adult world.

Dr. Lawrence Cranberg, a physicist in Austin, Texas, who wrote a letter on the subject of elitism to the *American Journal of Physics*, pointed out that elitism is a term borrowed from political science that broadly means rule by an elite.

"That has nothing whatsoever to do with nurturing an elite of talent," he said. "That so primitive a confusion exists even among us is dismaying and must be confronted. Physicists are like the miner's canaries. Their health and vigor is an early warning signal of the healthfulness of the air we breathe. And although some canaries are still singing, the native species is headed for mass extinction unless we act quickly and intelligently."

The infuriating irony is that the elitist argument is often made by people who themselves have been beneficiaries of Harvard or Wesleyan, or who want nothing better than to work at law firms like Sullivan and Cromwell. Their assumption is that schools should be exempt from the desire to concentrate special resources on the best and the brightest. To argue against elitism, as opponents use the term, is to argue that companies should not compete for the best workers, that colleges should not compete for the best students, films for the best actors, and publishers for the best writers. Instead it is to consign our society to a bland mediocrity in which everyone gets an equal chance to do a little bit of everything, but no one is encouraged to do anything well.

When asked about elitism, Leon Lederman shoots back, "What about the Chicago Bears or the Cubs? Are they not elitism? This is elitism of the intellect."

He also rejects the argument that specialized science schools rob schools of their brightest youngsters. A school such as Illinois Academy may rob one or two of the brightest kids from every school in Illinois. That certainly will not deplete any individual school. If society is willing to spend $15,000 for educating every handicapped child, $32,000 for housing every prisoner, why should it not spend tens of thousands of dollars on a youngster whose brain performs better than the run of the mill?

Among educators there has long been a considerable opposition to tracking. The argument holds that in a nontrack system the brightest students teach the slower ones how to read while the slower ones teach the brightest how to socialize or draw or sing. There is no doubt something to that romanticized notion, but many teachers are also aware of the problems inherent in this approach. In January 1990, the *New York Times* printed a letter from Elfie Israel, a Florida public school English teacher who had earlier taught in New York City. He argued that such "heterogenous groupings result in classes sinking to their lowest common denominators."

How can critical reading skills be taught if the bright need to explain the plot to others? When will there be time to study the nuances of meaning, the subtleties of language, the beauty of the words? Students, susceptible to peer pressure, are more likely to do less because our society does not value intelligence and perseverance. The bright do not want to be ridiculed, to be mocked, to be used— and so they will naturally do less, be accepted, and learn that that is the "American" way. I hope not.

Besides, there is also something to the notion that bright minds fire each other up, that a third-grader who is curious about Einstein will get more of a chance to explore his or her thoughts in a classroom where there are other students who are curious about Einstein.

Part IV

The Students

Chapter Eight

One Small Step for Mankind

Vanessa Liu wants to be an astronaut, quite specifically, the commander of the first international mission to Mars.

"It's the next frontier," she says, her eyes dancing simply imagining the journey. "On Earth, we've basically explored almost everything. If we establish a colony on Mars we can go to other planets."

But Vanessa has three strikes against her. For one thing she is a female seeking membership in virtually an all-male club. For another, she is Chinese-American while the astronauts are red, white, and blue—though mainly white—Americans. Most of all her mother thinks she's crazy. "My mom says, 'What happens if you go on the space shuttle Challenger and it blows up?'" Vanessa says. "I love astronomy so much that I'm willing to take that risk. I'd rather be a doer than a spectator."

So there on a crisp sunny day in early March, a day brimming with premonitions of spring, is seventeen-year-old Vanessa taking her first small step for mankind. She is standing in front of a mock-up of the space shuttle, which is perched on scaffolding inside a cavernous hangar of the Goddard Space Flight Center in Greenbelt, Maryland. Dwarfing Vanessa, the shuttle looks like a beached white whale except that it has been fitted with a new weather-research satellite that will soon be released into space. Goddard is where satellites are tailored to the shuttles and where the data they transmit is gathered and studied, and Vanessa is here to talk to NASA's scientists about what it will take to become an astronaut and command a craft like the shuttle. For Vanessa, Goddard is easily the best choice among the medley of scientific installations that have offered tours and professional conversations to the forty winners of the Westinghouse Science Talent Search.

Vanessa is slim, with a waterfall of long black hair down her back and a bright, eager-to-please disposition that conceals more than a few inner struggles. She is dressed in a trim red suit and brown loafers and dangling from her arm is an Instamatic-type camera. But she is not just a starry-eyed tourist here. She has information to pass along. A short walk from the shuttle installation is a "clean room," a huge alcohol-scrubbed, dust-free room where scientists in bleached white overalls tinker with satellites without worrying about dirt particles that might distort delicate optical instruments. Dr. Richard Fisher, a physicist who is devoting his life to studying the sun and who today is serving as one of Vanessa's escorts, tells her that the room is the largest clean room in the free world. But Vanessa has already seen the largest clean room in the entire world. It was on a visit to the Soviet Union in 1988 as part of a delegation of American junior high and high school students sponsored by NASA and an American science teachers association. She tells Fisher and her other NASA escorts that in the Soviet clean room the scientists wore plain clothes, not these foreboding and antiseptic overalls, though, she adds, the Soviet satellite was wrapped in cellophane to keep it clean. Since they've never been to the Soviet installation, they listen with keen attention to her descriptions. Fisher pays her back by advising her that, against conventional belief, electrical engineering, not astrophysics or aeronautics, will provide the best foundation for a career as an astronaut. And, over lunch in Goddard's cafeteria, Dr. Ted Gull, associate chief of the Laboratory for Astronomy and Solar Physics, offers her a word of cautionary advice: "This is not a forty-hour-per-week place. When a mission is going up, we work 100 hours and we do it because we love it."

That information does not phase her one bit. Her schedule in and out of Stuyvesant High School in Manhattan is as tumultuous as a mission launch every week. Still, before she leaves, Vanessa is teenager enough to ask the scientists to stand in front of the shuttle so she can snap their photograph.

While there is something wonderfully innocent and eminently

dismissable about a teenager's ambition to fly to Mars, with Vanessa one never knows. Perhaps it will not be some pipe dream. Vanessa, after all, goes after what she wants and usually gets it. Her dreaming is almost never idle.

She started to take piano lessons when she was seven and within a few years her teacher, Tung Kwong Kwong, a famous pianist in Asia, wanted her to travel around the United States giving concerts. (She never did.) She started to take ice-skating lessons and soon her instructor urged her to consider a professional career, even a bid for the Olympics.

"I used to dream of the Olympics," she told me, just a few weeks after an Asian-American woman, Kristi Yamaguchi, won the gold medal in figure skating. "Oh gosh, I would have to wake up at four in the morning and then skate after school and then I would have to drop all my other activities, which I'm not willing to. In the past I had that decision to make. I advanced really quickly. But then I realized I would practically have to give up my childhood and high school for skating. I just do it for recreation now. For the love of skating."

Similarly, this Renaissance teenager began work on a neurobiology research project at school—a scientific enthusiasm totally different from her interest in astronomy and space—and within two years she was in Washington battling for the 1992 Westinghouse prize money, and visiting Goddard.

What is it, then, that makes Vanessa Vanessa, that allows her to do so many things so well, that allows her to scale heights of achievement from which most teenagers recoil as if they had acrophobia. Ultimately, such questions remain a mystery. Still, there are a few telling personal facts and some hunches.

Vanessa is what the country folks in *Mr. Smith Goes to Washington* called pixilated, and she volunteers that she is an incurable eccentric. Breathlessly, she follows her whims and passions wherever they may lead her, and society, school, and her parents be damned (unless, of course, her parents give her too hard a time). In fact Vanessa has made a study of eccentricity and has given speeches on the subject as a member of Stuyvesant's speech team (a spinoff of its debating team). Over lunch in a coffee shop around the corner from Stuyvesant, she told me how she has spoken about "a king whose toenails were like around six inches long and he had to walk on crutches" and an "English author who was rather a rotund man and he would roll down hills to amuse people, to amuse himself."

"Eccentricity is actually something creative for people," she said. "Great things have been made by people who have not cared about what other people think about their eccentricities and society should not discourage people from their eccentricities and should actually encourage them to be different people."

At first glance, the traits Vanessa describes as eccentricities are rather trivial, not terribly offbeat. Vanessa has a habit of talking to herself. And she has these sudden bursts of energy. At odd hours. And often with her cherished cousins—thirty of them—in the Netherlands.

"My friends say, 'You're too crazy, Vanessa. Why do you do these little things?' When I was in Holland with my cousins, I was so awake one night I made my cousin drive a bunch of us in the middle of the forest and just walk in the forest. It was pitch dark and it was crazy. New York has so many street lights everywhere and it's dangerous. I thought it was really neat how it's so safe there that you can go out in the middle of the forest and not have to worry about being murdered."

But her true eccentricity, and what it is that is really important to say about her, is that Vanessa gets extraordinarily passionate about things, and then works very hard at them until she masters them thoroughly. Of course, she had a high average at Stuyvesant—a 97.5 average—and scored 780 on her math SAT and 670 on her verbal, a perfect score on each being 800. ("I wasn't concentrating very much on the reading comp," she apologized. "It's so hard. I didn't want to be there.") But she achieved that while captaining the girl's team in soccer, a sport she loves, and taking a strong role in the drama club, another of her twenty or thirty enthusiasms. "It's great how you can become things you are not," she says of the theater. "It serves as an inlet to myself, to discover myself." She even sometimes writes articles for the school newspaper. All in addition to her serious practice in figure skating at an East Side ice studio on weekends and the one to four hours per week of piano lessons at the Si-Yo Music Society, which is run by Kwong and her husband, the violinist Ma Si-Hon. (In the spring of 1992 she was practicing for a solo graduation recital that would take place a few weeks after her Westinghouse trip to Washington.) And, of course, she put in twenty hours or more per week at a laboratory at Mt. Sinai Medical Center to produce her winning Westinghouse.

How does she do all this? For one thing, Vanessa manages to thrive while sleeping comparatively little.

"Last term it was horrible. Last term I got an average four to five hours. I had so many things. After Westinghouse I had to do my homework, and study for tests and try to keep my grades up as well as do all of these other things."

And she has far more of that indefinable quality called energy—Is it psychological abandon? Is it high metabolism? Is it uncommon genes?—than most human beings.

Actually, Vanessa offers a rather parsimonious explanation. Her various activities have different seasons. She can play for the girl's soccer team in the spring and give speeches in the fall. Of course, that explanation does not quite account for all the homework and piano playing and figure skating and all the rest.

"They're all at different times and so it usually works out. Usually. It was really hard last year when I had to juggle soccer. What would happen was after soccer practice I would go up to the lab and I'd be really tired. I'd be so tired. But I do all this stuff on weekends. Like piano and figure skating. That's on weekends."

Whoo!

But Vanessa also has a rather discerning explanation for why she brings so much fire to all these pursuits. "What's good about these things is that all of these things are my own incentive," she says. "I'm pretty sure if someone had pushed me I wouldn't have wanted to do it. My parents encourage me but they weren't, like, 'You have to do this, you have to play the piano, you have to write an excellent paper for the Westinghouse, and do really good research.' They encouraged it but it wasn't extreme pushing. It was my own incentive, and I thought that was probably what made me stay through all of these things. It's because I love doing them all."

It is probably not too daring to say that Vanessa may also have been born with exceptional gifts, something that gets overlooked in the egalitarian rush to attribute success simply to the whims of economic status. Her mother, Sheung Mei Liu, says Vanessa has always had a remarkable memory.

"She knew all the twenty-six letters of the alphabet by the time she was thirteen months," Mrs. Liu said. "I bought her alphabet blocks. If I mention A or B, she get A or B. She didn't talk well but she knew."

Mrs. Liu is a rather impressive woman herself. In a matter of years after immigrating to the United States, she built from scratch a midtown Manhattan shop that manufactures crystal earrings and other costume jewelry for such customers as the Miss America Pageant. But more about her later.

Vanessa has also been blessed with a remarkably independent and enterprising spirit. Psychologists and biologists might debate what that is, but there seems little doubt that some children come into the world with a sense of great trepidation, clinging first to their mother, then to home, then to spouse, sometimes never really setting out on their own, while others are out and about almost from the time they can walk. They actively seek out unseen places, unfamiliar people, untried pursuits. The world for them is like a great carnival, with every ride or booth an invitation to enchantment. And so it seems for Vanessa, who tackles everything she does with zest and verve.

While I interviewed Mrs. Liu in the summer of 1992 in her small showroom, the phone rang. It was Vanessa calling from Berlin. That's right, Germany. I had forgotten that she was planning to spend the summer at the Free Institute of Berlin studying biochemistry. A solitary trip of that distance is unusual enough for a seventeen-year-old, but her mother mentioned that Vanessa was leaving Berlin on weekends and taking trains all on her own to Amsterdam to visit her cousins, the children of her father's three brothers and a sister who settled there.

"She's crazy," her mother said.

It was an affectionate rebuke. After all, it was Mrs. Liu who bought Vanessa her Eurailpass. And Vanessa had visited the Netherlands many times before. Mrs. Liu proudly showed me a note Vanessa sent from Berlin that said, "Please write/call/fax to me often, or else I'm just not going to bring back any form of chocolate. Ha!"

So Vanessa is exceptionally self-reliant. But ultimately what makes Vanessa Vanessa remains elusive. The very same mix of traits in another child would not yield someone of Vanessa's extraordinary accomplishments. Vanessa herself suggests in a conversation that gifts such as hers may also need the right surroundings and acquaintances, more nurture than nature. When we were heading out for Goddard Space Center from Washington's Mayflower Hotel, our taxi drove through a rundown section of town where we saw clutches of young men standing around a small park, neither working nor going to school. The contrast with Vanessa, whose industriousness would be rewarded that evening with a prize at the Westinghouse ceremony, was so glaring that I asked her why those young people were not in her shoes. She did not mention poverty. After all, she had once been poor also. She did not mention the fact the young men were black. She too was a minority. She did not mention marginality. Who could be more marginal than a Hong Kong immigrant?

"They succumb to peer pressure," she said of the young men. "It's based on your friends and the people you hang out with. If one of them expressed an interest in science, their friends would say, 'Oh, that's lame.' They're afraid of not being part of the group."

Yet, Vanessa's foreign birth has, no doubt, made affirmation by certain groups, perhaps even elite intellectual ones, very important to her. After all, doing well in science at a place like Stuyvesant does not exactly make one a maverick. And Vanessa is not really a maverick, perhaps exaggerating the feisty, crusty side of herself to disarm those who would see her as too much of a golden girl.

Vanessa was born in New York City in 1974, a period when New York was just beginning to experience its first great wave of Asian immigrants. Her parents were both from Hong Kong, though her mother's roots were actually in mainland China where Vanessa's grandfather had been an officer in the army of Chiang Kai-shek. Vanessa's father, Kai Yin Liu, came to the United States in the late 1960s to study sociology at the University of Oregon, then moved to California and then to New York in search of work. Mrs.

Liu had gone to high school in Hong Kong with her future husband and later taught music and singing in an elementary school in Hong Kong. But in 1972, she joined him in New York, partly to marry, but partly because she was aware that the British Crown colony, the banking and commercial capital of Southeast Asia, had no future. It was going to become part of China in 1997.

The early years in this country were painful for the Lius, a pain still evident in Mrs. Liu's doleful eyes and ironic smile. The Lius had left families thousands of miles away. They had little money. Most of all they were Chinese in a country that has always seen Asians as irretrievably alien. Indeed, Mrs. Liu's brother has refused to leave Hong Kong because he does not want to be a second-class citizen in the United States.

"No matter how good you are, no matter if you got your citizenship, they still consider you Chinese," Mrs. Liu says. "They yell at you on the street, they say, 'Go back to China!' When I had a retail shop on Sixth Avenue, if the customer become upset with you, they say to you, 'Go back to China!' When people meet Vanessa, even though she was born here, they say, 'You speak English very well.' "

Almost from her birth, then, Vanessa's parents saw that the only means of escape from this alienation, the only road toward a sense of place was through education. With all her greenness, Vanessa's mother had an impeccable eye for superior schools. She may not have known whether a program was whole-language or child-centered, whether it followed a Dewey or Montessori model, but she knew that it was prized by mothers in the playground. My own mother was a young refugee from Poland with a grade-school education, yet she found out very quickly that Bronx Science was the school New Yorkers esteemed, and it was there she prodded me to apply. It was not educational sophistication that was pivotal, just a fierce desire to have her child exposed to the best.

"When you have a child you will do that if you care enough," Mrs. Liu said matter-of-factly. "If you know education is important, you do everything to investigate what school is good, what teacher is good. Most Chinese parents are aware of this fact. When new immigrants come to this country, they ask which school district is the best, then they buy a house. In the Chinese papers when they advertise the rental of a building or a house, they always advertise, 'This is a good school district.' "

The Lius were living, as they still do, in Southbridge Towers, a mammoth futuristic nine-building complex tucked between Chinatown, City Hall, and the South Street Seaport in lower Manhattan, and Mrs. Liu sent Vanessa to a nursery school operated by Pace College. She learned that Public School 124 in Chinatown was the neighborhood's best elementary school, with a program for gifted students, and sent Vanessa there. Then she found out that Wagner Junior High School in upper Manhattan had a rigorous academic program for bright youngsters and sent Vanessa there. It was Wagner that sparked Vanessa's passion for space; a science teacher there established a "young astronaut program" and had students design a base for humans on the moon that relied on aquatic algae as the main source of oxygen.

At home, Mrs. Liu and her husband have always spurred Vanessa, sometimes in not-so-subtle ways. "We always encourage her," her mother said. "We always point to the Chinese paper or the English paper. Whichever article is about some youngster. We say, 'See how well they are doing. Can you do that?' And we inspire her."

The Lius' pattern of nurturing their children's talents, it should be said, is typical of many Asian families. In 1989, Dr. Herbert Ginsburg, a professor of psychology and mathematics education at Teachers College, Columbia University, conducting some international comparisons, found that neither teacher preparation, nor class size, nor the length of the school year explains why Japanese and other Asian children do so much better than Americans in math. Rather, he suggested, the key was the different attitudes of parents. American parents, he found, are far more ready to attribute mediocre work to a lack of innate ability, while Japanese parents and other Asian parents "believe all children can learn mathematics if only they try hard enough." While there is always the danger of creating national or continental stereotypes, it is fair to say that there are cultural commonalities in the way parents relate to their children that may explain the extraordinary strides of Asian youngsters after they immigrate here.

"Even if these parents," he wrote, "cannot themselves speak

English and therefore cannot help with homework, they nevertheless clearly convey the impression that success is both possible
and desirable. Such expectations seem to be a major impetus to
students' hard work and subsequent success."

In the Lius' household, there were, nonetheless, misgivings
about the direction Vanessa was taking, a very untraditional path
for a Chinese girl. The doubts were voiced from as far away as
Amsterdam.

"In my dad's part of family, they're really traditional," Vanessa
said. "When I had quote unquote brains, they're surprised. My
female cousins are not encouraged to do things. My parents play
a big role in telling my uncle and aunt that I'm going into science.
They start saying all the pros, they buy it, and they come to accept
it. I've experienced a struggle trying to go into astronomy. My
uncle and aunt want me to be a doctor. They're very concerned
about economic life—will I be able to support myself? My dad is
very into getting a job where you earn money."

Her father, she says, has often told her, "You're a girl. Why
do you want all these male jobs?" Vanessa, however, counts herself
lucky. Coming of age in the egalitarian New York City of the 1980s
and 1990s, she did not hear her teachers and classmates make
such comments, and that made her different from many girls with
a scientific bent growing up elsewhere in the country. That difference was striking in some of the breakfast conversations Vanessa
had in Washington with the other young women who won
Westinghouses.

Claudine Madras of Newton, Massachusetts, an astronomy buff
like Vanessa, calculated the rotation rate of an asteroid for her
Westinghouse. But thriving in science was for her an uphill struggle. "It's not looked upon well for a girl to do well in math," she
told Vanessa. She got a subtle, discouraging message that even
thinking about becoming an astronaut "would be out of the norm"
for a girl. To take some of those pressures off of her, she chose
to attend the Winsor School, an all-girl high school. Patricia Bachiller
of Scotch Plains, New Jersey, who explored how male zebra finches
learn their distinctive songs, said, "It's the students, not the teachers, who discourage you." That is why she believes girls are so

much quieter in science and math classes. "People look on science with awe," she said. "Girls are not encouraged to be brave."

Hearing these remarks, Vanessa joked, "I've been sheltered." For whatever the gender-tinged messages she received at home, there was never any doubt that Vanessa would have to make a success of herself. That, of course, was largely immigrant hunger, the extra soupçon that beyond Vanessa's brains and education propelled her to the top of America's teenage scientists. Even with girls, she said, immigrant Chinese have "adopted the American view that they have a well-rounded child. Education is a top priority and things like chores come second."

"It has a lot to do with culture," she told me when I asked why an immigrant family like hers could produce a Westinghouse winner. "In my family education is really stressed. We're not as lucky as people who have a foundation. We have to establish a foundation for the next generation."

Vanessa's mother sees this quality in subtly different ways. The children, she says, may not be driven by immigrant hunger, but they absorb the tacit lessons of parents who are so driven.

"In the families of the immigrants, they work harder," she says. "They know they have to struggle before they can succeed because they are newcomers. If you were born here, you take it much easier, and that kind of attitude influences the children. If a parent is very easygoing and enjoys life, then the child will not work so hard. Immigrants don't have that sense of security. You are in a foreign country. You have nothing."

As we spoke, Mrs. Liu was sitting across from me in the reception room of her costume-jewelry firm, which is on Manhattan's West 38th Street in the trimmings district just east of the Garment Center. This is a neighborhood where you can find a replacement leather buckle for a Burberry raincoat or the match of the sparkling button that fell off your black evening dress. The assortment of ragtag shops is stacked with bulky spools of ribbons in a Joseph's coat of colors and shades, with boxes of buttons in a plethora of sizes, shapes, and materials as well as bows, baubles, beads, tassels, sequins, and plumes. The people who run them appear to have prodigious memories that can locate, among a thousand boxes, precisely the half-inch purple bone button for which you were looking.

Mrs. Liu's shop, in a loft building between Fifth and Sixth Avenues, makes large gaudy earrings and necklaces of fine quality that she sells to the Miss America Pageant and other beauty contests and to such stores as Fortunoff's. Beyond the reception area there is a long narrow work area where fifteen or so young men and women, most of them Asian art students, sit all day at long tables quietly gluing tiny pieces of crystal onto balls and cubes. The only distraction for some is the music they hear through the earphones of their Walkman-type tape players.

"That takes a lot of patience," I say, as I watch one young woman carefully sticking tiny crystals onto a small ball.

"The Chinese are famous for their patience," Mrs. Liu answers.

But it was not just patience that built this impressive business so quickly. For one thing, Mrs. Liu, like Vanessa, works very hard, from 8 A.M. to 9 P.M. and often seven days a week. Characteristically, she says, she had good fortune, and learned to capitalize on it. "Vanessa and I are both lucky," she says. "We met the right people." Luck is a familiar Chinese explanation for many gifts. But I suspect the truth is a little more complicated than that. We all meet many people, but not all of us have the knack for capitalizing on those encounters. Vanessa, for example, is not afraid to engage people who share her passions; they respond to this tacit affirmation from her and are often eager to help her. She probably inherited that knack from her mother. One of Mrs. Liu's first jobs after arriving in the United States was as a bilingual secretary to a Garment Center manufacturer, Arnold Bernhard. He was so impressed with her that he helped her take courses in accounting at New York University. After a few years, she launched out on her own and rented space in a large store on Sixth Avenue for a small costume-jewelry counter. In 1988 she set up her own business, which bears the name Formart Corporation. Somewhere along the way, she taught herself some basics of jewelry making, management, marketing, advertising, sales, and the whole panoply of skills needed to run a successful business.

"I always said, 'You are not born to learn everything,'" she told me. "But if you put your mind to it and put your effort, you will learn. That's my philosophy."

If one wanted to find the roots of Vanessa's restless and roving nature, her father might be the best place to start. While Vanessa's mother doggedly built up her business, Vanessa's father, Kai Yin Liu, repeatedly shifted pursuits. A school principal in Hong Kong, he came to the University of Oregon to study architecture and sociology. But he tired of academia and moved to Manhattan's Chinatown, immersing himself in neighborhood organizations. He became the president of the Twin Bridges Neighborhood Council, an important community group that among other things strives to straighten out some of the teenage gangsters who molest Chinatown. He also worked as a reporter for a Chinese-language cable station. In recent years, he switched once again to the study of law, enrolling at Touro Law School in Manhattan. Mrs. Liu does not deny that her husband may harbor some political ambitions for which a law career might be useful. At fifty-two, he is doing his best to read while warding off two teenagers and the television they sometimes let blare. He also helps his wife in her business.

Surprisingly, neither parent has any yen for science. And despite her swarming family, Vanessa could think of only one relative who worked in science—an uncle who is a pharmacist.

Vanessa has a brother, Jason, who is nineteen months younger and with whom she shares a room. But that is about all they share. Jason is very bright but not quite as relentless intellectually. While he goes to Stuyvesant, he does not intend to undertake a research project. Far from craving a trip in space, he is thinking of a career as either a lawyer or pharmacist. Vanessa says he has even, at times, expressed disinterest in going to college, though his parents have firmly squelched such notions.

"Jason is very different," said Mrs. Liu. " 'If I can get a 92, I'll be very happy.' That's his attitude. 'I don't have to stay up all night to get a 98.' "

Vanessa puts it slightly differently, and perhaps more perceptively. "He's tried to have his own life because he's always been under my shadow," she said.

A psychologist might say Jason has chosen to identify with his father's more meandering nature or that he has chosen to be the foil to his aggressive sister. All of which shows that simply coming from a bright Asian family does not guarantee Westinghouses or any other trophies of intelligence. Complex, mysterious, even Freudian forces are still at work.

In contrast to some Westinghouse hatcheries, the Liu home is not particularly well equipped. Vanessa has an IBM-compatible computer that she uses largely for writing, a small microscope that has been overtaken by the professional ones to which she has access, and a collection of science books, particularly on astronomy. That is all. So Vanessa had to capitalize on Stuyvesant's synergy with the scientific establishment in New York City to produce her winning Westinghouse project.

The project's seeds were sown in her freshman year when she struck upon another in her string of intellectual passions—genetics. At the same time she was drawn to the idea of working on a Westinghouse project.

"The experience of just working in a lab as a high school student I thought would be really rewarding because it's so different," she said. "Normally people don't get that kind of opportunity until they enter college. I thought I would learn more than just reading a textbook or using the facilities we have at Stuyvesant. I wanted a hands-on experience of doing research."

The fact that a distant cousin, Angie Choy was a semifinalist several years before no doubt provided a competitive spur. (The Westinghouse does sometimes run in families.) Finally, one of Vanessa's incentives was the challenge of winning as a girl. "Besides the scientific challenge, there's the social challenge," Vanessa confided in Washington. Males, after all, still dominate the competition, with 204 males and 96 females finishing as semifinalists in 1992.

Vanessa went to Richard Plass, Stuyvesant's Westinghouse Svengali, and when she told him her range of interests, he directed her to Mt. Sinai Medical Center, which has a thick sheaf of names of scientists willing to take on young researchers. She jotted down ten laboratories whose work piqued her curiosity and settled on the first one, a neurobiology laboratory headed by two Germans, Drs. Jurgen Brosius and Henri Tiedge. These scientists probed her background and her fascination with neurobiology, then described their research. When she said she was interested, they had her plow through some topical articles. Soon she was sectioning rat brains into one-millionth-of-a-meter tissues and calling her mentors Jurgen and Henri.

"They treat everyone the same, as an equal, and they make it a point that everyone is called by their first name," said Vanessa. "I thought it was rather weird. But after a while I called everyone by their first name."

Her project is a part of the general study of how nerve cells transmit messages that instruct muscles to move, lungs to breathe, hearts to beat, the mind to remember. She bore in on one esoteric speck, the biochemical processes that occur at the junction between nerve cells. There an impulse or message begins its leap across a one-millionth-of-an-inch gap, or synapse, from one nerve cell to the hairlike branches, or dendrites, of another. Specifically, she investigated how proteins are made at the sites of the dendrites, proteins that may perhaps play a role in the transmission of messages. That is a counterintuitive idea since scientists have generally found that such proteins are made in the cell body, not in its branches.

"Maybe proteins are made when they're needed, wherever they're needed," Vanessa hypothesized.

That was indeed the case, Vanessa found. She studied microscopically thin slices of the brains of rat embryos and newborn rats, whose dendrites are still being formed in a process known as synaptogenesis. She found that the levels of one newly discovered and mysterious ribonucleic acid—BC1—rose and fell in rhythm with the development of dendrites. This finding of a correlation between BC1 expression and synaptogenesis suggests that, counter to the conventional scientific wisdom, there might indeed be a protein-synthesizing machinery in the dendrites.

What does it all mean for the human race?

"In the long run it would help sort out how memory works," Vanessa said. "It is associated with memory, long-term memory especially, which requires new proteins. Humans only use 10 percent of the brain and if we used that little what happens to the other percentage—there's rather a large percentage we don't use. And hopefully this would help with what happens during memory, how memory functions. It would help with Alzheimer's research."

As Vanessa is telling me this across a Formica-topped table in that crammed and clamorous First Avenue coffee shop, I feel that far less than 10 percent of my brain is working. But I do understand one thing. As intricate and bold as Vanessa's experiment is, her ability to pull it off does not tax plausibility. After all, she worked with a laboratory at Mt. Sinai that has been working on brain and nerve processes and she delved into one small portion of the larger research. Yet that, in fact, is the way virtually all scientists work.

The myth of the solitary biologist's suddenly discovering a polio vaccine or penicillin or DNA spirals is borne of America's romance with heroes and frontiers but has little to do with the collaborative realities of science. Most great discoveries are culminations of the incremental work of scientists in scattered labs, with each person's research providing another fiber in a weave whose design will not become apparent for a long time. Vanessa, with her smattering of advanced high school biology and chemistry, could join that adventure only because other scientists were there to help her over the rough and perplexing spots where her pristine knowledge proved inadequate. That circumstance does not take away anything from Vanessa's achievement. Rather, it should serve as an invitation to other young people to immerse themselves in research. At her tender age, Vanessa knows this completely.

"Scientists are international," she told me during the Westinghouse festivities. "They're not saying you have to do this for America. They collaborate. They copublish. They work together. The only scientific advances are through teamwork."

To get her project off the ground, Vanessa had to bone up on synaptogenesis. "I had to do a lot of literature research. BC1 is so new there's nothing on it. Basically my lab is on the frontier of discovery." But Jurgen and Henri were there to arm her with a quiverful of necessary lab techniques: how to section brain tissue, how to distill and treat water so that it is free of an RNA-killing enzyme, how to work with radioactive sulphur, how to bind a radioactive probe to the BC1 in the synapses so that its "expression" will appear on film.

"You see a picture of the rat brain and in some places it's really dark and you see the BC1 is really strong there," she said.

She worked at a "bench" she shared with two graduate students (cuts in research financing have crowded the laboratory) and did most of the jobs essential to the lab's operation. Practically the only task she didn't perform was actually killing the rats. "He did all the killing," she says of one of her mentors. "He'd get the rats and say, 'OK, here's the fresh brain.' "

What Vanessa brought to the lab was a lively, sponge-like mind and dogged perseverance. During her junior year, she went to the lab three to five days a week and stayed there on each occasion for an average of three hours. That meant she had to travel from her school at East 15th Street to the hospital at East 99th Street, a thirty- to forty-minute trip, and, after completing her research after nightfall, take the subway downtown again to her home near Manhattan's South Street Seaport, another thirty-minute trip. On days she had to section a brain, she had to remain at the laboratory until the procedure was finished—six hours—and not leave there until 9:30 at night. And, during the summer, she worked all day, five days a week. In short, she drove her parents crazy. Yet Vanessa did not think she was working particularly grueling hours. Henri often worked in the laboratory until 3 A.M.

"In doing some of these experiments, there is a time thing involved," is her sensible explanation. "You have to put things in for a certain amount of time and you have to adhere to that schedule."

All along, Plass, her Stuyvesant teacher, kept asking for papers and revisions of those papers, making sure she adhered to professional journal style. She completed her experiment in the summer and finished her last revision in the fall of the senior year, then submitted the paper to the Westinghouse contest. When I first interviewed her the following February, Vanessa had long finished her paper but was still working at the lab. She was gathering additional data so she could publish her work in a professional journal. And Henri was prevailing on her to work with him on a book—an atlas of the rat brain. No best-seller, to be sure, but a guide that will be helpful to other neurobiology researchers.

"I would have found it so useful," said Vanessa, "except there isn't one in existence. The brain is different at different ages."

Why couldn't Henri do such an atlas himself? Well, it turns out Vanessa, in doing her research, had already done much of the mapping, sketching the different contours of the brain at different periods of development. For Vanessa simply loves science, loves the intellectual paths science takes, the payoffs in discovery for the hard work she puts in. She and so many of her Westinghouse comrades get angry at the idea that science has to have tangible and immediate benefits, probably absorbing their indignation from older mentors frustrated with contemporary trends in government and foundation financing. Vanessa feels that science is legitimate for its own sake, and that the greatest discoveries arise from that whimsical and unchartable process.

"My project has no immediate application," Vanessa confessed the morning after the forty Westinghouse winners first displayed their projects. Her bright eyes were flickering merrily. "Science is a pursuit. The public always thinks that science has to have a direct application. Yesterday, at the Westinghouse display, I was so thrilled when someone said that the project is so fascinating. In and of itself."

Chapter Nine

Rabbit Run

Reading, Pennsylvania, is not a breeding ground of scientists. It has no special high school, no major research university. It is a rather humdrum city in the southeastern part of the state that flourished making iron cannons during the Revolutionary War and, later, servicing railroads and their commerce. Today, with 78,000 people, it is best known as perhaps the largest factory-outlet center in the Northeast, a place where shoppers from Virginia to Massachusetts pick their way through hangars full of discount blue jeans and irregular shirts. John Updike has made the towns around Reading his Yoknapatawpha County, familiarizing American readers with the region's "close-packed rows of semi-detached brick dwellings" and their "idle alleys and darkened foursquare houses."

Yet, Reading is David Haile's town, and David in 1989 confounded all the theories about early training for young scientists by winning a Westinghouse for contriving a new method of classifying butterflies. David is a tall, lanky teenager with blue eyes behind silver-rimmed glasses. He could be the earnest, diligent lad of Updike's boyhood novel, *The Centaur*, the son of a sweet-natured teacher in an unremarkable town. What makes David remarkable, though, is that he is a virtuoso at science and mostly self-taught at that. By age seventeen, he had already won dozens of state and national science competitions. The accountant in his blood prompted him to keep a log of his winnings, and when I interviewed him, these added up to $18,265 in cash and scholarships and an additional $23,000 in expenses-paid travel.

But David did not just emerge as a full-blown scientific genius from his mother's womb. There were forces in his background that seemed to steer him toward inventive science. Years of hard work and painful nurturing went into David, years when he was often lonely, when his parents had to brace him against self-doubt. I did not quite understand that until I asked Carol Haile, his mother, a capricious question and received an illuminating answer.

"Why do you think so many immigrants win Westinghouses?" I asked. "What does that say about American families and what they're doing wrong in raising their children?"

What she told me had the shining quality of an epiphany.

"I look at my husband and myself," she said. "We had to make it on our own. It was like we took a boat from another country and decided to start over in America. Neither of us was particularly close to our families for reasons that are painful to us. My parents were extremely abusive and so was my husband's mother. We came here with no money in our pockets. We started with less than nothing. My husband had to get an advance on his pay just to feed David. So we felt like immigrants. We were just off the boat."

Behind many Westinghouse winners, it seems, there is a story like that of the Hailes—stories of bruising struggles that have sometimes scarred the children yet toughened them and given them the enormous energy, savvy, and zeal needed to scale Himalayas like the Westinghouse. Stories like that of David Haile are about grit and discipline; they belie the popular notion that scientific stars are born as geniuses, touched at birth with radiant powers that soon emerge no matter what parents and teachers do. Yes, there may be a minimal genetic foundation necessary for success in science, but just as important are the implicit lessons that emerge from a life of struggle. Yet every life is a mystery. David responded resourcefully to the troubles that came his way; other kids respond destructively. No one has yet produced the surefire blueprint for successfully raising a child.

David Haile's parents both spring from large families, John from a poor Catholic family with six children in the coal-mining town of Shamokin in central Pennsylvania, Carol from a Lutheran family of five children in Pottstown, an hour north of Philadelphia. The two met as students at Bloomsburg State College in Bloomsburg, Pennsylvania, about forty miles southwest of Wilkes-Barre.

Toward her senior year, Carol discovered she was pregnant.

She was devastated. Her father had taught her that women who get pregnant "aren't worth much," she said. And so she thought about putting her baby up for adoption. But instead she and John chose to get married. Six months later, they gave birth to David, who was to be their only child. This was 1971, when the young sexual revolution's notions had not quite penetrated as far as and as deeply into places like Bloomsburg. She was an unwed mother and her ample belly so soon after a rushed wedding was the subject of vitriolic gossip. There was still hurt in her voice as she recalled being "laughed at" as she walked pregnant around campus.

"I had David in my senior year of college, and that was my big sin," she said. "I shouldn't have done that. But I'm done apologizing for having given birth to David."

As an infant and young child, David did not exhibit any signs of precociousness. He did not talk nor read remarkably early. But he did show one distinctive and auspicious trait. Like Vanessa Liu, he was fiercely independent. "If he didn't want to do something there was no way you could cajole or force him to do it," his mother said. "But what he wanted to do he would go at like gangbusters."

That independence acquired a lonesome edge in the fifth grade. The Hailes had already moved to Reading, partly because it put a substantial distance between them and their families. When their accounting business began taking off, they moved out of a rough quarter to a more affluent neighborhood of professionals on the city's western edge. They picked out a house in which they could also install their business, and they put David in Sacred Heart Elementary School, a Catholic school.

"The reason we bought this property is because we didn't want David coming home to an empty house," Mrs. Haile recalled. "We were always aware of his emotional well-being. My husband and I come from dysfunctional families and there were certain things David was not going to do without."

Yet it turned out that David was not readily accepted by the students. "He was ten or eleven—he would come home crying," his mother remembered. "I like to think the kids were all snobs. They were all upperclass." In fact, David discovered he had different interests than most of the kids he did know.

"David," his mother said, "used to put it like this: 'Mom, it's like this. At recess the kids are throwing stones at each other but I would take a look at the stone and study it.' He couldn't relate to the kids throwing stones at each other, he couldn't see any sense in it. He was more curious about the striations in the stone and where the stone was quarried. So his interests were different from the kids around him and that would increase his feelings of being different and alone. He wanted them to be more like him. He didn't want to be like them because he didn't see any sense in it."

David saw it more benignly: "I lived in a neighborhood without many children," he told me at the Westinghouse exhibit in Washington. "Those who were there weren't interested in playing with me so I devised my own world."

Devising your own world in America is not easy. The United States is an enormously social, even aggressively gregarious society. There is nothing more disheartening for some parents than an empty slot on their calendar of play dates, and children are put through Little Leagues more to meld them into a communal fabric than to get them to play competent baseball. Too often, what gets sacrificed is the tang or flair peculiar to a particular boy or girl. For the most intelligent and intriguing work is done far from the madding crowd, in moments of contemplation, in moments of wrestling with one's spirit.

David began his work by collecting things: electronic gadgets, popcorn boxes. Then he took on a variety of projects, things with a fixed goal that he could do in a limited time. He developed photographs, fooled around with his parents' computer programs, raised championship-quality goldfish that he entered at local fairs. If he received an electronic calculator for Christmas, it also turned into a project: he took it apart to find out how it worked. Soon he graduated to taking living things apart. He persuaded a butcher— one of his parents' accounting clients—to put aside some skulls and organs, which David duly dissected. And he ordered fetal pigs and frogs from a mail-order biological company so he could dissect them as well.

When he was in the sixth grade, David's parents bought what they call a "bug whacker," one of those purple-hued ultraviolet lamps that fries any insect it draws in. His mother said David had "a typical boy's interest in murder and mayhem," but what was not so typical was the intensity of David's fascination with the slain insects. He started collecting those as well. "The bigger and more colorful and more bizarre the better," his mother said. "Among the very first stuff he caught was a big brown beetle with two bright spots on its back, and it was like the greatest thing God had ever created."

David studied the insects around his neighborhood, stopping at neighbors' houses and telling them, "You have a neat insect. Can I catch it in your backyard?" He prodded his parents to take him on expeditions outside Reading where he could find more exotic specimens. Sometimes those expeditions went quite far afield—to Puerto Rico and California. But parents have an odd way of trusting their children's judgments about even expensive notions, and David's parents indulged his.

"Because David didn't have any friends, I would have to be his friend," said his mother. "I was not just his mother. I was his friend. He was the most important thing in my life and I never thought about it much as it was happening. I tried to make it as much fun as possible because he was just lonely. When he would not catch the bugs he wanted, I would try to bolster his ego. 'Well, not today, but maybe another time. Maybe the temperature was not right.' I was trying to direct him in a positive way toward keeping him enthused."

But Mrs. Haile also had some philosophical foundations for the encouragement she gave David.

"American youth spend too much time in frivolous pursuits," she said. "I don't think parents have much balance in their lives and therefore can't put balance in their children's lives. In our case, if he was interested in something, we would encourage that and participate in that and help make it interesting for him. We would make it a family project for him. If he wanted to go to a particular area to catch his bugs, we'd all go, take the family dog, make it fun, you know what I mean."

Mrs. Haile's efforts involved more than canny parental instincts. She has a college degree in secondary school education, and while she never used it to teach, she learned, she said, "the importance of keeping a positive mental attitude." Still she is not all sweet-natured nurturance. She admits she has tended to be somewhat critical, just like her father was with her. She sometimes chastised David for wasting time. Yes, she pushed him, something that parents are forbidden to do in this Feelgood Age that denies consequences of any sort, even death.

"I knew I was enormously active," Mrs. Haile said. "If he'd be watching TV, I wouldn't see that as constructive." And she remembered being somewhat disapproving when David, in the ninth grade, fell in love for the first time and "couldn't stick to his schedule."

"He did a lot of daydreaming," she recalled.

Still, Mrs. Haile kept driving him on his excursions, even at the price of having to pick off ticks that clung to her own body, and she let David move his expanding bug collection from his own room into the guest room. "I was asked why I would tolerate these insects in my home. People would say, 'I don't know why you put up with it. They're dead.' "

Indeed, David's projects have a way of chewing up much of his parents' home. Their two-story house in Reading was previously owned by a doctor who used the ground floor as his office and laboratory. David has already taken over much of the laboratory. A darkroom the doctor built has become the darkroom in which David develops his photographs of the microscopic wing scales of butterflies. The office has metamorphosed into his parents' accounting business, but David usurps the computers there to analyze differences in wing scales. Upstairs, the guest room has become his "bug room," the display and storage area for his collection of hundreds of butterflies and other insects. And of course there is David's own room.

"He just kind of took over the house," said Mrs. Haile. "Wherever we hadn't laid any claim to the territory, he would fill it with all of his projects and interests."

David began hatching his own butterflies from cocoons. And sometime around the seventh grade, David learned that Albright College, a local campus that has an enrollment of less than 2,000, was offering a course for high-school juniors and seniors in microphotography—the skill of snapping photographs through a microscope.

"David talked his way into it," his mother said.

Albright taught David microphotography, a skill that was to prove crucial to his Westinghouse, but his mother made the equally crucial sacrifice of agreeing to chauffeur him to and from the college. She and her husband were so busy working, she explains, their guilt was assuaged by David's immersion in his hobby. Microphotography is hard on the eyes. Most students, Mrs. Haile pointed out, tire after a half hour. David could stay with it "for three hours at a clip and never complain because he was just so excited at what he was seeing under the microscope." It was then, she said, "when it hit me that he really had a passion for what he was doing."

The following winter, a snowstorm closed the schools, and David's parents, partly to keep him amused and partly to pique his interest in medical school, bought him a trinocular microscope for $1,000. It could magnify objects to 400 times their size, and though it was a used Bausch & Lomb model, its third lens could be fitted with a semiautomatic Nikon camera. In a frenzy over his new toy, David examined all sorts of objects under its powerful lens and took pictures, pictures he developed in his darkroom. "You know how it is with a new microscope," he recalled. "You put butter, water, hair. I put a butterfly wing."

What he saw so fascinated him that it turned into his next, and most enduring, enthusiasm. For a seventh-grade project, David did a study of the tiny kaleidoscopic scales that give butterfly wings their distinctive beauty. Again, David worked feverishly at assembling the project, but he also had his parents' help. David's father built the backboards needed to display the project. Indeed his father was to apply that skill to the roughly fifteen fairs David entered in the next five years. According to his wife, Mr. Haile is also "very good at taking software and making it do what it's supposed to do." So Mr. Haile helped David with the computer tallies or analyses that had to be done. The family synergy was rewarded when David's seventh-grade project captured first place in his grade among the physical science projects displayed at the Reading-Berks Science and Engineering Fair, the regional science fair.

It should be noted that most Westinghouse winners seem to have parents who embroil themselves in their children's work, even if they do not quite understand it. The parents may not be able to help with mathematical formulas and scientific principles, but they can drive, something most sixteen-year-olds are not permitted to do, and they can hammer and paste, and they can intervene with school administrators, and they can set down some rules about bedtimes and strains on health. Whatever they can contribute takes some of the pang of isolation—as unavoidable as it is—out of the projects the youngsters work on. The youngsters get the reassuring sense that their work matters to the people who matter most to them. That kind of inspiration is at least as important as the flights of fancy we imagine geniuses have.

"When I did a science project," Mrs. Haile remembered of her girlhood, "I had to spend time to get the cardboard to stand up. I had no financial backing. I had no encouragement. So I said if my son has to do a project or assignment in school I'm not going to let him do it the way I had to do it. He's going to do it with resources." Indeed, Mrs. Haile was not too modest to admit, "If it had not been for my husband and me, none of this would have happened. I don't know why other parents don't do as much. I've been approached by other parents who complain, 'He sits and watches TV all the time. How do you get your son interested in these things?' But I say, 'Have you made any sacrifices here?'"

David continued to catch butterflies and to examine them under the microscope. Eventually, he collected more than 500 specimens and took 2,000 photographs, compiling thirty-six looseleaf notebooks of photographs and data.

"It would get bigger and bigger," his mother said. "He wouldn't know when to stop."

He kept entering science fairs, and he kept winning: He snatched the eighth-grade championship at Reading-Berks in 1985, a first place in the zoology division at the Pennsylvania Junior Academy of Science contest in Allentown in February 1986, grand champion at Reading-Berks in March 1986, a first place in zoology at the International Science and Engineering Fair at Ft. Worth, Texas, in May 1986, then another first place in the International Science and Engineering Fair in Puerto Rico the following year. The last fair also won him U.S. Navy scholarships worth $15,000. He kept winning and he kept traveling. The U.S. Army gave him a one-week, all-expenses-paid visit to the Smithsonian in Washington, the navy a ten-day all-expenses-paid trip to San Diego to visit naval research facilities there.

As a by-product of these achievements, David, his parents believe, attained a new maturity, acquiring many of the strengths he would have gained had he spent the years in more social pursuits.

"When he started winning science fairs, it was like a light bulb went off in his head," said his mother. "He got confident. He was somebody. He was noticed in a positive way. He was getting what he needed and he ran with it." David became a celebrity in his school, and "the girls were very interested in him."

In fact, when I interview him, David has so cracked through his solitary shell that he has formed a steady attachment to a girl named Margie whose ambition is to become a doctor. Yet his new social life does not seem to diminish the range and breadth of his enthusiasms. He has become an expert on military history and hardware. He has become an avid fan of Ray Bradbury and other science fiction writers, and a devotee of monster movies. He has built rockets. He has learned how to fly and become a student pilot. He manages to squeeze all these interests into a seventeen-year-old's day by setting a very tight schedule for himself. Of course, these accomplishments do not endear him to everybody. David is still sometimes the butt of jokes.

"They tried to influence me to get out of it," he remembers of some of his classmates. "They're saying, 'He's with his butter-flies.' Lots of students my age seem to be anti-science."

And sometimes, his enthusiasms and headstrong will collide with his mother's headstrong will. In the senior year, David makes plans to go to the prom with Margie and also decides that he has to rent a room for the night. He asks his mother about it. Mrs. Haile says her answer surprises him and it hurts him.

"We got into a big argument," she recalls. "He said all the kids were having parties. He wanted to get a room for the night, right where all the parties were. He got this idea that that's what you do. I didn't want him to be supervised. Well, he went ahead and got his room. He and Margie were traipsing around in the middle of the night, he and Margie and her older brother stayed out all night through all these parties. I told him I can't stop you from doing it. Afterwards, he told me, 'That didn't work out.'"

As his science projects grew more sophisticated, David hit on the idea of putting some of his butterfly-wing data through spreadsheet analyses on his IBM-XT personal computer. "I'm a scientist by nature," he explains. "I can't be satisfied with an unanswered question, so I started asking questions." David discovered that four basic measurements—length, width, a numerical value for complexity of design, and a numerical value for overall shape—could be combined into a single number that was unfailingly distinctive for every species. These numbers, then, could serve as genetic markers for families and subfamilies of butterflies and moths. Indeed, they could be used to differentiate one species from another.

If verified—and it has not yet been widely accepted—David's finding would be groundbreaking. Classification systems for butterflies are notoriously slow, relying on characteristics of wing-vein structure, nuances in genitalia, and other subtle distinctions that take weeks and months to analyze and confirm. Because of the time it takes, there is a ten-year backlog of new species waiting to be classified.

"In most classifications," David explains to me as he shows off his Westinghouse project in Washington to streams of visitors, "it can take two years. This can take two hours. It's kind of like fingerprinting."

It was this project, tried out at earlier science fairs, refined, and eventually published in *BASE*, a journal of original scientific work by young scientists, that became David's Westinghouse entry. The project soon preoccupied the family, and when David became a semifinalist—one of the nation's top 300—it consumed the family.

"We talked of nothing but that," said his mother.

She remembered vividly that she was at work when her husband called. "There's an envelope from Westinghouse," he said. "Should I open it?"

Mr. Haile opened it, and Mrs. Haile recalled, "He screamed. 'He's one of the top forty!' And I screamed. And we told everybody. David was just on top of the world. This was the pièce de résistance. The Westinghouse is like next to the Nobel. It's the best thing in science you can do without winning a Nobel. David had won everything you can win, but when he won the Westinghouse, nothing else mattered. This was it."

Chapter Ten

Fathers and Sons

"It's like a movie, really, when I start to think about it," Tamir Druz's mother, Bella, says of her life.

And, indeed, her life and the lives of her husband and two sons could make a movie, a story of epic sweep, a story that takes the family across three continents, from terror, squalor, and despair to comfort and security, with enough perils along the way to suit a half dozen Paulines. It even has a corny ending: one son, Tamir, wins one of America's most coveted awards for young men and women—the Westinghouse—and is congratulated by the president of the United States. It is a story with a message sentimental enough to have exasperated Louis B. Mayer and prompted him to use Western Union. The message is that struggle, and only struggle, gets you anywhere in this world.

"I never blamed anybody for my troubles; I solved them," says Tamir's father, Alexander Druz, with steely conviction. That self-reliance has been bred in Tamir's bones.

Alexander, a tall, solidly built man with a graying Douglas Fairbanks mustache, would be an armchair philosopher if he ever took the time to sit in an armchair. He is full of epigrams that were born of his tumultuous experiences: a birth in the Lvov ghetto, a clawing survival there through World War II, a youth under Stalinist Russia, immigration to Israel, service in the Yom Kippur War, a nervous journey to the United States, an anxious start in New York. His experience is written on his tongue. He speaks Polish, Russian, Ukrainian, Hebrew, and English. And this epic of a life has given Alexander a perspective on American life so unconventional it seems almost revolutionary. For example, when he talks about education from his hard-bitten outlook, he rejects almost all the

American reforms of the last thirty years, feeling that poor and troubled children have been pampered, to their true disadvantage, with free-lunch programs, bilingual education, and fewer academic requirements.

If anyone has grown up with obvious disadvantages it has been his son, Tamir, he argues. Tamir came to this country with no home, with parents who had no jobs, with no knowledge of English. And yet his school career—almost entirely at schools in the New York City public system—has been one of nearly unalloyed success, capped by the triumph of the Westinghouse, which he won as a student at Bronx Science in 1989 for an investigation of the relationship between creativity and skill in chess. The reason, when one looks closely at Tamir's origins and his life, is again the subliminal message of his parents' life about the rewards of struggle. Like his parents, he learned to adapt to whatever life brought his way and he too prevailed.

The story of Tamir Alexandrovich Druz begins long before he was born in Israel on October 12, 1971. It begins with his parents, who emerged from the nightmare that was Jewish Europe in World War II. Alexander Druz was born in Lvov. Until the war's outbreak, the city had been part of Poland, but it came under Russian sway as a result of the "nonaggression pact" through which Hitler and Stalin carved up Poland. The Nazis, of course, reneged and invaded the Soviet Union, including the formerly eastern Polish territory that embraced Lvov. They herded the Jews of Lvov into a ghetto and confined them there for two years until those who had not starved to death or died of disease were shipped off to concentration camps. Alexander was born in that ghetto and he and his mother survived there for nearly five years. Just before the last Jews were deported to the camps, a Gentile family found Alexander and his mother a room in the Aryan part of the city and secured them Christian identity papers. Many of their relatives perished in camps like Auschwitz. But Alexander and his mother, posing as Christians, made it through the war until they were reunited with his father, a theater producer who had been on tour in the Soviet Union when the war broke out.

Much later, as a young man, Alexander visited Auschwitz and took many photographs, which he keeps in a scrapbook in his home in the Bronx. He laid the scrapbook out on the coffee table and showed me the photographs, observing with bitter mockery that the aura of death still lingers about the place.

"You smell it!" he cried. "So many years after the war, you smell!"

Tamir's mother, Bella Druz, is a robust woman with red hair and large brown eyes who speaks all of her husband's languages and Yiddish as well. She was also born in Lvov, but in 1947, after the war had ended. Her parents survived the war because when Lvov was absorbed by the Soviet Union, they migrated to the relative safety of places farther east. Her father was stationed with the Russian army in the Ural Mountains; her mother worked as the principal of an orphanage in Kazakhstan. Her parents met in Kiev and married, then returned to Lvov, which remained in Soviet hands after the war. In 1956, when Bella was nine, the family was permitted to return to their native Polish territory and they settled in Wroclaw (known in German as Breslau), an industrial city in southwestern Poland famous for its 100 bridges over the Oder River. What is most salient about Bella's memory of the city is the war ruins. Children often played in the bombed-out buildings, and every now and then a child was killed by a forgotten mine.

From her father, Bella inherited a radiant sense of the importance of education. He had been raised as the only Jew in a Polish orphanage and was often beaten up by Gentile classmates, but from his youngest days he cherished learning. "Her father was very, very poor," Alexander Druz told me. "He didn't have money to buy shoes, and if he got money to buy shoes, he bought books."

Destiny, it seems, brought Alexander and Bella together. Both their families happened to be in Lvov in 1947, and on Passover, just before Bella was born, the parents met in a synagogue. During a toast, Alexander's father looked at Bella's mother, then amply pregnant with Bella, and said, "If you are carrying a girl, this will be my daughter-in-law." The story, a legend in the Druz household, is made somewhat less implausible by the fact that very few Jews were left in Lvov after the war.

Actually, the children did not meet each other for more than two decades, and then entirely by chance. In 1965, nineteen-year-old Bella took a trip to Odessa to visit a friend, who suggested she meet a young man named Druz. Bella recognized the name from her parents' conversations and consented to a date. The young man was indeed Alexander, and the date was such a hit that three days later they decided to get married. They called Bella's father in Breslau.

"This is Yeshia's son," Bella told her father.

"I know the family," her father replied, "but I would like to meet the boy."

Given travel restrictions, that was not a simple request. Bella resisted, and so her father wavered about blessing the marriage. "My father is like Tevye," Bella said, referring to the *Fiddler on the Roof* character. "On one hand, on the other hand." But when his wife prodded him, he consented to a wedding.

The betrothed couple journeyed to Alexander's hometown of Lvov and there they got married. They stayed for three days, then Bella headed back to Polish Wroclaw, where she was required to return. But at the border, Soviet guards accused her of smuggling and conducted a humiliating body search. When Alexander learned his bride did not arrive home, he headed for the border and found her in a small hotel favored by customs officials. He persuaded the officials to let her return to Breslau and even got to spend an additional night with her. Still, they remained apart for more than a year until he received permission to emigrate to Poland.

Soon after they were reunited, they decided to emigrate to Israel. "It was something holy for me," Bella says simply. She had learned about Israel in a Sholem Aleichem School for Yiddish culture in Breslau. The class had been taught by a woman who had been an inmate at the Treblinka concentration camp and had seen her children torn in half by trucks pulling in opposite directions. Hearing stories like hers, Bella decided she wanted her children to grow up in the safety of a Jewish land. In 1968, they received permission to travel. Three months before they left, Bella and Alexander gave birth to their first son in Breslau. They named him Ari, after Ari Ben Canaan, the hero of *Exodus*, Leon Uris's novel about the desperate struggle of Holocaust survivors to penetrate British-occupied Palestine. They were, after all, making an exodus of their own.

The Druzes lived in Israel for seven years, mostly in Kiron, a town outside Tel Aviv. Alexander worked as a technician in a dental lab and as a correspondent for Kol Yisroel radio, the state radio station. Tamir was born there. But Alexander and Bella soon found themselves restless again. Like many other Israelis, they were disillusioned in the letdown of the Yom Kippur War, in which social fragmentation and overconfidence in Israel's leadership were to blame for the frightening setback of the first few days. The roller-coaster inflation of the Israeli economy and the lure of American success were also spurs.

"Suddenly you think maybe you're missing something and you want to try it before you get older," Alexander says.

In 1975, they made it to the United States. For the first two months, they lived in a transient hotel, the Hotel Wellington in midtown Manhattan, until they found a one-bedroom apartment in the Sheepshead Bay section of Brooklyn. Druz paid the rent by working in a dental lab for $142 a week, a piddling sum even then.

"On this salary we were supposed to live four people," Alexander said, "and we did it. We even saved money, and the children were clean and healthy and we never used food stamps and any other help from the government, and I'm proud of this."

Alexander even had some coins left over to buy his children a toy or two. "I always bought toys that can develop them," he says. "I couldn't afford it, but I looked for bargains, sometimes fire sales. I tried always to buy something that can educate, that can give them something.

"I came without language—no single word—and it was OK. I never blamed anybody for my troubles. I solved them."

The legends of the Druz family—the anguished tales of the war years and the more picaresque sagas of the aftermath—are stories of resourcefulness, tenacity, patience, courage, and will-power, of inventive solutions to almost insurmountable predicaments, of resilience in the face of unimaginable loss. These qualities, honed by the menace of death and destitution, served the Druzes in the years ahead. And their children were to absorb them with Bella's milk, if not literally then in observing their parents cope with the trials that were to come. The parents grappled with Nazi Poland and the Stalinist Soviet Union. The children struggled with Manhattan and the Bronx. Both more than managed. Indeed, researchers studying Holocaust survivors are beginning to find that their ordeals, far from defeating and demoralizing them, hardened most for the rough lives ahead and yielded an astonishing record of regeneration, even triumph.

I found myself drawn particularly to the story of Tamir and his parents because my parents also are survivors of the war, having fled from Nazi Poland to the tenuous security of the Russian interior. They endured hunger and typhoid and other miseries, then returned to Poland only to learn that their families had perished, their worlds destroyed. They had to spend the years after the war in displaced-person camps before finally coming to America. Even then, I remember my parents and we two small boys living in a single room in the Capital Hall Hotel on the West Side of Manhattan for two weeks, knowing almost no one in New York City and frightened by the scale and tumult of the place. Yet, I also remember my parents venturing out to find apartments, track down job leads, locate other survivor friends, scour stores for savory foods at thrifty prices. They had no large goals in mind, just the simple need to cling to a foothold. Perhaps their prime inducement was terror at what would happen if they could not put it all together. But there was a determination my brother and I and a sister who came along later never forgot. Today, he is a doctor, she is a psychologist and I am a journalist, and we are still restless souls, who never seem to have done enough. Often, I wish I were more complacent, but I am also glad that my parents etched into us the knack for survival.

After a life of working for other people, Alexander now owns a dental lab near the home he also owns in the Pelham Parkway section, crafting crowns and bridges for dentists. Bella, who briefly studied pharmacology, now counsels Russian immigrants for an organization called the North Bronx Association for New Americans, part of the Bronx Jewish Community Council. Though Brighton Beach in Brooklyn remains the most popular destination, more than 500 Russian families live in the north Bronx, finding the rents somewhat cheaper. When immigrants come here, they are generally put up in small midtown hotels until they find apartments and jobs, and Bella helps them through the perplexing and intimidating phenomena of America. Russians, for example, are accustomed to stores with empty shelves. They find themselves overwhelmed by the cornucopia of America's supermarkets, by the need to distinguish among a dozen brands of coffee that each come in percolator, drip, and automatic grinds, as well as caffeinated and decaffeinated. "Do you know how many times they buy what they don't need?" Bella says of the refugees she helps. "She is opening the box and she sees it's not what she thought."

Her agency also tries to break down barriers between Soviet newcomers and young professional Americans who have forgotten that their grandparents and great-grandparents also clawed their way to build lives here. They try to acquaint Americans with Russian mores. For example, Russians, coming from a country with relatively few telephones, have a custom of simply dropping in on friends. Americans find themselves startled by such unexpected visits. Bella tries to familiarize each group with the other's habits.

"So they wouldn't feel these people are weird," Bella explains.

Tamir's parents have been telling me the story of their lives in the snug kitchen of their home, a two-story brick house on a quiet street of similar houses off Pelham Parkway. The memory talk is interrupted only by the clinking of the cups of tea Bella serves. I ask Alexander what he did to raise such an exceptional son as Tamir, and he answers with candid puzzlement.

"It's hard to say what I did," he says. "The most they did by themselves. We always tried to direct our children. It was always free, it was never pressure. I never checked homework; I asked. If he said yes it was yes. Between us and our children, it's friendly. We love them and we respect them. You cannot fool a child. I don't have the experience of children lying to us. If he tells me, 'Father, I don't feel like going to school,' I say, 'Fine, stay home,' and the same with the big one."

Tamir, sitting nearby, has been listening to the conversation intently, here and there greeting a remark by his parents with a skeptical eye. It turns out that he does not fully buy his parents' claim to tolerance of his idiosyncrasies.

"When I wanted to go to film school, you said, 'No,'" he protests.

"I say be whatever you want, but be good," Alexander reffirms, laughing.

This is, more or less, true. Even Ari, Tamir's twenty-year-old brother, has been given a long leash. He is studying at Hunter College, trying to decide between careers in either industrial design or commercial art. He has his parents' support for either path.

"It doesn't matter," Alexander said. "We would like him to be happy. The most important thing is that you have a profession that you enjoy doing. This is the biggest part of your life. Education opens the door for the future. Money comes and goes, but what you know, whatever you know, it's important. You can always make a living."

Alexander cherishes the gift of schooling, treats it with a respect bordering on awe. In the long morning that we spent together, he took pains to show me an album of family photos. Curiously, there were many of either Ari or Tamir simply standing in front of a school. Alexander explained that he makes sure to take a picture of his sons in front of every school they attend. He does this the way other fathers might take pictures of their children next to a trophy. For Alexander Druz, the act of merely attending school is a triumph to be prized.

Tamir received virtually his entire education in New York's public schools. He came to the United States when he was three and a half years old and for a single year attended a preschool class at a Brooklyn yeshiva. Afterward he went exclusively to public schools—to P.S. 96 on Pelham Parkway, nearby JHS 135, and to Bronx Science. His elementary and junior high schools were not among the city's dwindling bastions of middle-class whites. Most of his friends were black and Hispanic. Yet his family did not abandon the schools the way many white working-class families have done. Alexander Druz is the greatest defender of public schools. His son, he said, has had "good teachers, good laboratories, good sports facilities."

"No private school can afford to get things like this. Some parents blame teachers, the schools, education. I think it's foolish. If children want to study, they have all the opportunities in public schools. It's not true you have to pay. I have a friend who pays $5,000 a year for private school and he's not the greatest student. It's a waste of money. Parents who blame public schools, they're supposed to blame themselves."

Alexander did not seek out one of the board of education's bilingual Russian programs for his sons. Like most Russians, he does not believe in bilingual education. (According to statistics for the 1991–92 school year, only 865 of the 5,332 eligible Russian children were enrolled in bilingual classes, roughly 16 percent. By contrast, 59,401 of the 88,894 Spanish-speaking children were in bilingual classes.) American teachers did not teach his son in Russian, and yet his son mastered all his subjects and learned to speak English fluently, while retaining his Russian.

"They're looking for an excuse," he says of proponents of bilingualism.

Bella is even struck by how many American children are brought to school by bus. "Who heard in Russia bringing by buses to school?" she says. "In Russia children are walking ten miles to school."

"Americans are used to luxury," Alexander interjects. "It makes them more harm than good. It's not needed. I give you an example of a Dr. Birnbaum. A patient says, 'It's going to snow, I can't come for the appointment.' She lived on the second floor of his building. He was on the first. This is America."

"Children are getting everything too easy," adds Bella. "They have school. They have lunches. When I go to school, mother give me a piece of bread and smeared something on it."

"There's too little hardships," said Alexander. "Children wear fifty- or sixty-dollar sneakers. My children don't wear fifty- or sixty-dollar sneakers."

Alexander and Bella Druz reared their children with a European-bred philosophy that stressed individual responsibility rather than the community's obligation to take care of floundering souls. It is the same philosophy that the American pioneers brought with them to the frontier but that seemed to get lost as life in this country grew exceedingly comfortable. And Tamir has absorbed this Carborundum-tough stance. When Tamir was in Washington for the Westinghouse awards banquet, he happened to visit American University on a gray chilly morning. Sleet began falling and he heard a secretary in one office say that all college classes were being canceled. Tamir had to laugh at such indulgence.

"I look up and I see a few drops," Tamir says, with his father's biting sarcasm.

When I met him, Tamir, whose name in Hebrew means tall and stately like a palm tree, was a tall, lean young man, with the slightly awkward bearing and the soft facial hair of an adolescent. There was still a discernible coarseness to his speech, the telltale brand of his immigration. Yet, there was an impressive core of iron. Beyond the credos he received through his father's moralizing, there was a stronger message that came through in how his father and mother behaved. Yet if you ask Tamir what role his parents played in raising an enormously successful student, Tamir will say, "There's no concrete thing they did. It's what they didn't do. They didn't put any limits on me. They didn't force me to go to sleep at eleven o'clock when I wanted to do something. My parents tried to make me more responsible, but I don't think it worked very well. Self-reliance is something I think I lack. I don't think I'd be able to make it through the Amazon."

He hasn't been forced to test himself in true hardships, he argues to my utter disbelief, because his parents made it possible for him not to have to go to work to earn an income.

Tamir, really, is as self-sufficient as his father. He has terrible homework habits, preferring to rise at 3 A.M. or 4 A.M. to do the previous night's homework. "I'm lazy," he says. "When I get home I don't feel like doing anything. I like to save work for a while." Often he will lie down on the carpet to do his assignments, spreading papers across the floor in a jumble that only he can understand. But he never misses his assignments, his parents say.

Tamir may not be able to make it through the Amazon, but his accomplishments in the public schools were quite dazzling. Tamir had a 96.5 average through four years of high school, with a 97.2 in the first half of his senior year. He achieved that average while taking three college-level courses in history, Spanish, and chemistry. He was in the top 1 percent of a school whose students are among the brightest in a system of almost one million pupils. On the SAT, Tamir scored 760 out of a possible 800 in math and 710 out of a possible 800 in English.

"I wouldn't have won a Westinghouse if I hadn't gone to Bronx Science because I don't have the amount of self-reliance to actually initiate the process," Tamir told me, displaying again his striking streak of perfectionism. "Whereas at Science the technicalities were solved. All I had to do was join the social science program [run by Carol Nash] and then I was guided through. This was the project you might consider and this was the place you might go. All I had to do was actually do the project."

A small challenge, of course.

Tamir speaks Russian but did not take it in high school. Not only did he take all his subjects in English, but he took four years of Spanish, including the advanced placement class. He points out that only 20,000 Americans have learned Russian. Two years before the collapse of the Soviet Union, he told me, "If Moscow opened up and we wanted to persuade Russians of the dangers of Communism, we couldn't communicate with them. It's American arrogance. I go to France and I expect people to speak English."

Tamir is a voracious reader. "Since he was small," his father said, "he read everything he could put his hands on. If he had a good book, you will not move him from the place."

"I can't tell you anything about fairy tales or nursery rhymes," Tamir added. "I wasn't exposed to it. I would read what I could pick up. I'd read a manual on how to fix a TV."

Now, he combs the Fordham Road library—the main Bronx branch—or the 42d Street library for books about his many obsessions. When I interviewed him, Tamir said he had been reading several books about the Holocaust, an interest born no doubt of his parents' and grandparents' experiences.

Tamir has a small, narrow room on the first floor of his parents' house. Compared to rooms of so many American youngsters, with their dazzling sound equipment and posters of rock-'n'-roll stars, his room seems almost monastic. There is a neat desk, a few chess trophies, a small globe, several science magazines. His parents told me he had been fond of classical music from an early age, but Tamir confided that he liked country music, "music that tells a story, that has a smooth melodic rhythm," and rap.

As a Russian at a school that draws the top students from one of the world's most diverse cities, Tamir has an international range of friends. They appear to share many values and perspectives that they themselves see as quite different from those of more rooted

American youngsters. Tamir spoke movingly about how immigrants are the last believers in the promise of the American frontier, in the idea that struggle and hard work will reap rewards in a country of such open possibilities.

"In a sense we're more American than the Americans," he said, sagaciously. "We actually believe in individualism, in going out and making your own way."

Reflecting his own views, he also told me that his Chinese friends "appreciate modesty," something they don't sense very often in Americans. "They don't like arrogant Americans," he said. "They call them poseurs because they walk around with Banana Republic T-shirts. Most Americans don't have the work ethic, and recent émigrés from Asian countries are more modest and respect the work ethic more."

Nonetheless, Tamir does allow himself one vice: chess. He can be consumed by the game, challenging classmates at Bronx Science, the old men at the stone chess tables on Bronx Park East, or the accomplished players at the Manhattan Chess Club. "Chess is sort of a status symbol among some people," he says. "It's your way of showing you're better than someone. Instead of doing the community pool hall, it's like the community chess club. You're trying to be at the top of the heap."

In typically adolescent fashion, Tamir acquired this passion for chess out of fascination with the talents of another young man, Anatoly Drubman, also a Soviet émigré. The two boys first met in Bronx Park East when they were both in junior high school. Drubman was beating several old men on the stone chess tables near Lydig Avenue, the main shopping strip of the Pelham Parkway Jewish community. Tamir, then more of a casual player, asked Drubman for some chess books and began seriously studying strategies of play. The following year Tamir played in his first tournament, but won only one game out of the eight he contested. "I was totally crushed," he said. "It was a real ego destroyer. But I left that tournament determined to study more. It was a vicious cycle. As I lost I wanted to be better."

Drubman was the star of the Bronx Science chess club and in 1989 was the top-ranked under-eighteen player in the United States. Tamir, though, became good enough to play second board on the

Bronx Science team. Drubman became something of a hero figure for Tamir, a maverick whose iconoclasm and rascally ways Tamir admired. "The main thing in life for him is to excel in some game," Tamir said. Drubman even loves checkers and a bevy of Oriental games. He is the kind of person who when the SATs are given in May will run off to the Kentucky Derby. When Drubman first entered Bronx Science, he cut many classes and alienated his teachers, but he was brilliant in chess, "a wunderkind, a child prodigy," Tamir said. "I was intrigued by this, that he could have all these faults, and yet he was admired and held in high esteem." One gets the sense that Drubman embodies a devilish Mr. Hyde figure that is seething inside Tamir's conventional Dr. Jekyll, but that he fights consistently, and successfully, to suppress.

Along the way, Tamir grew curious about what makes chess players good. And when he decided to do a project in psychology or political science for the Westinghouse, it was not surprising that chess seemed to sweep him into its magnetic field once more. Looking around for a topic, he attended a conference at Fordham University for students interested in working on science projects. There he met Dr. Robert Reynolds, a Fordham psychologist who also happened to be the U.S. champion in correspondence chess, where chess players battle each other through the mail. Their conversation soon turned to a project that might combine chess and psychology. Reynolds agreed to become Tamir's mentor.

By "begging and grovelling" at chess clubs, Tamir ultimately found nineteen expert chess players who were willing to submit to a test he designed to measure their creativity. Collating the results, he discovered that the strongest players have one approach in common. They are divergent thinkers who look for many possible solutions to a problem instead of focusing on a single strategy and forcing it to succeed. They examine a variety of initial moves and their consequences rather than perfecting a neat single sequence of moves. They tend, in Tamir's phrase, to look "broadly rather than deeply." That finding became the core of his winning Westinghouse project.

When it comes to planning his own life, however, Tamir is not above using a sequential approach. He already has mapped his career several moves ahead. He wants to delve into international business and eventually get a graduate degree in business administration. But first he will attend Cooper Union's engineering school, a school he chose over both the University of Pennsylvania and New York University because it is free. "I don't want my parents shelling out $80,000," he said. Moreover, this callow seventeen-year-old is already savvy enough to have determined that a background in engineering will bolster his opportunities in business.

Ever the internationalist, Tamir also knows that in addition to the English, Russian, Spanish, and Hebrew that he already speaks, he will be studying Chinese. "China will be the largest economy in the next decade," he explains.

Like many children whose parents abandoned Communist countries, Tamir is a political conservative. He describes himself as a neoconservative, though he is far too young to have ever had a previous incarnation as a liberal. When we spoke in the spring of 1989, he planned to work as a volunteer in what turned out to be the feeble mayoral campaign of Ronald Lauder, a conservative Republican and the heir of the Estée Lauder cosmetics fortune. Tamir believed then—some would say prophetically—that the United States was sinking fast and had entered a decadent stage of capitalism where "we don't build the wealth, we transfer from one company to another or one person to another."

"I'm pretty scared about what's going on in the world," said Tamir. "There's a total disintegration of the United States and the allies. I just think this country is going nowhere and we need people who have a social conscience, a real social conscience, people like our president [George Bush], who don't feel an obligation to support any cause just because it's labeled humanitarian."

No mushy idealism for him. Indeed, Tamir, like his father, had a pretty steely outlook, one that was particularly striking for a seventeen-year-old. But it was an attitude hardened by a hard life, a life that taught him that everything valuable—including a Westinghouse—is earned.

Chapter Eleven

The Right Stuff

I've always been very curious about the world, and I can't understand how someone is not curious.
                    —*Jenny-Yi Lin, a 1989 Westinghouse winner*

The brain is like a muscle. The more you work it, the more you exercise it.
                    —*Divya Chander, a 1989 Westinghouse winner*

There is a popular myth that youngsters who can handle the advanced thinking required by a Westinghouse practically emerged from the womb reading sentences and adding numbers and by the time they started first grade they were comfortable with Newtonian physics. But remarks like Jenny's and Divya's suggest that something far less magical, and more manageable, may be at work.

Yes, there are some children who almost fit the popular stereotype. Christopher Skinner, the first-place winner in 1989, did know his multiplication tables by the time he started first grade, though a very good Montessori program and a mother who read to him as she rocked him in the cradle did not hurt. Still, the surprising revelation from interviews with dozens of Westinghouse winners and some of their parents is that most winners displayed no particular signs of precocity. They learned to read and to do simple arithmetic in school, just as their more ordinary classmates did.

If they did manifest any precocity it was in such qualities as curiosity, enthusiasm, diligence, discipline, and an appetite for exploration, not in the breadth of their knowledge or the intricacy of their reasoning. They were, of course, fortunate that those qualities were encouraged, not snuffed out or sidetracked.

David Haile, the 1989 winner from Reading, Pennsylvania, was fascinated by the insects that dropped dead beneath his parents' outdoor bug whacker, and his parents let him delve deeply into how those insects were strung together. J. Patrick Crosby, from Evanston, Illinois, a 1992 winner for a project on the contact time of colliding spheres, always pried into how things worked, starting with his baby toys. When he was seven years old, he spent two days taking a toy robot apart. The inspiration for his Westinghouse project also came from a game—the pool table in his basement. Benjamin Abella, the third-place winner in 1988, recalled that "when I got a microscope in the third or fourth grade, I pricked myself so I could look at my own blood." No one interfered. As these youngsters followed their impulses, exploited the books and objects and plants and animals and people that were available to them, they indeed became precociously knowledgeable. But one wonders what might have happened had their parents tried to channel their energies into more conventional projects or required them to spend more time making the right kind of friends.

It would be presumptuous to attempt to explain the secret of the Westinghouse winners' genius. There is mystery at the core of all human character. Every youngster who wins a Westinghouse is an individual with a unique story and a distinctive blend of parentage, heritage, upbringing, experience, and schooling. Beyond the fact that so many attended the rising number of special science schools, there are no clearcut common denominators among these children. But there are some qualities many of them share in abundance.

One trait that Westinghouse youngsters seem to observe about themselves is their sense of wonder.

"As a little girl I was amazed that a plane flies," said Ana Pavich, a bashful 1989 winner who was born in Santo Domingo, the capital of the Dominican Republic, and raised by an adoptive aunt and uncle in New York. "I saw a rose open. God, it's so amazing. I'll never lose the wonder of it."

Once their interest has been piqued, the winners are also extraordinarily ardent about what they do. Teenagers, of course, are expected to be ardent. Most youngsters show their zeal for rock stars, cars, dating, or sports. What is different about these winners is the subjects of their passion. Divya Chander talks with great zest about chaos, a relatively new realm that is only on the margins of her scientific interests but still one she finds intensely provocative. David Haile's affection for butterflies is almost palpable. So is Jordan Ellenberg's for the magic of numbers and Rowan Lockwood's for the enigma of dinosaurs and Claudine Madras's for the wonder of the stars and planets. These youngsters have an almost insatiable hunger for the subjects that intrigue them.

Again, there are youngsters who can talk with equal zest and authority about batting and earned run averages or the subtle shadings of a Bruce Springsteen performance. What separates the winners is their early exposure to science and to intellectual inquiry.

Had Christopher Skinner, who explored an age-old problem in number theory, been born among peasants cultivating maize in El Salvador, he may, with all his genes, have flowered into a cunning, even prosperous farmer, but chances are small that he would have developed into a mathematical wizard. In a culture where books are uncommon, his mind may not have been allowed to savor the elegant motions of numbers. The fact that so many Westinghouse winners are children of scientists and physicians sometimes leads to the assumption that they have inherited brilliant genes. In fact, their parentage may say as much about environment as about genetics. Dinnertime conversation at Westinghouse homes bristles with scientific conundrums and is bounded by the discipline of evidence and precision. If something sparks these children's curiosity, there are books to plunge into right in their living rooms. If the right books are not available, they have parents who will shepherd them to the right library. Their parents are not intimidated by microscopes and laboratory chemicals. In most cases, their parents enjoy watching their children re-enact the inquisitive adventures of their own childhood. They relish the affection their children display for a field that had given them so much pleasure. Perhaps they even enjoy watching their children plunge into warrens of knowledge that they themselves never had the leisure or money to pursue. A father surprised by how much his daughter knows about the habits of birds or the ways of dinosaurs may be correcting a childhood gap that his own parents never had the time to fill. Without entirely rehashing the nature-versus-nurture debate, it seems logical that both are factors, that a striking intelligence results from a robust upbringing as well as robust genes.

In fact, most Westinghouse households are not headed by doctors or scientists. But, usually, they are homes that cherish certain old-fashioned qualities of character. Diligence and resourcefulness are prized in everything, from what gets put on the dinner table to the pursuit of a career. There is an insistence upon and an appreciation of excellence. A mother may display it in her ardor for a passage of Mozart played by Isaac Stern, and the child may replicate it in an admiration for the achievement of Marie Curie.

There is also an insistence upon duty and responsibility. The father may burnish those qualities in his children by the way he makes it to work on time every morning. The child may reproduce it in the care taken to show up punctually at the laboratory and make certain that the experiment's mice are well fed. In homes like these, children discipline themselves almost without questioning. They learn to make the most of every hour.

Leafing through the short biographies of the 1989 winners, one is struck by how much they have managed to squeeze into their short lifetimes. In addition to the work he does on butterfly classification—the equivalent of a full-time adult job—David Haile breeds finches and goldfish and he's learning how to fly airplanes. Divya Chander writes fiction. Celeste Posey, a North Carolinian who developed a method of mapping restriction sites on DNA, is an avid piano player, a member of her high school's Latin club, and a participant in her church's puppet ministry.

Christopher Skinner is a backpacker and a chess player. Rowan Lockwood is one of the top divers for her age in Illinois and leads the flute section in her high school band. Jordan Ellenberg, the mathematics prodigy, juggles. Jason Felsch of Rochester, Minnesota, is the principal cellist in the John Marshall High School orchestra. Daniel Allen Sherman of Columbia, Missouri, whose Westinghouse research was in molecular virology, won a varsity letter in wrestling. Thomas Westcott of Midwood High School in Brooklyn, who worked on an enterprising system for recording the proliferation of osteoarthritis in the spine, holds a black belt in the

martial art of Tae Kwon Do. Mahbub Majundar of Washington
State, whose research project explained how the greenhouse effect
might further deplete the ozone over Antarctica, won first place in a
national writing competition on the U.S. Constitution. He personally
received that prize from President George Bush at the White
House, making him probably the only Westinghouse winner in 1989
for whom a presidential encounter was old hat.

Tamir Druz of the Bronx calls himself lazy because he tends
not to do his homework right after coming home from school,
preferring to play chess or work on one of his multiple projects.
That Tamir wakes up every morning at 4 A.M. to prepare his lessons
for the next day may be unconventional. Nevertheless, it is
disciplined.

These habits, this impassioned diligence, are naturally put to
use in a project like the Westinghouse. Julie Tsai, a Bronx Science
junior who entered the 1990 contest but did not win, did not run
home and turn on the TV when her school day was over. Four
days a week, she took a subway from a station near Bronx Science
in the North Bronx to the East Side of Manhattan—a trip of forty-
five minutes to one hour—and walked several very long and, on
wintry days when the wind blew off the East River, very chilly
blocks to Rockefeller University. She arrived about 3:45 P.M. and
for three hours studied DNA in fruit flies. Then just before 7 P.M.,
she headed home to Bayside, which is across the river and on the
other end of Queens, more than an hour away. When she got home
what was waiting for her was the day's homework. She knew that
if she did not maintain an exceptional school average, she could,
because of the contest's rules, lose out on the Westinghouse no
matter how exceptional her project.

That willingness to cleave to a project, despite the strains of
travel and the truncated time for pleasure and rest, is fundamental
to success in the Westinghouse. Students who cannot commit
themselves that tenaciously to the work required by a Westinghouse usually cannot complete a winning project. That is not to
say that students have to become monks taking vows of self-denial
and obedience. But they must be able to keep their sights trained
on the completion of the project. Winning projects are too intricate
to be knocked off in a few weeks before the deadline.

"Results sound exciting," said Divya Chander, "but the actual work is tedious and boring. You need the ability to dedicate and become part of something."

"We the winners are just ordinary people," she added, a bit too modestly, but still to the point. "Our difference is motivation."

Indeed, winners tell of having to repeat the same procedure dozens of times to get enough results to make an experiment valid. They talk of the drudgery of recording data day after day while no clear pattern emerges. They talk of following fruitless leads. They recall, sometimes with laughter, sometimes with anguish, the maddening frustration of seeing weeks of work wiped out by the sudden demise of their fruit flies or bacteria. But, they learn, as the song by Dorothy Fields and Jerome Kern goes, to pick themselves up, dust themselves off, and start all over again.

We are a society that insists on prompt gratification. The idea of waiting on a one-hour line to buy a stick of butter, as Russians do as a matter of daily routine, is repugnant to us, and should be. We expect speed as a matter of course, and those expectations intensify year after year. We are slowly growing accustomed to thawing a roast in ten minutes in a microwave, having our latest missive speed across an ocean in a few seconds via fax, and seeing a hit movie on our home VCRs within months. Science and engineering, of course, deserve the credit for much of this remarkable revolution. But the paradox is that scientific discoveries do not emerge in a culture of haste. Scientists will even tell you that the federal government's insistence on spending research dollars on projects that promise quick and sure results is crippling America's ability to make the truly significant findings that alter our lives.

The cures for cancer and AIDS, the next great leap in extending life spans, the development of a useful space station, the invention of a clean-burning automobile engine, will not originate in the frenzied tempo typical of American life. Our overly technological world is, ironically, spoiling our children's ability to do science. It is robbing them of the idea that scientific talent and accomplishment require the leisure of time and a tolerance for mistakes and delay.

Again, the Westinghouse winners are wiser on this subject than any outside observers.

"We're a society interested in the immediate result," says Christopher Skinner, "and numerous problems have no immediate application."

Children we are likely to regard as ordinary show impressive patience and diligence when it suits them. They may have the fortitude to spend an entire night waiting to purchase tickets for a Madonna concert. They will hang around the neighborhood gas station for hours and become so familiar with the workings of an engine that they can make a nuclear physicist whose car has stalled feel like a dummy.

The fact is there is a lot of industry and perseverance out there. As a parent, I know how maddening it is to try to channel a child's interests into something I regard as constructive. I have been a pretty miserable failure at distracting my daughter from the Saturday morning cartoons. And she is only six. Yet channeling such native energy cleverly is the primary challenge most parents face. Perhaps one of the reasons we are so struck by the number of immigrants who win Westinghouses is that their achievement seems such convincing testimony to the wasteful habits of American life.

Part V

The Families

Chapter Twelve

The Huddled Masses

Immigrants have always won a remarkable proportion of the Westinghouses. From the 1940s to the 1960s, many of these champions were Jewish children whose parents had sought refuge in America before or after World War II. By the 1970s, an increasing number of the winners were from China, Taiwan, Japan, or India. While America has always been a nation of immigrants, they still constitute a relatively small proportion of the population. Yet in 1989, to take just one typical year, more than one out of every four winners was foreign-born, as indicated by this list put out by Westinghouse officials:

Mahbub Majumdar, Richland, Washington	Bangladesh
Peter Nigrini, La Habra Heights, California	Canada
Rowan Lockwood, Evanston, Illinois	Canada
Ana Pavich, New York City	Dominican Republic
Tamir Druz, New York City	Israel
Lucy Shigemitsu, New York City	Japan
Al Avestruz, New York City	Philippines
Wai Ling Ma, New York City	China
Jenny Lin, New York City	Taiwan
Rose Du, New York City	Thailand
Vladimir Teichberg, New York City	Soviet Union

In addition, that year, winner Divya Chander of River Vale, New Jersey, was the American-born child of Indian parents, and Ray Wang of Allentown, Pennsylvania, the child of Chinese parents.

The number of immigrant winners dipped to four in 1993, but that is considered a statistical fluke, and many of the winners were children of recent immigrants.

Most of the immigrants come from New York City, so someone might argue that immigrants win awards because they attend New York City's vaunted science schools. But one can argue the reverse just as forcefully, that New York City does so well in the Westinghouse because it has been a favored haven of immigrants. Whatever argument one chooses, it is apparent that the experience of immigrating seems to instill some qualities in children that seem well suited to success in a trial like the Westinghouse.

What are those qualities? To satisfy the cynics, let me start off by conceding there is probably a lot of truth to the popular theory that immigrant children are driven frenetically by guilt and obligation. The young Westinghouse winners admit it themselves.

"I want to make my parents happy," said Hong Huynh, a Vietnamese immigrant living in San Diego who at sixteen won a 1988 Westinghouse. "They gave up their home, furniture, everything, so I could be here. I don't want to disappoint them."

Hong and his parents fled Vietnam in 1980 on a crowded boat, searching for a better life. The struggle they went through to reach America and put down roots here was a brutal one, and scenes of anguish seared their way into Hong's soul. He feels he wants, if not to repay his parents, at least to see them find some gratification for their efforts. His is a common refrain among immigrant children, not just Westinghouse winners, but it is certainly echoed by many of the winning immigrants.

"You don't want to let down your family," says Johannes Schlondorff, a Bronx Science student who immigrated from West Germany with his parents. He won a Westinghouse in 1990 for his investigation of the chemistry involved in the movement of cilia, the hair-like structures found on many organisms. Even Johannes's biology teacher, Carol Greene, who has shepherded many winners through the Westinghouse ordeal, credits the immigrant experience for the extra spark and drive that immigrant children bring to their efforts.

"The parents made sacrifices to come here," she says. "They

didn't say it, but their children felt it. Sometimes they left their own parents behind. That inspires kids. They feel an obligation."

Immigrant children see their parents' strain and worry and fear, and they do not want to aggravate that suffering. They do not want to do anything wrong that might bring their parents pain. They may even have an exaggerated sense of needing to do everything right, which can produce a welter of problems of its own in guilt and resentment. They may also feel a desire to redeem their parents' lives, to make up for the years lost in a Cambodian prison or in a refugee camp in Thailand or the years lost by the Holocaust. "My parents had no chance to make something of their lives," they might say, "but I will make up for the waste of theirs."

Many immigrant parents, unfamiliar with the nostrums of a Dr. Spock, also push their children harder than American parents do. There is a greater urgency to do well, a sense of making up for time lost in lingering too long in the old country, or in the travails of lengthy journeys. There is a sense of needing to hurry to catch up. There may also be a mistaken notion on the part of some immigrants that living in America is an honor that must be vindicated, that if they fall short this country may chuck them out as peremptorily as their previous country might have.

Immigrants may also come from a culture where education is precious, a privilege to be treasured. Americans, by contrast, have had generations of compulsory schooling and wide access to college and have come to regard education as a birthright. They sometimes scorn it as something cheap and trifling. Foreign-born young people do not.

"There's always discrimination against immigrants, and the way you can overcome that is through education," says Patrick Purdon, of Chula Vista, California, a Hong Kong native and a 1992 winner for a project on evolution in cypresses. "It's a struggle for dignity. A struggle for survival. If you're an immigrant you have to have some unique skills in order to survive." He remembers that, as an immigrant who felt isolated and marginal, he used his gift for schoolwork to his advantage. "Kids ignored you," he remembers. "When you're a little kid you want to have some attention. So you need to prove yourself." Sometimes, he was given attention he did not like, singled out by students who subtly found ways of pointing out his ethnic differences. But he used his academic talents to battle such prejudice as well. "Once I got into a high level of academic achievement, nobody messes with you," he says.

Their old-country sense of education as a privilege even gives some immigrants an exaggerated notion of how well their children should perform in school. Then too, many immigrants come from schools where the level of teaching is far higher than in the United States. Their children often find courses in math and science here much simpler than those they were taking back home.

These reasons—guilt, obligation, fear, cultural displacement—are all rather grudging explanations for the success of immigrant children. I prefer more sanguine explanations, ones that may yield some lessons for nonimmigrant children as well.

My own belief is that immigrant children do as well as they do because they are accustomed to struggle, thrive on it. Watching their parents, they absorb the notion of struggle like Zwiebacks and milk. They see life as a perpetual challenge, and are not afraid of or indifferent to taking it on. The obstacles that must be cleared on the way to a Westinghouse may daunt them, but not defeat them. Hard work is something they expect, not dread. In fact, deprived of hard work, they may grow bored and restless, as if life was being played at the wrong tempo.

"In my household, work is something everyone does," said John Abraham, a Stuyvesant high school senior and a child of Indian immigrants who won a 1992 Westinghouse for an enzyme research project. "I don't have to be pushed. There's a natural feeling that work is good. In America, people work just to get by."

Whatever they achieve has greater value to them because they had so little when they started. Divya Chander, a striking young woman with raven hair and green eyes, was born in America just one year after her parents arrived here from New Delhi. She remembers the crowded apartments she grew up in in Queens and Manhattan until her parents established themselves and settled into their own house in River Vale, New Jersey. Her mother, Dr. Praveen Chander, is now director of renal pathology at New York Medical College; her father, Dr. Naresh Chander, is a pulmonologist. Divya articulated the lessons she has learned quite concisely on a visit we took together to the National Institutes of Health (NIH).

"Opportunities for education for kids in this country come too easily and they don't value it as much," she said. "There's a lack of discipline. Kids in this country are not expected to be responsible for their education and morals. I know a lot of intelligent kids capable of entering something like this and winning. It's hard work that turns them off. They're interested in instant gratification and don't understand long-term goals. They'll study for a test because they can see the immediate effect. But something that requires a year's work, that is not sure, where they don't know whether they'll get results they want, they won't do it. Science requires lots of dedication, effort, and sweat. Discovery is fun but it can come at the end of a year and there's a lot of tedium in between. You go to a lab, things don't behave the way you want them to. Organisms have a way of doing what they want to do. Science can be a frustration."

Immigrant children seem to cope better with that frustration. They have seen their parents in a jam before, clinging to the edge of a cliff, terrified and desperate. Terror and wretchedness and defeat are all familiar to them and they are not as paralyzed by such emotions. On the contrary, their response is to fight, to maneuver, to wriggle their way out. They are comfortable with hardship, and more than a few seem to crave it. When Divya was told she had to submit a paper for Spanish class on the same day that she would be in Washington receiving her Westinghouse honors, she did not protest to her teacher or have her parents step in. She went to Washington and stole every minute she could to finish that paper. When she and I and a group of Westinghouse winners went out together by subway to NIH at Bethesda, Maryland, she sat on the train huddled over a notebook writing the Spanish paper, squeezing in some extra moments of work. Later, while some of her friends were out sightseeing, she continued writing in her room until she finished the paper.

Immigrant children seem less afraid of being resourceful, of coming at problems sideways or discursively, like Julie Tsai, the charming Bronx Science student and Taiwanese immigrant who called up Rockefeller University pretending she was a graduate student to find out the names of scientists working on genetic regulation. An American student whose parents were doctors or academics might have been more willing to call up a professor directly, but Julie got the job done anyway. And it is the knack of getting the job done, of working her way around obstacles, that probably gives her an edge over American-born students when the research begins.

Jenny Lin, of Columbia, Maryland, a 1989 winner, slender with long black hair, was born in Taiwan and came to America at the age of four. Her parents are well-educated professionals: her father, Dr. Ruey Lin, was a doctor for the Institute of Public Health in Taiwan; her mother, Feng-Ying Lin, was a research coordinator for the Agency for International Development. Jenny attends a private school, the McDonogh School in Owings Mill, Maryland. Her life does not seem to have been a deprived one. Nevertheless, the pang of being a newcomer, an outsider, someone different, seems to have propelled her to her own distinctive heights. She is first in her class of 136 students. She already speaks Mandarin and Japanese but is taking French and has started Russian. She has a strong need to keep striving and credits that engine for her success in the Westinghouse. For her project, she developed a way to isolate and measure free protein S, an anticoagulant in the blood. (People with low levels of protein S have a higher incidence of heart attacks.) The measurements are useful in the diagnosis of thrombosis.

"Immigrants feel that because it is not their native country they have to try harder to succeed," she said.

Immigrants bring the illuminating perspective of outsiders to this country. While most Americans still have a complacent sense of America's dominance in the world, many immigrant children are already developing a sense of angry disappointment, as if the prize they sought so hard to attain—American citizenship—is not worth what it once was. In my interviews with them, they seemed more keenly sensitive to the decline in America's world position relative to Japan and Europe and somewhat indignant about the smugness of too many Americans who ignore reality or surrender without a fight.

"Native-born people always have the notion that we're number one," said Tamir Druz, the Bronx Science chess whiz who was born in Israel of parents raised in Poland and Russia. "But we're not number one anymore. The new generation doesn't understand American development. They think it's just there, but unless we start working to establish what we have, we won't get out of this rut . . . . The frontier made America what it is. Every time they felt tied down, they could become pioneers. Immigrants have a frontier. America is like our new West."

And, he might have added, the opportunities available to immigrants, in education, in careers, in comfortable life-styles, stand out there shining like the nuggets of gold in California that must have beckoned to the pioneers of another day, inspiring them to risk the rugged mountains and desert trails of the nineteenth-century West. For immigrants, the chance to win a $40,000 college scholarship is not something to be taken lightly, something whose worth can be calculated against the probability that Dad will figure out a way to pay for college anyway. The Westinghouse is seen by immigrants as a marvelous chance, fully worth a year or more of afternoons spent in a lab rather than in front of the television set. For many immigrants, it is an ideal that transcends individual acclaim, that becomes an affirmation of their families, of their people.

In glorifying these immigrants as the embodiments of the American dream, care must be taken. With Asians particularly, the myth of the model minority has been two-edged: it has produced both admiration and resentment. And even as we Americans slap ourselves on the back about how open a society we still are, we goad and sometimes derogate others—black or Hispanic—who for complicated reasons have not been able to pull themselves up by their bootstraps as quickly. As Ronald Takaki pointed out in his 1989 history of Asian immigrants in the United States, *Strangers from a Different Shore*, there have been plenty of drawbacks to the model-minority myth. Asian applicants have been barred by silent quotas at several colleges and graduate schools, and those who get in have sometimes been the targets of racist assaults. Stereotyping educators and employers have too readily steered Asians into the sciences and into technical fields, ignoring or snuffing out the poets and artists. Too readily viewed as passive, Asians have been excluded from the top managerial ranks even as Americans trumpet the efficient management and robust productivity of Japanese plants. The Asian success story has also allowed Americans to overlook Asian immigrants who are not doing well and bypass them in government or charitable assistance programs.

Nonetheless, America has for the most part realized that immigration has been its fountain of youth, its source of new blood, new spirit, and new ideas that has allowed the country to reinvigorate itself, make itself over from generation to generation.

Ana Josefina Pavich, a shy student at A. Philip Randolph High School in Harlem, was born in Santo Domingo in the Dominican Republic and soon given up to an aunt and uncle in New York City, Mr. and Mrs. Branko Pavich, who formally adopted her and gave her their surname. Ana seldom sees her birth mother and, when asked questions, is protective of her mother's privacy except to say that her mother felt there would be more opportunities in America.

At Randolph High, Ana is president of the Future Physicians' Club, captain of the Academic Olympics team, editor of "Science Times," and a National Hispanic Scholar Awards semifinalist. For her Westinghouse, Ana did her research at Columbia Presbyterian Hospital in Manhattan in an NIH program for minority students. She examined the development of neurotransmitters—the chemicals that pass messages from nerve endings to the brain. She claims that she disproved the hypothesis that neurotransmitters are produced earlier than peptides, proteins that can also act as neurotransmitters. She showed that the peptide galanin is manufactured at least as early as neurotransmitters.

"Americans tend to be egocentric," she told me in Washington as she showed off her Westinghouse exhibit to visitors at the National Academy of Sciences. "They really feel that the United States will remain number one without any input from themselves. You have all these immigrants coming here trying to make your country stronger."

Ana, who wants to become a child psychiatrist, is sometimes disheartened by the lack of hope among so many young Hispanic children in New York, by the flamboyance of the drug and fast-money culture, and by the lack of competing exemplars in math, science, and other fields. Like so many immigrants, she is on a mission that seems to go beyond herself, to take in her entire people.

"I see myself as a role model for Hispanic people," she said. "There's not enough Hispanic people in top positions who can say, 'See, look, we've overcome all the odds and we made it.' "

Ana has already made that list grow one important name longer.

Chapter Thirteen

What's Bred
in the Bone

When Kevin Heller was a toddler on Long Island, he happened upon a string bean in the kitchen of his home and asked his mother, "Where do string beans come from?"

Many parents might have replied that they came from the local supermarket or from a farm. Kevin's mother took Kevin out to their backyard garden, broke open a string bean and planted the beans in the ground.

"We waited to see it come out," Kevin recalled, somewhat breathlessly. "It was a unique learning experience."

Kevin told me that story as we sat perched on top of a shoeshine stand in Washington's Mayflower Hotel waiting for the start of the 1989 Westinghouse awards dinner, where Kevin's project on corn genetics was among the forty winners. Kevin, at the time a slight, self-possessed boy of seventeen, was anxious and giddy as he anticipated whether he would place among the top ten money winners, and I was in a rush to soak up information about Kevin's life. And so as the shoeshine man snapped his buffing cloth over our shoes to bring out the extra luster, neither of us made an elemental connection between the string bean story and Kevin's Westinghouse project.

Kevin had investigated the effects of temperature on the jumping genes of maize, or Indian corn. Jumping genes move from one part of a chromosome to another and can disrupt the functioning of the resident genes. Kevin showed that abnormal temperatures create white stripes in corn offspring because they induce a jumping gene to disrupt the standard functioning of the chlorophyll gene. His experiment, of course, was far more complicated than the one he had done with his mother in a backyard more than ten years before. The jumping genes investigation was carried out at the Cold Spring Harbor Laboratory, home not only of James Watson, who taught the world about the DNA double helix, but also of Dr. Barbara McClintock, who won a Nobel Prize in 1983 for her experiments with jumping genes.

Still, the backyard experiment and the Cold Spring Harbor project were fundamentally linked. Both involved genetics, the way one generation transmits its essence to another, not just in the way string bean begets string bean but in the way Kevin's mother was able to pass on her intuitive feel for science to her little son.

Success in the Westinghouse contest is often about what one generation transmits to another. Schools are crucial in turning out compelling projects, but homes are just as essential. Behind the winners are parents who are deeply concerned about who their children are, how they are growing, what excites them, what hurts them, what paths make sense for them, and what paths may require some gentle adjustment. Many of the parents, to be sure, are scientists or doctors who innately managed to transmit a love of what they do to their children, who were able to pass along a good grounding in scientific knowledge and some rigorous habits of mind. But I was impressed by how often parents of Westinghouse winners who did not have advanced degrees still had a strong visceral sense of what would help their children flourish.

Most important, what these parents seem to have in common is a style of child-rearing that allows children to trust their own curiosity, a style illustrated by Kevin Heller's mother when she planted the string bean in reply to his question. Actively or unwittingly, such parents encourage a willingness to question, to be skeptical of authority, to have confidence in one's own doubts and puzzlement. Too many children grow up thinking that what is written on the printed page is gospel, that what a scientist or a doctor says must be true, that all the major mysteries of life have been answered. These children may do well on standardized tests like the New York State Regents, but they will not become scientists.

In fact, the most important questions in science are still unanswered. We do not know how the universe began or where it is going. We do not know how life was created and what still animates it. We know almost nothing about how the mind thinks. We are only beginning to understand the fine chemistry of reproduction. We know almost nothing conclusive about how our emotions work. And millions of details about all those issues and hundreds of others remain elusive. There is plenty left for science to do, much more in fact than the legions of scientists can handle. But too many of our children are raised believing that humankind pretty much has got the universe down pat, that life is without mystery. They are raised with a faith in some imposing central authority of knowledge that contains the solutions to all of life's riddles. They are raised to believe there are some perfect people out there who will still all doubts, soothe all anxieties. They turn our scientists and doctors into deities, until a disaster like the explosion of the space shuttle Challenger forces them to see scientists as the groping, tinkering, doubt-plagued, and occasionally gravely mistaken human beings they are.

In talking to the Westinghouse winners, I also found parents who managed to be there for their children in a host of small but significant ways. I found parents who drove their youngsters to laboratories or, as did the mother of David Haile, the butterfly lover, chauffeured them to forests to find specimens for their research. I found parents who helped their children build exhibits and scrounged for books and materials. Most important, I found parents who took the time to listen and show some interest. They may have found the work arcane but they sensed it was valuable. Some parents worked extra hard at inspiring their children, like the parents of Janet Tseng, the second-place winner in 1988, who made a point of showing her newspaper clippings about very intelligent people. But generally, I did not find parents who maneuvered their children into their own unfulfilled pursuits. I did not find a crop of stage mothers and fathers.

Two 1992 winners from Stuyvesant High School both give their mothers "99 percent of the credit" for simply leading them toward that selective school. Zachary Gozali, who did a neuroscience project, says his mother, Harriet, decided to move from Wisconsin to New York City so he could apply to Stuyvesant. And Michail Leyb

Sunitsky, who labored in number theory, says his mother, Raisa, now a mathematics teacher at Baruch College, learned in Leningrad that there were three selective schools in New York City. When they arrived here, she made sure he applied and took the entrance test to Stuyvesant.

The parents of Kevin Heller, whose high-polished shoes took him to a seventh place worth $7,500, were always there with the things he needed. Charmed by his interest in astronomy as a second-grader, they bought him Golden Books on the stars and planets and then a telescope. In junior high school they bought him a microscope. He used that microscope in his first official project, an investigation of the impact that stresses like banging noises have on protozoa. He discovered that when the banging got loud the protozoa on his slide would contract from their trumpet-like shapes into little balls. Soon, he was addicted to microbiological research.

By 1988, when he was working on his Westinghouse at Cold Spring, he had moved beyond any equipment his parents could afford. Still they found ways to be there for him. Every morning his father drove him from their home in Dix Hills through the punishing citybound traffic of the Long Island Expressway then, in an eight-mile northern detour, through clogged local streets to Cold Spring Harbor. Then retracing his path south, the father returned to the murderous traffic of the expressway so he could be on time for his job as a pharmacist for a drug-supply company.

Divya Chander finished in tenth place in 1989, a few paces behind Kevin, for her examination of the detailed process by which bacteria invade the tissue of a host. Although she lives in New Jersey, she had to do her research at New York Medical College in Westchester County, across the Hudson River and a substantial drive north. New York Medical is the same college where her mother, Dr. Praveen Chander, is the director of renal pathology. But Divya did her research after school and on weekends, and her mother could not leave work to pick Divya up at home in River Vale and drive her back to Westchester. So she did the next best thing. She taught Divya to drive.

"She sat with me, I drove," recalled Divya. "She had chronic heart failure. If your parents won't support you when you're young, you won't get too far."

At the two-day exhibit of the Westinghouse projects at the National Academy of Sciences, Jenny Jen-Yi Lin boasted perhaps the most professional-looking display. An explanation of her effort to develop an effective measurement of free proteins in the blood was illustrated and handsomely printed in white against a stark black background. Jenny's mother, Dr. Feng-Ying Lin, is a research coordinator at the Agency for International Development and was able to advise Jenny on where to get the printing done with professional flair.

But chores are just a small part. Almost every Westinghouse winner I interviewed or read about remembered small things their parents did from infancy that started them on the road to science. Divya's parents, as recent immigrants from India, simply read to her every night, launching her on a lifelong habit. "By two and a half or three, I could read," she said. "As soon as I could speak, I could read."

John Abraham, the 1992 winner from Stuyvesant, remembers that his parents did not object when he started taking apart his toys from the time he was in the crib. "I took wheels off a toy car to see how to put it back together," he said. "Instead of just pushing the car, my parents encouraged me to take it apart. That's the kind of attitude I grew up with." Another 1992 Stuyvesant winner, Zachary Gozali, remembers how, when they lived in Wisconsin, his mother started a summer program that brought professors from the University of Wisconsin to teach elementary school children, including Zachary, about basic physics and creative writing.

Meredith Albrecht, a 1988 winner from Evanston Township High School in Evanston, Illinois, recalled in an interview with *U.S. News and World Report* that, when she was five, her father, an anesthesiologist, encouraged her to work in his laboratory. Her mother, a former nurse, introduced her to math workbooks. Together, the parents laid down firm rules. TV was simply not allowed on weekdays. Meredith had to tape weekday shows like "MacGyver" and watch them on weekends. Internalizing such discipline, Meredith by seventeen was able to put together a project with the daunting title: "Effect of Geometric Variations in the Dispersed Phase on the Thermal Diffusivity of Composite Materials."

Of course, the children of doctors and researchers have an

extra edge, absorbing their love of science from their home ambience. Andrew Gerber, a 1989 winner for a project that studied the impact of certain drugs on the brain, remembers that when he was about six his father, Dr. Donald Gerber, a researcher in arthritic diseases, bought him a bell and dry-cell battery.

"When you grow up in a household where science is the only thing, it's as if you grew up in a house where your father is a soldier and you wanted to go to the army," Andrew said.

Erica Klarreich, a Brooklyn teenager who studied the process by which white blood cells engulf bacteria, remembers her father, Paul Klarreich, a math teacher at Bronx Community College, bringing home books of logic puzzles when she was seven or eight years old so she could hone her reasoning powers. One puzzle, she recalls, went something like this: "If you have three people and one always tells the truth, one always lies, and one sometimes tells the truth and sometimes lies, how can you find out which is which?"

But most winners do not spring from families of scientists and doctors. They are children of accountants and dental technicians, teachers and architects and real estate salesmen. They grow up in cluttered apartments in the Bronx or in spacious suburban homes. Parental systems of discipline and reward vary. Tamir Druz's father doesn't mind that Tamir skips homework in the evening. He knows that Tamir works best getting up at 4 A.M. and sprawling on the living room rug. Meredith Albrecht's parents are more traditionally firm. In this day and age, they actually reward their three children with cash for good grades.

"You get $5 for an A in an advanced placement course," said Meredith. "If you get a C in a regular course, you have money taken away. Gym grades don't count. None of us ever did well in gym."

Still, these families do have much in common, and one ubiquitous strand seems to be a stress on self-reliance, sometimes to a fault.

Divya Chander's mother informed her about the Westinghouse competition but required her to arrange her own laboratory placement, even though, with her position at New York Medical College, she could have easily persuaded a colleague to become Divya's mentor.

"She didn't want to get it for me because it would kill the purpose," Divya said. "There had to be initiative involved."

There are some homes where the Westinghouse award has been passed from one generation to another. They become part of the family lore just like the perfect jackknifes and one-and-a-half twists became part of the lore of Olympian diving families like Kelly McCormick and her mother Patricia McCormick. Kurt Cuffey, of State College, Pennsylvania, came from a long line of Westinghouse winners. His father, Dr. Roger James Cuffey, a paleontologist at Penn State, won a Westinghouse in 1957, and an aunt, Hazel Rita Schubert, an opera singer, won a Westinghouse in 1960. Starting when Kurt was five, Roger Cuffey took the family out West just about every summer to study mountains and valleys in Colorado, California, and New Mexico and explore the prehistoric secrets they held. So it was not that surprising that Kurt's brother, Clifford, won a Westinghouse in 1986 for analyzing fossilized brachiopods (small, clam-like shellfish) and explaining how their structure helped them adapt to the rough aquatic habitats that existed 400 million years ago. And Kurt's Westinghouse project also touched on paleontology—a study of how glaciers changed the shape of Montana's valleys. Clearly, the family consumes paleontology and Westinghouses like some families eat Wheaties for breakfast.

All told, there have been at least thirty-four families that have produced more than one winner. There have been eight groups of brothers, four groups of sisters, eight groups of brothers and sisters, two father-son combinations, one mother-daughter combination, and one father-daughter combination. In addition five Westinghouse winners have married five other Westinghouse winners. The Westinghouse, in other words, either runs in families or spawns new ones.

Without trying to make these exploits sound like baseball heroics, it is interesting to note that one Taiwanese family, the Kuos of Queens, produced winners in three consecutive years: John Shu-Shin Kuo in 1985, Mark Huan-Fu Kuo in 1986, and David Feng-Ming Kuo in 1987. They are the children of Dr. and Mrs. Hsien-Tsung Kuo, Taiwanese immigrants, and all three brothers attended Bronx Science.

"I was ecstatic," Mark said in a *New York Times Magazine* profile of the family. "It's only half a dream, to win yourself. But having your brothers, too. It's really incredible. I was thinking right away that I bet no other family ever did it before."

The work of the two eldest boys was in microbiology. John, a fifth-place winner, studied a jumping gene in a microbe to see if the gene reproduced itself as it shifted. Mark used many of the same techniques in examining how a certain DNA fragment—known as Tn5—transposes itself. But David's work was in mathematics.

If the Kuo boys' triple crown is phenomenal, the explanation lies partly in a phenomenal upbringing. The Kuo boys practically raised themselves for several years and learned to take care of each other. They came to America without their parents in 1976 when John, the eldest, was just nine. They lived with relatives for two years before their mother, Mei-Hui Kuo, finally came over. Their father, who had been a surgeon in Taiwan, did not arrive until six years later in 1984, and he had to weather a wrenching dip in his self-image by taking work as a respiratory technician.

"The years that we spent without our father forced us to be independent at an early age," John Kuo said in the magazine profile. "And of course we realized what our parents had to go through, to remove themselves from their familiar surroundings to bring us here for a better education."

The brothers goaded each other to ever higher levels of achievement, with the older brothers teaching the younger ones the subjects they were learning. John and Mark, for example, realized that David's was an uncommon mathematical mind and they taught him geometry and trigonometry when he was just in junior high school. Mark said that John, the eldest, "sets a goal of excellence and we try to attain it. I try my hardest and David does better than that."

Social scientists who have studied the phenomenon of families like the Kuos attribute their habits of diligent hard work and their yearning for excellence to the distinctive culture of Asian families. It is not surprising, therefore, that another Asian family is also one of the Westinghouse legends. Mr. and Mrs. Ming Yuan Lo of Queens produced three winning children, two brothers and a sister.

Cecilia Lo, a Bronx Science senior in 1971, studied the aging process in protozoa, testing a hypothesis that aging is accelerated by the release of certain enzymes in response to environmental stresses. Martin, also a Bronx Science senior in 1971 though two years older than Cecilia, worked in astrophysics, examining the dynamics of an expanding universe and its moving galaxies in light of the "big bang" theory. Six years later, it was baby brother Andrew's turn, and he studied a bacteriophage, a virus that invades bacteria.

Richard Feynman, the quirky and brilliant theoretical physicist, was an apostle of skepticism. He distrusted authoritative knowledge unless he could prove it himself, and on his office blackboard were the words "What I cannot create, I do not understand." That refreshing irreverence once gained this master of an esoteric field an uncommon national spotlight. In the wake of the Challenger shuttle disaster, he exposed how insufficiently resilient were the shuttle's O-rings in the icy weather of launch day and he did it in a way the most unscientific American could understand. At nationally televised hearings, he simply threw a piece of the ring's rubber into a cup of icy drinking water and showed how brittle—and vulnerable to vapor leaks—it had become. Yes, he had a distinctive genius that could virtually leap at solutions to problems that had frustrated other scientists. But Feynman could also make such breakthroughs because he did not idolize scientists and engineers and he knew the absurdities they were capable of.

That iconoclastic attitude was bred in him by a father who, like Mrs. Heller raising Kevin, taught him to trust his own eyes, to be suspicious of authorities, and follow his own intuitions until those proved flawed. In Feynman's second volume of memoirs, *What Do You Care What Other People Think?*, he tells of the time his father sat him on his knee and showed him a newspaper illustration of the pope acknowledging the bows of the faithful.

What's the difference between the pope and the others? his father asked. "This difference is the hat he's wearing. But this man has the same problems as everybody else: he eats dinner; he goes to the bathroom. He's a human being." Feynman wryly buttresses the anecdote by noting that his father knew of what he was talking: he was, after all, in the uniform business.

Feynman's father actively discouraged his son from memorizing names of things, and indeed, Feynman boasted throughout his life that he was "blessed" with a poor memory. Feynman's father preferred to cultivate an inquisitive, searching, and sometimes skeptical attitude rather than a reliance on received knowledge. Feynman recalls his father's visits on summer weekends to the family's Catskills cottage and the walks in the woods the two would take. Memorizing the names of the birds they saw, his father said, would get Richard nowhere.

"You can know the name of that bird in all the languages of the world, but when you're finished, you'll know absolutely nothing whatever about the bird. You'll only know about humans in different places, and what they call the bird. So let's look at the bird and see what it's *doing*—that's what counts."

Feynman's father noticed a bird pecking at its feathers and asked Richard why the bird was doing that. Richard guessed that the bird was straightening its feathers. The father pointed out that if that hypothesis were true the bird would stop pecking after it had rested on the ground for a while. The boy could see that the bird continued to peck, so he tried another hypothesis. Eventually, the father showed the boy that birds peck at lice and he used that information to teach the boy something about the food chain: birds are nibbled on by lice which are in turn preyed on by mites which are themselves exploited by bacteria. "So you see, everywhere there's a source of food, there's some form of life that finds it," the father told him.

The details of the food chain, Feynman observes in the memoir, may have been flawed, but the principle was not. In his own sometimes ham-handed way, the father taught him deep principles of science and, more important, taught him to notice things and trust his eyes, not the authorities. Feynman went on to share a Nobel Prize in 1965 in a field known as quantum electrodynamics, but according to science writer Timothy Ferris, he arrived at an explanation of the spin of an electron by the serendipitous route of his own playful mind. At a Cornell cafeteria, he saw someone throw a dinner plate into the air and was intrigued by the relationship between the plate's spin and its wobble. He decided to calculate it, and that relationship became a foundation for his atomic theory.

Feynman's eyes were spectacularly open. So in his memoir, Feynman thanks his father for the "love and interesting discussions" that opened his eyes.

"It has motivated me for the rest of my life, and makes me interested in all the sciences," wrote Feynman, who died of cancer in 1988. "I've been caught, so to speak—like someone who was given something wonderful when he was a child, and he's always looking for it again. I'm always looking, like a child for the wonders I know I'm going to find—maybe not every time, but every once in a while."

Christopher Skinner's parents nurtured a similar independence of thought in him, allowing him to trust the value of his own intellectual meanderings. Christopher was the first-place Westinghouse winner in 1989. In doing so he defied many stereotypes. He was not from Bronx Science or Stuyvesant, not even from New York. He was not Asian, not even an immigrant. Christopher emerged from Little Rock, Arkansas, in the nation's Bible Belt, and he was the son of devout Baptists. Despite the redneck stereotypes held about that region, Christopher's parents seemed to bring to child-rearing the same viscerally understood principles of Richard Feynman's father or Kevin Heller's mother.

Christopher is the son of Dr. Robert and Raynell Skinner. The father is a professor of neuroanatomy at the University of Arkansas Medical Center. Mrs. Skinner spent her time raising four sons and did so proudly. "I was fortunate enough to stay home with the boys," she told me. By most measures, she did a credible job. At the time I interviewed Christopher, his brother James was a college student majoring in Greek and French and teaching himself Hebrew and Arabic. Christopher, the second oldest, was a whiz in mathematics. And the twins, Andrew and Stephen, were budding artists. The four boys chose widely divergent fields, but they all shone.

"I read to them even when I held them and rocked them,"

Raynell Skinner told me. "We read out loud as a family and I encouraged all of them to read."

Christopher was clearly born with a rare mind. At one year old he talked in simple sentences. By the time he came out of a Montessori preschool program and headed toward kindergarten, he already knew his multiplication tables and could do long division. His mother, who majored in preschool education during her two years of college, credits the Montessori method for Christopher's precocity. At a nursery program, the Montessori-trained teachers allowed Christopher to study everything in the room and pursue his own instincts until he finally seized on numbers. The teachers did not bar Christopher from learning addition even if the conventional wisdom is that three-year-olds are not supposed to learn addition. Of course, there were other children in Christopher's program and most of them did not demand to learn addition.

For elementary school, Christopher went, not to a special school, but to his neighborhood public school in a state that is among the bottom of the country in per pupil spending. "The dollars are not always the most important thing," Mrs. Skinner says. "Christopher has been very fortunate to have very good teachers, teachers who have not felt threatened by a child who wanted to do independent research. They said, 'Can I help you? Can I find something for you?' "

Mrs. Skinner likes that approach because it happens to square with her own. "Our philosophy is that we believe a child can learn most anything he comes in contact with if it's explained at the level he's at right there. We also feel there are periods of time when a child is more interested in one thing and needs to be able to go with that as far as he is able to."

Christopher continued to be intoxicated with math. "His idea of relaxing was to drink a soft drink and look at his Daddy's college algebra book," his mother said. Still, he learned literature, science, geography at his own rate, reading on his own in a habit his mother had bred in him. And Mrs. Skinner prudently set some boundaries, exhorting him to finish other subjects before math.

In part, Mrs. Skinner's approach has been inspired by her strong Baptist faith and her spiritual understanding of Christopher's genius. "We firmly believe this is a gift from the Lord and we believe each child comes with a talent and it is their duty to develop that talent," she says. The Lord, she suggests, will lead Christopher toward what his life's work was meant to be. All his parents need to do, she says, is to be alert to what may be needed to help Christopher get there. So, she has created an ambience that permits Christopher to flourish, an ambience dictated by Christopher's own needs, not hers to raise a genius.

In fact, Mrs. Skinner is insistent that her boys be "well-rounded," that they not lose perspective on the rest of life. She encouraged Christopher to join the Boy Scouts and play tennis and racquetball. And, of course, all her boys are active in church. (The Skinners actually belong to the more traditional wing of the denomination, the one that firmly believes in the inerrancy of the Bible. She thinks there is a public stereotype of Southern Baptists as reactionary and backward. But in fact, she says, Southern Baptists are "well educated and in all walks of life.")

In seventh grade Christopher started at a public junior high school that has a magnet program in science, and in the summer right after seventh grade, his parents sent him to a talent program at Duke University in North Carolina. By the time he was fourteen he had moved so far in math that no Arkansas junior high school could offer him any content he hadn't already encountered. The school district decided to let Christopher skip ninth grade and move on to Hall High School, the neighborhood high for western Little Rock.

Mrs. Skinner had always resisted such promotions. "Ever since he began school, I've heard 'Let's advance him,' " she said. "I have seen too many students advance at a young age and have problems." But this time she relented because it was Christopher, not his teachers, who came to her asking to skip a grade.

"It was his idea," Mrs. Skinner said. "If he looked at the pros and cons and still wanted to do it, we felt he was ready to do it."

Christopher's teachers immediately let him take a half dozen college classes at the local University of Arkansas campus, in such subjects as calculus and discrete math. (No one at the university, however, worked with number theory, and Christopher had to do much of his research out of state in the summer, especially at the Research Science Institute at McLean, Virginia.) Christopher finished first in his high school class of 428 students. He got a perfect 800 score on his SAT in math and a 720 on the verbal portion. Christopher used his analysis of a classical mathematical equation named after the fourth-century B.C. mathematician Diophantus of Alexandria to win first place in the 38th International Science and Engineering Fair in Knoxville, Tennessee, and then to take first place in the 1989 Westinghouse. The equation—$apX + bqY = c + dpZqw$—contains four unknowns that can be satisfied by an infinite number of values. Chris demonstrated mathematically that there were, in fact, upper boundaries to the possible solutions, a feat that dazzled the Westinghouse judges.

How did a boy from sleepy Little Rock beat out all those egg-heads from the fast-paced, big-city science high schools?

"The resources are there," Christopher told reporters. "You're going to have to try a lot harder."

Christopher exudes a dogged self-sufficiency and that trait was evident in the way he chose a college. Christopher could probably have embellished his resumé with a name like Harvard or Princeton. But Christopher liked the math program at the University of Michigan. That confidence and trust in his own instincts were cultivated in a home that valued autonomy, personal initiative, and responsibility, values that ultimately may prove more important than his genes. Michigan is now the place where he hopes to earn his Ph.D. and start on the road to becoming a college math professor.

"For me it's the right decision," Christopher says simply.

Part VI

The Contest

Chapter Fourteen

The Westinghouse Candy Store

Every year around December, Carol Luszcz, the director of the Westinghouse Science Talent Search, calls her sister, Veda, to help with the contest. Luszcz asks Veda to take a week off from her regular job because Veda has proven herself adept at one skill crucial to the Westinghouse. She is nearly flawless in making sure the various components of each of hundreds of student entries wind up in the right folders.

The Westinghouse contest, despite its national reach and Fortune 500 connections and Nobel Prize prescience and rich scholarship awards, is really run like a family candy store. A nucleus of five full-time staff members screens and processes the entire nation's applications. They may, near the end, call in prominent scientists and academics to evaluate the applications—and Luszcz's sister to pitch in—but basically the year-round operation is small and close-knit.

"We work incredible hours," says Luszcz, a handsome blond woman who directed the program from the mid-1980s until she left after the 1992 contest. "I try to forget about sleeping by the time December 15 rolls around."

The Westinghouse awards have gotten more publicity than almost any other high school event, but most of that attention has been focused on the brilliant winning students and their mighty schools. Relatively little has been written about how the contest actually works. Yet a closer scrutiny makes the contest seem less intimidating for anyone—student, parent, or teacher—interested in plunging in.

Every August, the staff of Science Service, the Washington-based organization that runs the contest for the Westinghouse corporation, mails out thin brochures to every one of the roughly 20,000 high schools in the country and to another 20,000 teachers, administrators, science supervisors, or college mentors. The brochure announces the contest that will climax the following March, explains its rules, and provides examples of winning entries from the previous contest. By August, though, it is too late for most students to launch a successful project. Most likely entrants have already been working for months, some for years, and many have displayed projects in local or international science fairs.

Still, teachers could certainly get the ball rolling for projects a year and a half into the future. But in fact every year fewer than 2,000 students enter the contest—about one student for every ten schools in the nation—and many of those students come from a narrow spectrum of schools, places like Stuyvesant and Bronx Science. Sadly, the reason for this tepid response is that most students, even most science-minded students, are not aware of the Westinghouse's existence. In some parts of the country, school administrators may figure the brochures are junk mail, a promotion for the Westinghouse corporation perhaps, and drop them into wastebaskets. Even teachers who have heard of the contest may not have the time or inclination to nurture a bright young prospect or two. And many may feel their schools are not up to competition on a national level. But all these educators are doing their students a great disservice. High schools with strong science programs are not the only ones whose students win scholarships that range up to $40,000.

Fundamental to every science project is a worthwhile idea. Ideas comes from many sources, from personal experiences, hobbies, influential relatives, spinoffs from a mentor's research, illuminating conversations with science teachers, or pure epiphanies.

Stacy Benjamin, a tall young black woman from Queens, was drawn to a project on race because of a series of confrontations in New York in the mid-1980s that were capped by a gang attack on three black men in the Howard Beach neighborhood in her borough. Like many New Yorkers, Stacy was angered, hurt, confused. She decided to design a test of whether New Yorkers were really biased in their judgments by sampling the reactions to crime of a racially mixed group of residents. Did witnesses to the same crime respond differently when the assailant was black than when the assailant was white? Would they have responded differently if the race of the victim had been changed? Behavioral experiments have become increasingly popular in the Westinghouse, and Stacy could have shaped hers in many different ways. But she wanted to capitalize on a passion for film and video that she shares with her sister, who manages a local theater called the Black Spectrum.

Stacy staged an armed robbery of a grocery store in which the clerk shoots the robber. She filmed the scene four different ways, changing the race of the actors so that in one version the clerk was black and the robber white, in another the clerk was white and the robber black, and in two others both clerk and robber were of the same race. She showed the different versions of the film to a total of 222 subjects and asked them to evaluate the seriousness of the crime and decide whether the clerk was justified in shooting the robber.

The results confounded her expectations. People pretty much had the same opinions about the crime, whatever the race of the victim or the robber. Race, she concluded, did not affect perceptions as much as age, educational level, and other factors.

Scott Schiamberg of Okemos, Michigan, a slender, earnest young man, chose to work in cancer research because his cherished grandfather died of lung cancer in 1985. "So it was in my mind to work wherever I could to find a cure for cancer," he told me. Scott, the son of an ecology professor at Michigan State University, collaborated with researchers at the university who were preparing two synthetic inhibitors of an enzyme, sialic acid, that fosters cancerous growth.

Rowan Lockwood, a tall blond young woman from Rockford, Illinois, and a student at the Illinois Mathematics and Science Academy at Aurora, had been fascinated with dinosaurs since childhood. "Their size and the idea of anyone living so long in the past," she explained. "It's a different world. It doesn't relate to our world. That's why it was so intriguing. You'll never be able to check up on your research and find out what really happened."

One magazine article about pterosaurs, the flying dinosaurs, irritated her because it claimed they were clumsy, wobbling gliders, not the soaring beasts she had imagined. The article didn't make sense to her because she knew the pterosaur thrived on fish, a rather fast prey, even snatching them out of the water. Rowan also knew a thing or two about takeoffs and landings and midair acrobatics. She happens to be one of the twenty best springboard divers in her state. For her Westinghouse project, she decided to compare the pterosaur to heavy living birds that still can soar and swoop such as the condor and albatross, and she constructed a mechanical model that could account for a pterosaur's more graceful flight. She showed how the pterosaur could have made the erect, bipedal running takeoffs necessary for long-distance flight by holding its winged front feet up and swept back to gain lift.

Impressed Westinghouse officials said that Rowan's project is "believed to be the first to combine data from morphological research with an analysis of the energy requirements for takeoff using principles of physics."

Pat Crosby, a 1992 winner from Evanston, Illinois, is an ardent pool player, accomplished enough to sink a whole rack of fifteen balls in an unbroken series. One day, listening to the click of the balls on his basement pool table, this tall lanky lad wondered how long the balls were in contact every time they "kissed" and whether that time fluctuated with such factors as the angle of the collision. He set up a complicated apparatus of swinging steel balls, using an oscilloscope to measure head-on collisions and glancing collisions, and tried to confirm the results with a graphic model created on a Cray supercomputer. The work, guided by Evanston Township High School's master physics teacher, Robert Horton, took twenty months, and scientifically, Pat's analysis was very impressive. Still, none of this will help his pool game.

"Sometimes I don't think it helps when you think about the shot too much," he said. "It's something intuitive you should just trust and not worry about."

Ideas, then, come from everywhere—from family traumas to annoying magazine articles—and the genesis can be quite mundane. Once a field is chosen, students narrow the topic to a workable problem, a small sliver of a larger research question. Some students are more adventurous. Like David Haile, who came up with the computerized system for classifying butterflies, they may devise a new method for doing something. Or like the 1989 first-place winner, Christopher Skinner, they may advance a new theory and demonstrate how it might work.

Research projects can be in mathematics, physical science, biological science, engineering, or behavioral science (psychology or sociology, for example). The projects can involve laboratory work or field work or theoretical research. Library research is not acceptable. The ideas and the data must be generated by the student. Some projects are performed on expensive equipment like an electron microscope that students may find at a cooperative local laboratory, but many of the best are made from materials scavenged from the teeming discount stalls along Manhattan's Canal Street or from Dad's basement workshop.

The Westinghouse contest does not discourage help from teachers or professionals. Here's what their brochure says: "There is no such thing as a 'self-educated' person. You know what you do now because you have received counsel from innumerable people during your lifetime. Exhaust every possibility or help from books, magazines, technical journals, and people as you work on your project and plan your report." Of course, most projects these days are done in consultation not just with a high school teacher but with a professional scientist or college professor. However, Westinghouse officials require both student and adviser to fill out a questionnaire that is used to determine how much of the work was the student's and how much came from the input of the scientist.

A consulting scientist will be asked some of the following questions: How did the student get the idea? Was the project assigned, was it picked from a list of research topics, did it come out of discussion with a scientist, did it arise from some work in which the student was engaged, or did the student suggest it? How independently did the student work on the project? What parts did the student do and what parts did he or she receive help on (in the experimental design, choice of techniques, use of special instruments, etc.)?

Students do not bring their entire experiment down to Science Service in Washington. Rather, they submit a concise report that is written with virtually the same strictures as a professional scientific paper. The report must include a short introduction describing the background and purpose of the work, a section laying out the research techniques and the results, and a short concluding discussion. Carol Luszcz points out that the scientists who review the projects are experts in the field and don't need volumes of exposition on a project's scientific background. Westinghouse asks for double-spaced reports of "about 1,000 words long," though officials admit that the word limit "means less than 2,000," and in fact no one is disqualified for exceeding even that limit. (Recent application forms allow papers up to twenty pages long.)

The research report accounts for about 75 percent of the judges' score, according to Luszcz. The remaining 25 percent is based on a student's class ranking, scores on such standardized tests as the SAT, and the cogency of responses on a personal questionnaire that each student must fill out. The eight-page sheet asks questions that might be found on a typical college application: the occupations students aspire toward, the foreign languages they read, the subjects they like most, their extra-class activities, the awards and scholarships they've won, their hobbies, their summertime activities, their parents' occupations, the people who have had the most influence on them.

But it also asks five questions designed to probe a student's curiosity, inventiveness, initiative, and work habits.

"Do you discriminate between pertinent and nonpertinent evidence in solving a problem?" goes one question that tries to ferret out an entrant's approach to science. "Have you ever made a discovery that was exciting and new to you? How did it come about and what was it?" is the wording of a question that gauges inventiveness. A sixth question asks students how they got their ideas, who supervised the research, what help was given.

All parts of the application must be received—not postmarked—by early December. That's where Luszcz's sister comes in, making sure the project report, the personal questionnaire, the teacher or mentor recommendation all converge in a single student's file. The files are then sorted into twenty-one categories and assigned to appropriate experts for evaluation. The categories are worth listing because they give a sense of the breadth of science that student projects cover.

Astronomy and meteorology
Biochemistry and molecular biology
Biology (which includes zoology, botany, microbiology and paleontology)
Biophysics
Computer programming and cybernetics
Ecology
Electronics
Engineering
Geology (which includes seismology and archeology)
Health
Mathematics
Medicine and dentistry
Organic chemistry
Physical chemistry
Physics and geophysics
Physiology, animal and plant
Plant pathology
Psychology
Social science (including anthropology, economics, political science and education)
Sociology
Veterinary medicine

Each file is reviewed by two "evaluators," preliminary judges familiar with the field the project is in. The total corps of twenty evaluators ranks the research reports and the personal question-naires. If there is a significant discrepancy between the rankings of the two evaluators, says Luszcz, a third expert is called in. Though they are paid only a small honorarium for their work, the evaluators may read 60 to 100 files apiece. Why would scientists spend this amount of time reading high school research reports?

"I think they like to see what students are doing," said Luszcz. "They want to encourage youngsters. They feel this is a worthwhile project. It's definitely not for the money."

The scores on the personal questionnaire and the research report are averaged together in a formula that gives the research paper 75 percent of the weight. These scores are then ranked and the top 300 are chosen.

Then J. Richard Gott takes over. Gott, the Kentucky-ripened mid-fortyish professor of astrophysical science at Princeton who himself won a Westinghouse in 1965, is now the contest's chief judge. He culls through the 300 semifinalists and picks the 120 that he feels are most compelling, original, and inventive. It is those 120 that will be scrutinized by a panel of eight judges that he heads.

"We look for who is most likely to be a scientist," says Gott. "Our job is like comparing apples and oranges. There is no one major thing that we are looking for. It's like evaluating any scientific paper. How important was it? How significant? What is the overall promise as a future scientist?"

The judges scrutinize the reports to verify that the student followed correct scientific procedures, that the data support the claim the student is making, that the sample studied was really large enough to justify the conclusions. They look for signs of resourcefulness and the fine discrimination that marks a true scientific intelligence. The judges try to make sure the work was clearly accomplished by the student. If they are uncertain, they may call the scientist who worked with the student. They never call the student.

By the time the judges get down to picking the final 40, the quality is usually so strong that nuances make the differences. The ability to communicate scientific concepts, the ability to transfer thinking from one scientific field to another, the ability to apply and not just memorize concepts, the rigorousness in examining experimental results, all these subtleties shade the judges' selection. When the evaluators turn to the personal data sheet, they look for evidence of a deep and abiding passion for scientific inquiry, evidence that the student will persist in science and will make a contribution to whatever specialty he or she chooses.

The names of the top-forty winners from the field of 300 semifinalists from the field of 1,700 or so applicants are announced in late January, and in addition to convulsions of sheer joy there are broader waves of disappointment, hurt, and anger. The Westing-house is a human system and is vulnerable to human foibles. A student who does not grab the two evaluators' attention may not be named a semifinalist even though other evaluators reading the project report might have been more intrigued. Different people, after all, have different tastes. How many Nobel Prizes have also proven controversial?

One consolation for students who are let down is knowing that, for the forty winners, the ordeal is not over. Though they are each assured of winning at least $1,000, those forty have to journey to Washington in March for another round of judging, this one with some capricious and quirky aspects that the contestants have not encountered before. That final trip decides the nation's top-ten winners, including the winner of the $40,000 scholarship.

Chapter Fifteen

The Last Dance

"How would you play Ping-Pong on the moon?"

That question may seem more pure whimsy than an effort to test raw scientific thinking. But it is the kind of question put to students in the dizzying final round of the Westinghouse contest, and it suggests the flavor of that event. The final round is part science fair, part Sphinx-like riddle, part whirlwind tour, part beauty contest, and part graduation exercise, and it is all played out in five hurly-burly days in the nation's capital.

Those who have made it to the top forty have finished in the money. They are designated winners, and most colleges would be so pleased to get a winner they would not make picky distinctions between finishing fourth and twenty-fourth. The honored students should be able to relax and savor the flighty, eccentric questions of the judges with a sense of humor.

But, for students at this level of play, finishing in the top forty may not be enough. So there is a fevered race for first place and for the other top-ten spots, a race that is fueled, quite baldly in some cases, by money. After all, thirty students will receive scholarships of $1,000 apiece, but ten others will receive prizes ranging from $10,000 to $40,000, a considerable leap in value. Four will get scholarships of $10,000, three will receive $15,000 each, and the top three will receive $20,000, $30,000 and $40,000. Since tuition, room, and board at the nation's very best colleges cost more than $80,000 for four years, even the top Westinghouse scholarship will buy only half a college education. But that is still a lot, and the cachet of being one of the forty Westinghouse winners, and particularly finishing among the leaders, can unlock thousands of other scholarship dollars, so intense is the competition among colleges for these students. Christopher Skinner, the sixteen-year-old Little Rock mathematician, was offered $60,000 in various academic scholarships, in addition to his top Westinghouse prize, worth $20,000 in 1989. (The amount was doubled the next year.) That total would more than pay for studies at his choice college, the University of Michigan.

The forty winners are also treated to a five-day trip to Washington with a stay at the lavish Mayflower Hotel. In 1989, the winners met President George Bush and appointments were arranged with other dignitaries. Divya Chander, who dreams of becoming an astronaut, got to meet Sen. John Glenn of Ohio, the first American to orbit the Earth. The five-day fiesta also features an evening of dinner and theater; the 1992 finalists were treated to Stacy Keach's performance of "Solitary Confinement" at the Kennedy Center. And there is often a lecture such as the one given in 1992 by Glenn Seaborg, the Nobel Prize–winning nuclear chemist and chairman of Science Service. Students such as Vanessa Liu who are on the threshold of their own scientific careers, who may daydream of breakthroughs that will alter civilization, have been dazzled by such talks. Seaborg, then eighty years old, told the students about his role in the discovery of the elements plutonium, americium, curium, berkelium, californium, einsteinium, fermium, mendelevium, and nobelium. "This is what the periodic table looked like in World War II, and then I changed it," was the way an awed Vanessa Liu summed up his talk.

The core of the trip, though, is two days of hard work. These high school students have to show off their gizmos, molecular models, photographs, and charts to thousands of visitors who flood the cavernous Great Hall of the National Academy of Sciences. The atmosphere is more reminiscent of one of those Picasso or Matisse blockbuster exhibitions than the contemplative ambience one might expect around esoteric science. The exhibitors are crowded together along the walls of the hall and around a makeshift center island. Each student seems to be festooned with a clutch of interrogators. For three hours on a Saturday in March and another three hours the next day, the winners stand there and explain, and explain, and explain their projects and field hundreds of queries from the frivolous to the personal to the provocative. Some do it with a pitchman's flair, others seem overwhelmed and very, very young. Mouths and throats get desert dry, hair gets mussed, faces grow waxy, and feet get sore.

These youngsters are not just facing any audience. Many of the 2,000 visitors are scientists in the Washington area who have come to know that the Westinghouse exhibit is a yearly opportunity to revel in the robustness of their profession, to learn what scientific mysteries excite young people, to appreciate very tangibly that young people are still excited by science. If well exploited, the scientists' presence could bring some future advantage, and connections can be made that will bloom years later. Every now and then, a recruiter for a scientific company tries to lure one of these college-bound youngsters into taking a summer job that might later pay off in a first-rate hire.

Here's what visitors would have seen in 1992.

Edward John Newman of St. Anthony's High School in South Huntington on Long Island, is showing off a revolutionary new bicycle wheel that he invented at the tender age of seventeen. Instead of the typical wheel's thirty-three thin metal spokes, Edward has built a wheel of just four spokes. But each spoke looks like the flaps on an airplane's wings and is made of a tough black aerospace composite called Kevlar. With the wheel set on a table, Edward, a bicycle racer for his school, demonstrates how adjusting the flaps in mid-rotation can, like a windmill, capitalize on cross-winds and reduce drag. A cyclist can increase speed by three to eight miles per hour. "I'm meeting with Du Pont to discuss production possibilities," he confidently tells one visitor.

Pat Crosby of Evanston, Illinois, the gangly six-foot pool player, towers over his contraption of steel balls and steel wires. Mounted behind him are oscilloscope charts and diagrams generated by a Cray-2 supercomputer that suggest how complicated was the physics behind the contact times of colliding balls.

Patricia Bachiller of Scotch Plains, New Jersey, also flaunts intricate charts filled with sinuous lines, but these track the pattern of chirps made by finches, specifically the fourteen males of the zebra finch species she studied. Patty, a slender young woman with shoulder-length mahogany hair and dark brown eyes, tells visitors how she discovered that the length of the tunes, the arrangement of notes and pauses, and the relation between lead-ins to a song and the songs themselves, are distinctive to families, passed down from father to son to grandson. There are minute variations among siblings, but larger commonalities. These patterns help females distinguish their kin and help fathers recognize their sons in the wild.

Nearby is Vanessa Liu, in a black, floral-patterned dress and small purple earrings. She politely offers one woman visitor a printed synopsis of her project, but the woman goads her, "How about you telling me about it, instead of my reading it?" Vanessa goes through what by this point in the exhibition has become a singsong about the working of nerve cells and how synapses are formed and the impact of her secret chemical, BC1. But the visitor has more global interests.

"How did you become involved in the topic?" she wants to know. "So who was your mentor? How long did it take you? Where did you get the time? Who funded this? Are you going to be publishing it?"

Posted next to Vanessa, and appropriately so, is Claudine Madras, an animated seventeen-year-old from Newton, Massachusetts, with dark curly tresses. Like Vanessa, Claudine tells patrons that she also wants to be an astronaut and wants to be part of the first manned mission to Mars.

"Vanessa and I are going to be co-commanders," she says. "It will be a fabulous journey."

Claudine had the heady experience of doing research that contributed to a historic scientific project. She calculated the rotation rate of an asteroid, 951 Gaspra, by tracking shifts in its brightness through a telescope at the Lowell Observatory in Flagstaff, Arizona. Her data, as well as those compiled by professionals, were used by NASA in planning a picture-snapping flyby of the asteroid by the Galileo spacecraft as Galileo whizzed toward a rendezvous with Jupiter. Not only were her calculations accurate, but she was able to predict what contours Gaspra would actually have, a prediction confirmed by the flyby on October 29, 1991.

One exhibit that seems to engage most visitors—probably because it is comparatively easy to understand—is a study of generosity by Boaz Weinstein of Brooklyn's Midwood High School. Boaz, an aspiring psychologist, asked fifty-six children at the Bean Sprout

Nursery in Brooklyn's Park Slope to draw pictures. Half were promised a payment of ten pennies for a fine picture. The other half
were promised nothing, but given the same ten-cent reward. Boaz
then asked the children to make a contribution toward the purchase of a wheelchair for a handicapped child. He found that those
who had not expected a reward were four times more generous
than those who made their drawings knowing there would be a
payment at the end. The first group averaged a four-cent gift compared to one cent for the second group. The second group, he
concluded, viewed the payments they received as "earnings" for
hard work and so were more stinting, while the first viewed their
payments as bonuses and were more open-handed.

It is not difficult to understand why Boaz would be intrigued
by the mysteries of why some people give while others withhold
and what social, psychological, and economic factors may shape
such attitudes. Though he does not confide his story to the visitors,
Boaz, a genial youngster with a curly head of sand-colored hair, is
the adopted son of a Brooklyn machinist and his wife. His mother
raised five of her own genetic children, but she made a career out
of being a foster parent and became so attached to the infant Boaz
that she formally adopted him as her sixth child.

"Your mother and father are not the people who bring you
into the world," Boaz says. "It's the people who take care of you
all the time, who are there for you when your're sick in the night.
I consider the Weinsteins my natural parents. It's an even more
special love between parent and child because you were selected
for who you were."

Boaz credits the circumstances of his adoption with spawning
his interest in the psychology of human behavior. He was caught
in an agonizing tug of war that honed his relational and diplomatic
skills. While Boaz was in the Weinstein's care, his natural parents
fought to regain custody. But the natural father died of cancer
when Boaz was seven, and Boaz's natural mother relented and
surrendered Boaz when he was ten.

"I used to have people constantly talking to me about how I
feel about everything," Boaz told me. "And the way that I feel and
other people feel is very interesting to me. I'm a very introspective

person. If I see somebody has a problem I like to find out what it is."

With three much older sisters and two brothers, Boaz has learned how to handle himself in crowds, and the Westinghouse exhibit is a comparative pushover. With a display of charts that trace the variances in altruistic behavior, he gently explains to one visitor after another that stockbrokers have been found to be more charitable than doctors because "they play with other people's money and don't have the same possessiveness."

"The doctor figures he worked for every dollar," he tells a visitor.

How did you come up with this idea? another asks.

"The idea started by observing my mother," Boaz replies. "She likes to gamble on Lotto or numbers and after she wins she becomes more generous."

"Why did you give these kids ten pennies, why not dollars?" another visitor asks.

"Because I didn't want to go bankrupt," Boaz shoots back.

One of the most surprising aspects of the long Westinghouse weekend is how quickly these young scientists, most of whom have never met before coming to Washington, form close friendships. Ideas bring them together. One morning over breakfast at the Mayflower, Claudine Madras, Vanessa Liu, and Patty Bachiller candidly discussed the sexism they had experienced in American science, while some young men at the other end of the round table gently offered a running commentary. The three young women were complaining that their skill in math and science was not esteemed by their peers because they are female.

"It's not a source of pride that I won the Westinghouse," said Claudine, adding that she was shielded from many inequities because she attended the all-girls Winsor School.

"Why are you letting yourself be a victim of society?" interjected Adam Healey, the son of *New York Times* editor Barth Healey, and a tall, wiry youth who contrived a new method for detecting the Lyme disease antibody. "Women have to realize they should be going into science as much as men."

It's difficult to remember at times like these that these are teenagers, but when all forty winners gather on a chilly overcast morning at the foot of the Capitol for a group portrait, their adolescent awkwardness becomes apparent. As the photographer moves them around into a parabola to squeeze all forty and the Capitol dome into the photograph that will be used for next year's Westinghouse brochure, it's clear that some of the young women are not accustomed to high heels and others did not leave enough time for their hair to dry. Some young men's faces are still layered with peach fuzz and others are not quite comfortable with the fit of their growing bodies. These youngsters may have done research that few adults can match, but they are not yet adults.

For many of these budding scientists, the most exhilarating act of the five-day circus is the chance to meet with working scientists in the government research laboratories that saturate Washington. Even those who do not find that prospect exciting welcome a break in the tension before the night of decision.

In 1989, I followed Divya Chander through a day of appointments with scientists at the National Institutes of Health (NIH) in Bethesda, Maryland. Divya, the child of immigrant Indian scientists, moves as comfortably among them as Kirk Douglas's sons must have moved among film stars when they were young. For her Westinghouse research, she investigated the mechanism that allows bacteria—specifically the salmonella germs responsible for food poisoning—to pierce the tissue of its prey.

Divya took the sleek D.C. Metro train from the Mayflower to Bethesda, and it was on that ride that Divya gave me a quick sense of the intensity that won her the prize by opening a spiral notebook and dashing off the final pages of a Spanish paper. When we arrived at the Bethesda station, there was a steep Everest of an escalator that took us out to the sun-drenched streets. She swiftly climbed it, impatient with the escalator's sloth, while I huffed and puffed. At the 500-bed NIH Medical Center, the world's largest hospital devoted solely to research, Divya snaked her way through a maze of corridors to the offices of Al Rexroad, a staff science writer who had planned her day. On his office wall, she saw a poster about the new frontiers in chaos and observed breezily, "Chaos is great!" the way some youngsters might extol a poster of Madonna. Ever the teenager, she wondered where she could get a copy of the poster.

She and Rexroad then launched into a discussion of the genetic basis of mental illness and thought disorders and the work of Dr. Julius Axelrod, a resident scientist who won the 1970 Nobel Prize in medicine for discoveries of how brain neurons communicate with one another. Neither chaos nor Julius Axelrod's work were related to Divya's Westinghouse research, yet she easily held up her end of the conversation.

Soon it was time to visit Dr. Seymour Kaufman, a neurochemist at the nearby National Institute of Mental Health who has done the leading work on phenylketonuria, or PKU, a metabolic disorder that results in mental retardation. Because of Kaufman's thirty years of steady work with this arcane disease, the 400 children born each year with PKU can be treated.

"PKUs are otherwise healthy," Kaufman told Divya. "They are rather healthy idiots."

The two talked almost as equals, not as middle-aged mentor and adolescent student. Indeed, Divya has such a quicksilver mind that there were times I wondered who was intimidating to whom. Kaufman told her how he gave up $10,000 of private art lessons so he could train in biochemistry at New York University with Nobel winners. He even confessed that he ventured into PKU, not because he wanted to save children, but because it was "a fascinating area of chemistry."

"Scientists are piqued by questions that challenge them," he said.

Kaufman said that when he began his study more than thirty years before, it was known that PKU was caused by an abnormality in the process by which phenylalanine, an amino acid, is converted to tyrosine, another amino acid. This conversion took place in the liver. Why then should a defect in that process affect the brain, Kaufman wondered.

"How does the brain talk to the liver?" was how he phrased the question for a mesmerized Divya.

Through his research, Kaufman discovered that a chemical called biopterin and two enzymes played a critical role in the liver conversion process and that biopterin and one of these enzymes were essential ingredients in the synthesis of the brain's neuro-transmitters as well. A lack of biopterin would therefore impede brain functioning. To underscore his point, he told Divya that people who have Alzheimer's disease may also have experienced a decrease in biopterin.

Much of what he said went right by me, but Divya took it all in without a blink.

"I'm familiar with the morphology of Alzheimer's disease," she told Kaufman.

Although the Nobel Prize–winning Axelrod could not make it that day, one of his young associates, Chris Felder, ended Divya's visit by shepherding her through several labs. The NIH, which provides one-third of all the biomedical research money spent in the United States, likes to have youngsters like Divya around.

"Young minds ask fresh questions," Felder said. "The questions get stale after a while and you need new minds to ask new questions."

Divya, a lively person in any environment, seemed securely in her element. After all, she too had done scientific research. She deserved a place among these laboratories and clinics.

"All these labs look the same with test tubes and glass jars crowded up to the ceiling," she confided as we ended our visit. "Research sounds exciting but the actual work is tedious and boring. You need an ability to dedicate yourself, to become part of something. I'd wake up in the morning and say, 'God, do I have to go to work today?' But once you're there you get caught up in it."

The last lap of the Westinghouse race is the part around which some of the richest lore has grown up. Each student submits to four interviews, including a one-on-one with a judge, an interview with a psychiatrist, and gentle interrogations by two panels made up of three judges each. The judges ask questions that are designed to see if the students can approach problems that have nothing to do with their Westinghouse project in an inventive yet rigorously scientific manner. The questioning allows the eight judges to make the fine distinctions needed to sieve out the top ten.

"Students are asked questions they couldn't know an answer to," says Dorothy Shriver, the contest's associate director, "but they are asked to use their imagination."

For example, when Tamir Druz, the young chess expert from the Bronx, was asked, "How would you play Ping-Pong on the moon?" he believed the question called for an understanding of what adaptations might be needed for the moon's air-free, low-gravity environment. Tamir was aware that on the moon a ball would sail and drop more slowly, and so he answered that the Ping-Pong table would have to be much larger, the net higher, and the paddles broader. And, of course, the players would have to wear pressurized suits.

Ping-Pong was also the subject of a question put to Divya Chander. "How many Ping-Pong balls can you fit in this room?" she was asked. The question called on her to work with volume in two shapes—a box-like room and a ball. That is a skill that comes in handy in molecular biology and astrophysics.

The judges were aware that Al Avestruz, a Philippine-born student at the Bronx High School of Science, fabricated a thin film that can be used in creating superconducting electronic devices. But they asked him a question that seemed to have little to do with applied physics. "If a person is born on one continent, dies on another, and is buried on a third, what can you say about his or her wealth?"

There is no right answer, but the judges were interested in seeing how deftly he thought about the problem. Alexander the Great, Avestruz remembered, was born in Greece, died in Asia Minor, and was buried in Egypt. Yet, most people who leave their countries for other continents do so to escape poverty. Still, to have themselves buried on a third continent for sentimental or other reasons would require some means.

"They want to hear you think out loud," says David Haile, who was asked the same question. "They're scared of selecting a jack of one trade."

Haile, the young butterfly connoisseur, was quite impressed by a question asked by Dr. Glenn Seaborg, the Nobel Prize–winning chemist who is also a judge. Seaborg wanted to know the structural formula for glucose. Haile was forced to explain why carbon bonds with hydrogen and oxygen in the particular pattern it does and at discrete locations.

"It's an entire year of chemistry rolled up in one question," Haile said.

Kevin Heller also enjoyed puzzling out a deceptive chemistry question. The judge told him that in the previous year the United States had produced 36 billion tons of sulphuric acid and 15 billion tons of ammonia. "Which," the judge asked, "produced more molecules?" The answer was ammonia because there are more molecules in a single gram of ammonia than there are in a single gram of sulphuric acid.

Not all the questions are tricky. Many are conventional. "Draw an amino acid," for example. Others simply allow the judges to delight in the brisk liveliness of the students' minds. "Define luck," was a question put to Vanessa Liu in 1992. "Luck is not just a matter of fate," she replied. "Luck is preparing for fate." "What was the greatest invention?" Stuyvesant's Zachary Gozali was asked. He recalled Mel Brooks's shtick as the 2000-year-old man and was dying to answer, "Saran Wrap." But his reply was: ink and paper. "It gave mankind the ability to record ideas."

The contestants are always asked to explain how various devices work. In 1989, students were interrogated about the operation of a photocopier and a diesel engine. The aim is to see whether students understand the scientific principles behind these machines. These device questions have become so routine that Bronx Science warns its competing students to bone up on several pivotal ones.

It is not essential to get the answers right. Students are judged by how they look at a problem, whether they can pick out its key elements and structure a coherent answer. David Haile was asked, "Why is it hard for a helicopter to operate in Peru?" by a judge who noticed that David's hobby was aviation. In fact, David knows quite a bit about the mechanics of aviation, but he was not aware that Peru is a high-altitude country where thin air would complicate helicopter flight. Nevertheless, he believes he impressed the judges by analyzing factors such as temperature and humidity that might also affect the flight of a helicopter.

Everyone meets with the shrink, who in recent years has been

Dr. Stuart Hauser, a Harvard psychiatrist. According to Dorothy Shriver, the psychiatrist tries to find out whether students are "stable, whether or not they're able to deal with life in general." The psychiatrist may, for example, try to gauge whether a student has any interest in sports to see if he or she is well rounded. The officials do not quite say so, but they seem eager to make sure the top winners will be able to represent the Westinghouse contest in public appearances and in the national television and press interviews to which winners are subjected.

Chapter Sixteen

The Envelope, Please

Sometime during the four days in Washington, the judges get together in one of the hotel's rooms and choose the top ten winners and two alternates. At this level of competition, making distinctions between a fifth- and sixth-place winner is as much voodoo as precise calculation. But somehow the choices are made, and they are announced at the annual Monday-night banquet at the Mayflower's Grand Ballroom.

The guests at this banquet include leading scientists in the Washington area and business people, government officials, and academics who have been associated with the contest over the years. The men come in tuxedos, the women in luminous evening gowns, and scattered among them as they gather for predinner drinks are the gangly teenagers whom this evening is honoring, a few of them in formal attire as well. Many of the students mingle easily with the adults; others, like standard-issue teenagers, enjoy the illusion of being among adults, but mingle only with each other. One or two collect autographs from stellar scientists or from one another. The forty winners seem effervescent but nervous.

After the more than 400 guests sit down for dinner, the forty winners are introduced. Each climbs a small stage at one end of the cavernous ballroom, takes a bow in the spotlight and then joins one of the adult tables. Even with all the glitter and prominence in the room, each winner has been assigned to serve as the center of entertainment for a separate table of adults.

What this evening is really about is made clear in the 1989

opening speech by Edward Sherburne, Jr., the director of Science Service. He points out that with all the money that is being targeted for students who cannot read or write, the "needs of high-ability students get tossed out." There is a folk wisdom that these students "can get along on their own," but Sherburne insists this notion is false. Each winning student was helped by a teacher, or a school program, or a mentor outside the school.

"The old saw that genius will out is just not true," he says.

Moreover, he says, "these students give back to society a lot more than they receive." The subliminal message is that, in the competition for scarce federal dollars, the influential and government-connected scientists in the ballroom must use their influence and government connections to see that more money goes to programs for scientifically gifted students.

In following speeches, Seaborg jests that the projects are becoming so sophisticated that the "judges do their best to understand what is going on." And John Marous, then the chairman and chief executive officer of the Westinghouse Electric Corporation, centers his remarks on the idea that "quality may be the answer" to most of America's problems. Yet in their efforts to capture the soul of the contest and the pleasure of research, all the adult comments pale next to a succinct remark by Vladimir Teichberg, a Russian immigrant from Bronx Science who has been chosen to speak for the gang of forty.

"All of us have experienced the excitement of doing what no man has done before," he says.

The keynote address belongs to Leon Lederman, who was awarded the Nobel Prize in physics the autumn before. What is most germane about Lederman this evening is his role in founding the Illinois Mathematics and Science Academy, which opened in 1986 but has already placed a budding authority on pterosaur flight, Rowan Lockwood, in this ballroom. Lederman has been a champion for a greater public effort to nurture the country's most talented youngsters, and he opens his speech by calling Lockwood and the thirty-nine other students sprinkled around this room "the nation's crown jewels, the nation's most precious resource."

The gifts of such young people must be cultivated, he argues, and generously so. America is experiencing a decline in the public's knowledge and understanding of science. Only one in ten Americans, he says, knows that the Earth revolves around the sun once every 365 days. Such a regression is a "prescription for disaster" at a time when world competition requires an ever more sophisticated grasp of science. America is doing little to stem this tide. Expenditures for scientific education and research are shamefully low. Yet, it is scientific research that ultimately contributes to the growth of the nation's economy and to the enrichment of its culture.

But Lederman's talk does not have the leaden flavor of a jeremiad. "Most people think the two neutrinos are an Italian dance team," he banters in Henny Youngman style. And he informs his audience about the Einstein watch: "It not only tells you the time, its tells you why." And then, he shpritzes on, there were the two theoretical physicists who got lost while mountain climbing. One paused to look at a map, and after several minutes of studying, told his comrade, "See that peak over there. That's where we are."

Laughter rolls across the audience with each of his jokes. But for forty students scattered around this room the tension is building, for the envelope-opening moment is drawing near. The voltage is the kind that only high school kids yearning, praying for an award, can create, and the contest organizers make sure to string out the tension by announcing the winners in reverse Miss America contest order

Richard Gott, the chief judge, steps up to the lectern as a spotlight bathes him in yellow. Gott first discloses the name of the second alternate. It is Simon Zuckerbraun, a computer whiz who attends Bronx Science and researched mathematical permutations. The first alternate is Daniel Sherman, a Columbia, Missouri, teenager who bore in on DNA sequences in viruses. The tenth-place winner is, yes, Divya Chander. Her bacteria investigation has finished in the money, $7,500, and she strides confidently up to the podium, her royal-blue dress glistening in the spotlights.

Ninth place goes to Andrew Gerber, the Brooklyn lad whose father has helped develop other Westinghouse winners. Eighth goes to Andrew Jackson, of Medfield, Massachusetts, who contrived a new kind of spectrograph. Seventh belongs to Kevin Heller, of Dix Hills, New York, whose mother planted string-bean seeds in their backyard when he was a toddler to show him where string beans come from and who grew up to investigate jumping genes in corn.

The sixth-place winner of $10,000 is Allene Whitney, of Helena, Montana, who discovered a quicker way to detect the toxicity of a species of blue-green algae. Her discovery will not only be of great help to ranchers whose cattle drink such algae-infested water, but it also proved that a seventeen-year-old girl from Montana who did much of her research in a science summer camp can hold her own with the pluggers from the Bronx. Fifth place is awarded to Celeste Posey, the quiet tow-haired girl from North Carolina whose award for DNA research brings the first taste of glory to the North Carolina School of Science and Mathematics. Fourth place—and the third $10,000 award—goes to Stacy Benjamin, who investigated the impact of race in how people evaluate crime and punishment.

The winner of the $15,000 third-place award is Richard Christie, at fifteen the youngest of the forty yet not too young to work with postpartum female rats in a project that investigated interactions between the nervous and immune systems. Second place, and another $15,000 check, goes to Jordan Ellenberg, the teenaged comic who makes mathematics as spellbinding as magic.

The suspense has peaked in the ballroom. Who will win the top award, don the unofficial mantle of the country's top science student? There are still plenty of contenders left over from Bronx Science, Stuyvesant High School, and the other chic New York schools. Surely, it will be someone from one of those schools. Gott allows only the tiniest pause for dramatic effect, and then he calls the name of the victor, the winner of the $20,000 grand prize.

"Christopher McLean Skinner of Little Rock, Arkansas!"

Smiles light up the room. Christopher is the sixteen-year-old son of the devout Baptist couple who acquired his sophisticated grasp of mathematics by plundering the courses of a local college and who offered an approach to solving an historic puzzle of an equation. A short young man with tousled brown hair, oversized glasses, and braces, he has remarkable poise for his age.

Now, in his moment of triumph, Christopher strides to the front of the ballroom and turns to the audience, with all those taller girls standing behind him. A big grin of pleasure lights his face. Applause fills the room, with much of it coming from the thirty-nine other winners. Christopher is popular with his colleagues here. "He's not just smart, he's nice," Kevin Heller tells me later.

The top-ten youngsters pat each other on the back or bear-hug or kiss as the other forty winners stream from tables around the room and join them. The young men flash brave smiles. Tears glisten in several of the young women's eyes. This moment they have all been working toward for more than a year is drawing to an end. Tomorrow, they will all have to return to their hometowns and get on with the quotidian reality of senior life—finishing off their courses, making final decisions about college, bracing themselves to leave home for most of the next four years.

Still, for the top-ten winners the evening is only three-quarters over. They meander upstairs to the Westinghouse press room, and with reporters sprinkled around the room to listen, they dial home to tell parents and teachers their news.

"Oh, mother, I'm so excited, I can't believe it," gushes Allene Whitney to her mother in Montana.

Divya Chander is so frenetic she mistakenly dials the laboratory in which she did her winning project, then she reaches home. But her mother already knows. As happens every year, word of the top winners has been leaked just at the start of the banquet to one of the national wire services, and a New Jersey reporter has already called Divya's home to get the family's reaction.

"I just made it," Divya tells her mother. "I made number ten. I'm stunned. Are you?"

Kevin Heller gives his parents in Long Island a scorecard. "I kid you not," he says. "Only three people from New York and no one from Science or Stuyvesant."

As he waits for his turn at the telephone, Andrew Gerber of Brooklyn leans back in his chair, intoxicated and slightly fatigued with this victory. He answers reporters' questions as if he has been doing so all his life. One reporter asks him what is the value of the award. This seventeen-year-old looks around the room at the other winners talking on the telephones and says with a grand flourish:

"These are the future chairmen of physics and math departments around this country."

Out the windows of the Mayflower Hotel, a soft snow is falling, tinted to a pale yellow by the street lights. Andrew gets his shot at a free telephone and calls his mother to tell her of his $7,500 scholarship. His mother is delighted, of course, but she is also anxious to see that her son gets home safely. She has heard about the snow in Washington and she cautions him not to take his scheduled flight. He is, after all, still her child. But emboldened by his experience as a winner, Andrew has taken the liberty of making safer arrangements on his own.

"Don't worry," he says. "I'm taking the train."

For David Haile, the young butterfly aficionado from Pennsylvania, the evening has a wistful, bittersweet quality. His parents are perhaps the only ones there for the awards dinner. The Westinghouse discourages parents from attending the Washington events, but the Hailes spirited themselves into the Mayflower the night before the awards dinner on the pretext of helping David lug his displays and notebooks back to Reading. On the night of the dinner, they find they cannot help taking a place in the balcony overlooking the floor. They see their still-tender sprout among the nation's leading scientists, among the tuxes and gowns of the evening, and that gives them a rush of pride, a rush made more poignant by the hardscrabble lives they themselves have lived.

They hold their breath as the moderator announces the top-ten prizewinners. David's name is not among them. From their balcony perch, they see their son's crestfallen face, his mute disappointment as his name is skipped again and again and again all the way through the announcement of the top $20,000 prize to Christopher Skinner. From below David spots them as well. In a semaphore of his reaction, he shrugs his shoulders. Sometimes you miss the brass ring, the shrug seems to say.

The crowd, with many guests still percolating over this bright crop of youngsters and their phenomenal personal achievements and the remarkable, pessimism-defying achievement of their schools, streams out of the ballroom. David's parents come down to the lobby level and they spy David in the crowd and collect him.

It had been a long haul, but there are other long hauls ahead. For David and the hundreds of other youngsters who enter the Westinghouse do their research more for the sweet pleasure of discovery than for the money.

"Now, Mom," he says. "Let's go home and be normal."

Chapter Seventeen

Lessons

To a science teacher in Averagetown, U.S.A., the odds of harvesting a Westinghouse scholar or two must seem daunting indeed. The teacher must compete for the precious plaques with counterparts at Bronx Science and at the growing number of state-operated, dormitory-equipped science high schools. All these schools, the teacher reckons, probably have state-of-the-art laboratories, computers that rival the acrobatics of the human brain, trained researchers, access to teaching hospitals and universities. What is the point of competing?

There are nuggets of truth among these anxieties, but they are vastly exaggerated. As we have seen, Bronx Science, Stuyvesant, and Midwood do not have state-of-the-art laboratories, just clever, well-thought-out research programs. Their teachers are for the most part pedagogical lifers and not refugees from cutting-edge research institutions. The access the schools have to research institutions is a result of relationships they have artfully cultivated over the years, as well as simple geographic proximity. Moreover, lots of students who do not attend schools like Bronx Science capture laurels. Young people like Christopher Skinner manage to put it all together though they hail from what a Bronx Science sophisticate might consider a hayseed town.

The moral in all this is that thoughtful planning, willpower, and tenacity are far more important than equipment in the pursuit of the Westinghouse or, more important, the scientific acumen such programs breed. True, there are few cities, let alone suburban and rural communities, that can sustain special science schools, that have the money to finance them and populations large enough to grow a schoolful of science-minded students. But virtually all of the country's high schools have science teachers and laboratories. With a science teacher and a laboratory you can mount a research program that commits itself to training boys and girls in the basic procedures and attitudes of scientific inquiry, that aspires to reward young scientists with the gratifying lilt of discovery but also arms them with the humility to know that the rewards come after countless hours of deadly work. Mounting such a program takes a decision by principals, parents, and community officials that schools should be turning out as many prospective scientists as football players. That decision is harder than acquiring the right equipment.

We don't expect to turn out piano virtuosos by putting them in front of a piano at eighteen. But somehow our schools function as if we could turn out scientific virtuosos by starting them on research projects in college or graduate school. The remarkable schools I've profiled are, unfortunately, rarities. Most schools operate as if they expect their kids to pick up a flair for science through happenstance or osmosis. Things seldom work that way. Children need to be taught to do research just as they are taught to play the piano. Most may turn out to be weekend dabblers just as most piano students end up dilettantes who bang out a few chords of Gershwin at a family get-together. But the effort, in both cases, is not wasted. There is something priceless in the ability to create a mood or draw out an emotion by skillfully unraveling a row of eighty-eight black-and-white keys. Similarly, there is something invaluable in the habits of mind, the disciplines of work that result from scientific research. These habits are fundamental to law, business, journalism, not just science and mathematics. Imagining an explanation for a phenomenon, articulating it, devising the conditions under which it can be tested, demanding precision, acknowledging errors, all of these are talents of scientific inquiry translatable to numerous human endeavors.

Once the merits of a research program are appreciated, setting one up is not that difficult. Brooklyn's Midwood, as we have seen, takes 300 freshmen and gives them a half-year course called Science Research Methods for five periods a week. Students learn how to formulate hypotheses, create frequency graphs, operate triple-beam balances and micrometers. Every high school in the country, even the smallest, has the capacity to instruct its students in these skills. But too many schools are satisfied to spend their time imparting the standard biology and chemistry syllabi. Research, though, is the fun part of science, the part that allows for cunning and wonder.

A commitment to a research program does demand shifts in the academic program, in teacher deployment. But most curricula have some slack in them—study periods, hygiene courses perhaps—that can permit waivers for a selected number of students. After all, high school principals find ways of juggling the curriculum when a football championship is at stake.

At some point, training in research methods must turn to actual research. Many students don't know where to begin, feel daunted by the array of fields available for experimentation, and have trouble focusing on a single idea. A skillful teacher knows how to narrow the range of possibilities, even suggesting some questions worthy of inquiry. There are booklets put out by federal and state science agencies, by science magazines, by textbook publishers that are chock full of experiments that students can work on or adapt in a standard school laboratory. Crafty science teachers have learned to acquire uncommon materials by raiding local manufacturers eager to obtain a little public good will.

Fairs and exhibits help perk up interest in a science program, and many schools around the country already have these. The more aggressive schools submit projects to state and national contests. Sure, the projects should be done for the sheer challenge, but the inducement of a little glory never hurt. The same inducements are used in athletics, after all. For more advanced research projects, high school laboratories may not do. But enterprising science teachers at schools like Midwood have fashioned ties with private labs or colleges. There are now senior and community colleges near virtually every sizable town in the United States and most are equipped with high-powered microscopes, advanced computers, telescopes, spectrometers, chemical analyzers, all of which can be harnessed for science projects. Much of this equipment sits idle for long periods when it can be used to delight and inform a young high school student with a yen for the jolt of discovery. Inventive science teachers can search their areas for agricultural cooperatives, state parks and forests, hospitals, zoos and wildlife preserves, and chemical and biological plants where helpful professional researchers can be found. It is hard to think of an area of the country so isolated that it is not near one such facility. Many businesses are interested in cultivating prospective employees and don't mind the small investment of watching over a high school student. Many scientists welcome an extra hand in the laboratory. They remember when they were young and frightened and clumsy and were shepherded along by an experienced adult, and many want to repay that patronage by helping young people.

When my wife was a doctoral student in psychology at Columbia University, she corralled six Barnard seniors to help her on her dissertation project. The project centered on the varying abilities of mothers to separate from their toddlers, separation crucial to the development of a child's sense of independence. Her students gathered her data by observing videotapes of encounters between mothers and their toddlers as they said good-bye and rating the mothers for the quality of care and the comparative autonomy they gave the children. They spent scores of hours working for no remuneration, but what they learned in return was how to observe, how data are collected, how a project is put together, what planning is involved, what materials are needed, how much time an experiment takes. Several went on to use the same videotapes for their own discrete science projects. It is safe to say that they developed an ease with scientific projects, suffering less of the paralysis that strikes graduate students when confronted with large-scale research.

In recent years, clever high school teachers and parents have learned to steer promising science students into training programs run, typically in summer, by colleges, private and government research institutions, or federal agencies like NASA. There are now scores of them all over the country, many that put high school students up in college dormitories, charging only for housing and meals. Science Service, which manages the Westinghouse awards, has since 1982 published an annual *Directory of Student Science Training Programs for High-Ability Precollege Students*. The 1993 edition contained listings for 490 programs in almost every state and a dozen foreign countries. There were openings for thousands of students. Roughly half the programs consist of classroom instruction, but the other half involve research.

The School for Field Studies, a Massachusetts-based organization, offers students an opportunity to study the behavior of bottlenose dolphins in the Gulf of Mexico. The Foundation for Field Research, a California-based group, gives students a chance to do research on rare bears of Arizona. The University of the Pacific has a three-week residential program of research and courses in genetic engineering. Colorado College offers an outdoor seminar in the geology of the Rocky Mountains for students who can handle camping and hiking in rugged terrain. Project Oceanology, based in Groton, Connecticut, has research programs in oceanography, both after school and during summers, for commuting students. The Smithsonian Institution offers summer research programs in computers, biology, veterinary science, botany, physics, marine science, archaeology, and geology. NASA sponsors 160 summer research apprenticeships at most of its installations, all for free.

For the adventurous willing to brave more exotic places, the Foundation for Field Research allows students to work on an investigation of tool use among chimpanzees in west Africa. The School for Field Studies invites students to look at conflicts in ecological management in the Himalayas. Israel's Weizmann Institute of Science sponsors an eclectic research program for seventy-five students, with some slots reserved for Americans.

In cultivating young scientists, home is also a crucial part of the equation. My experience with Westinghouse winners and their families suggests that the basic operating principle is to follow the child's curiosity. Overly pushy parents who try to wrench a scientist out of a baseball player will probably wind up with neither. A child who is interested in biology finds ways of letting parents know. By the time David Haile's parents got him a microscope, that was an obvious rather than an inspired choice.

What parents can do is create an atmosphere where inquiry is as natural as play. I draw that observation by watching my daughter. When she was three and a half years old, we took a vacation in Martha's Vineyard and she found a small fiddler crab on the edge of a tidal pond and put it inside her yellow pail, filling the pail with brackish water. She wondered where it would sleep, and so she found half of a small clamshell and put it inside the yellow pail as the crab's bed. She asked me do crabs sleep at night or in the day. (I had already explained to her about nocturnal animals.) She wondered what it might eat, and she was concerned that we do everything we can so that it might live in her pail and not die. We talked about the water the crab would live in, and I suggested that she keep the brackish water, rather than change it for faucet water, because that was more familiar to the crab. She wondered whether ants or spiders might crawl into the yellow pail and eat the crab, and I had to explain to her that ants and spiders would probably not survive the salt water.

My daughter's curiosity is natural to most children. Sustaining that curiosity is one of the greatest challenges adults face. It is a shoot that can easily perish. I have no proof, but I bet that parents who have the patience to listen and respond to this endless stream of questions probably have a better shot at creating an inquisitive adult than parents who don't. One reason perhaps that so many Westinghouse winners spring from doctors and scientists is that these professionals may feel less anxiety in coming up with answers to their children's questions. They like thinking about science. But all parents can work on ways to keep their children's curiosity bubbling. Kevin Heller's mother showed him that if you put the beans from a string bean into the ground it would produce another string bean a few months later. Boaz Weinstein shadowed his father as he went about the house repairing lawn mowers and other machines, and Boaz learned some principles of mechanics.

Will my daughter win a Westinghouse one day? Probably not. Though if you think about it, the odds of winning a Westinghouse are a lot better than some other contests of life. But even if she does not enter, I hope she will have the schools and teachers who can keep her curiosity vigorously alive, and I hope I have the patience to do my part. And if that happens, I believe she will develop some pleasurable and fulfilling ways of thinking about the life around her, about the inexhaustible wonders that will sustain her through the years.

Appendices

I. Major Honors Achieved by Former Westinghouse Winners

Honor	Date Awarded	Name	STS Year
Nobel Prize (Physics)	1972	Leon N Cooper	1947
Nobel Prize (Physics)	1975	Ben R. Mottelson	1944
Nobel Prize (Physics)	1979	Sheldon L. Glashow	1950
Nobel Prize (Chemistry)	1980	Walter Gilbert	1949
Nobel Prize (Chemistry)	1981	Roald Hoffmann	1955
Fields Medal (Mathematics)	1966	Paul J. Cohen	1950
Fields Medal (Mathematics)	1974	David B. Mumford	1953
MacArthur Fellowship	1982	Frank Wilczek	1967
MacArthur Fellowship	1983	Richard Stephen Berry	1948
MacArthur Fellowship	1984	Arthur T. Winfree	1960
MacArthur Fellowship	1985	Jane Shelby Richardson	1958
MacArthur Fellowship	1987	Robert Axelrod	1961
MacArthur Fellowship	1987	Robert Coleman	1972
MacArthur Fellowship	1987	Eric Lander	1974
MacArthur Fellowship	1987	David B. Mumford	1953
National Medal of Science	1967	Paul J. Cohen	1950
National Medal of Science	1983	Roald Hoffman	1955
Albert Lasker Basic Medical Research Award	1979	Walter Gilbert	1949
Albert Lasker Basic Medical Research Award	1987	Leroy E. Hood	1956

II. Westinghouse Winners Who Are Members of The National Academy of Sciences

Name	Affiliation	STS Year
Adler, Stephen L.	Institute for Advanced Study, Princeton, NJ	1957
Axelrod, Robert	University of Michigan, Ann Arbor, MI	1961
Berry, R. Stephen	University of Chicago, Chicago, IL	1948
Breslow, Ronald	Columbia University, New York, NY	1948
Chilton, Mary Dell	CIBA-GEIGY Corp., Research Triangle Park, NC	1956
Clark, George W.	MIT, Cambridge, MA	1945
Cohen, Paul J.	Stanford University, Stanford, CA	1950
Cooper, Leon N	Brown University, Providence, RI	1947
Crothers, Donald M.	Yale University, New Haven, CT	1954
Davidson, Eric H.	California Institute of Technology, Pasadena, CA	1954
Felsenfeld, Gary	National Institutes of Health, Bethesda, MD	1947
Gilbert, Walter	Harvard University, Cambridge, MA	1949
Glashow, Sheldon Lee	Harvard University, Cambridge, MA	1950
Halperin, Bertrand I.	Harvard University, Cambridge, MA	1958
Hoffmann, Roald	Cornell University, Ithaca, NY	1955
Hood, Leroy	California Institute of Technology, Pasadena, CA	1956
Karplus, Martin	Harvard University, Cambridge, MA	1947
Martin, Paul C.	Harvard University, Cambridge, MA	1948
Mather, John N.	Princeton University, Princeton, NJ	1960
Mumford, David B.	Harvard University, Cambridge, MA	1953
Richards, Paul L.	University of California, Berkeley, CA	1952
Rosenblatt, Murray	University of California, San Diego, LaJolla, CA	1943
Sessler, Andrew M.	University of California, Berkeley, CA	1945
Solovay, Robert M.	University of California, Berkeley, CA	1956
Sternberg, Saul	AT&T Bell Laboratories, Murray Hill, NJ	1950
Streitwieser, Jr., Andrew	University of California, Berkeley, CA	1945
Tinkham, Michael	Harvard University, Cambridge, MA	1945
Wilczck, Frank Anthony	Institute for Advanced Study, Princeton, NJ	1967

III. Westinghouse Awards—Top High Schools: 1942–1990

School and Location	Winners	Honors	Scholarships/ Awards
Bronx High School of Science New York, NY	118	949	$260,200
Stuyvesant High School New York, NY	70	449	$199,450
Forest Hills High School Forest Hills, NY	42	217	$ 70,950
Erasmus Hall High School Brooklyn, NY	31	180	$ 9,600
Evanston Township High School Evanston, IL	27	158	$ 25,000
Benjamin N. Cardozo High School Bayside, NY	25	145	$ 44,250
Midwood High School Brooklyn, NY	24	142	$ 35,850
Jamaica High School Jamaica, NY	19	206	$ 13,750
Martin Van Buren High School Queens Village, NY	16	102	$ 14,850
Brooklyn Technical High School Brooklyn, NY	14	115	$ 27,050
Central High School Philadelphia, PA	11	46	$ 16,400
Abraham Lincoln High School Brooklyn, NY	11	80	$ 1,850
Hunter College High School New York, NY	9	37	$ 21,050

School and Location	Winners	Honors	Scholarships/ Awards
Lyons Township High School La Grange, IL	9	66	$ 11,700
New Rochelle High School New Rochelle, NY	9	108	$ 8,550
Coral Gables Senior High School Coral Gables, FL	9	58	$ 6,250
North Phoenix High School Phoenix, AZ	9	55	$ 1,500
Phillips Exeter Academy Exeter, NH	8	15	$ 9,550
Melbourne High School Melbourne, FL	7	35	$ 28,250
Newton High School Newtonville, MA	7	10	$ 16,600
Ramaz School New York, NY	7	39	$ 10,850
Niles Township High School-West Skokie, IL	7	27	$ 7,500
Columbus High School Marshfield, WI	7	8	$ 3,500
Stephen Austin High School Austin, TX	7	31	$ 2,050
Woodrow Wilson High School Washington, DC	6	28	$ 9,850
Wakefield High School Arlington, VA	6	16	$ 7,400
Princeton High School Princeton, NJ	6	15	$ 6,000
Nova High School Fort Lauderdale, FL	6	41	$ 5,250

School and Location	Winners	Honors	Scholarships/ Awards
James Madison Memorial High School, Madison, WI	6	24	$ 3,500
Alhambra High School Alhambra, CA	6	40	$ 3,000
McLean High School McLean, VA	6	44	$ 1,750
Eugene High School Eugene, OR	6	8	$ 900

DATE DUE

BRODART, CO.   Cat. No. 23-221-003

28 33 842/